Traditional Ecological Knowledge
and Natural Resource Management

Traditional Ecological Knowledge
and Natural Resource Management

Edited by Charles R. Menzies

UNIVERSITY OF NEBRASKA PRESS   ·   LINCOLN AND LONDON

Chapter 6, "The Case of the Missing Sheep: Time, Space, and the Politics of 'Trust' in Co-management Practice," by Paul Nadasdy originally published in a slightly different form as "Reevaluating the Co-management Success Story," in *Arctic* 56, no. 4 (December 2003), 367–80. Reprinted by permission of the publisher. ¶ Portions of chapter 6 originally appeared in "Knowledge-Integration in Practice: The Case of the Ruby Range Sheep Steering Committee," in *Hunters and Bureaucrats: Power, Knowledge, and Aboriginal-State Relations in the Southwest Yukon* (Vancouver: University of British Columbia Press, 2003), 181–221.

© 2006 by the Board of Regents of the University of Nebraska ¶ All rights reserved. ¶ Manufactured in the United States of America ¶ ∞ ¶ Library of Congress Cataloging-in-Publication Data ¶ Traditional ecological knowledge and natural resource management / edited by Charles R. Menzies ¶ p. cm. ¶ Includes bibliographical references and index. ¶ ISBN-13: 978-0-8032-3246-4 (cloth : alk. paper) ¶ ISBN-10: 0-8032-3246-2 (cloth : alk. paper) ¶ ISBN-13: 978-0-8032-8319-0 (pbk. : alk. paper) ¶ ISBN-10: 0-8032-8319-9 (pbk. : alk. paper) ¶ 1. Indigenous peoples — Ecology—North America. ¶ 2. Traditional ecological knowledge—North America. ¶ 3. Conservation of natural resources—North America. ¶ I. Menzies, Charles R. ¶ GF501.T73 2006 ¶ 304.2089'97—dc22 ¶ 2006016235 ¶ Designed and set in Quadraat by R. W. Boeche ¶ Image on title page © Andrei Tchernov/iStockphoto.

Contents

Introduction

Understanding Ecological Knowledge

Charles R. Menzies and Caroline Butler

From before the time Raven stole the sun and shed light on the world below, the Gitxaała people have lived in their territories along the north coast of British Columbia. Gitxaała laws (Ayaawk) and history (Adaawk) describe in precise detail the relationships of trust, honor, and respect that are appropriate for the well-being and continuance of the people and, as importantly, define the rights of ownership over land, sea, and resources within the territory. However, since the arrival of the first K̲'mksiwah (European) in Gitxaała territory in the late 1700s, new forms of resource extraction and expropriation have appeared that ignored, demeaned, and displaced the importance of the Ayaawk and Adaawk in managing the Territory of the Gitxaała. The new industries—forestry, fishing, and mining—relied almost completely upon K̲'mksiwah science for the purposes of management and regulation.

One of the major failures of mainstream resource management has been a lack of attention to the long-term implications of resource extraction practices. This has led to spectacular cases of resource depletion and habitat loss (see, for example, Rogers 1995). The local-level ecological knowledge held by people like the Gitxaała, rooted in an intimate and long-term involvement in local ecosystems, can be a crucial tool and source of knowledge for long-term sustainability and immediate resource conservation. During the last two decades the value of traditional ecological knowledge (TEK), such as the Ayaawk and Adaawk of the Gitxaała, has been increasingly recognized as important (Battiste and Youngblood Henderson 2000; Griffith 1999; Sillitoe 1998).

TEK has a strong potential to contribute to more effective and sustainable approaches to forest management in particular and natural resource management in general. A central strength (and weakness) to TEK is the fact that it is locally developed. Thus TEK can provide highly specific and detailed information crucial for the management of local ecosystems (Berkes 1999). It is important to recognize that this strength can also be a weakness in that locally developed knowledge is often difficult to translate beyond the immediate context. However, this should underscore the importance of documenting, recording, and analyzing TEK in detail in many separate locales. Ultimately, the value of TEK lies in the very fact that it is associated with a long history of resource use in a particular area and is therefore the cumulative and dynamic product of many generations of experience and practice (Berkes 1999; Menzies this volume). It is this aspect of TEK that is best able to provide alternatives to the dominant models of resource management that are in fact relatively new, externally formulated, and rarely site-specific in the way that TEK is.

Despite the growing awareness of the importance of TEK for natural resource management, the current regulations and practices in many regimes still do not provide effective formal mechanisms for the integration of TEK into active management. Beyond limited mechanisms regarding consultative processes with First Nations, for example, regarding cultural heritage (culturally modified trees, burial sites, and former village or camps sites), the knowledge inherent in the Ayaawk and Adaawk is still largely ignored by the dominant models of resource management.

This collection aims to demonstrate, through case studies of local-level ecological knowledge and its application, the powerful benefits and lessons TEK can offer for sustaining ourselves within the context of our environment. This introduction sets the stage for the more specific case studies that follow by first describing the research project that gave impetus to this collection and then reviewing the key elements and aspects of TEK. Although the separate chapters in this volume have their genesis in a variety of different projects, their authors share a recognition that local peoples who rely upon harvesting fish, animals, and plants for their survival, such as the Gitxaała, have much to offer to K'mksiwah science.[1]

Forests for the Future: Scope and Objectives

On a recent trip to Prince Rupert, Menzies had an opportunity to speak with the former Liberal Party Member of the Legislative Assembly (MLA). Within the confines of the airport's lounge, the conversation turned to the nature of the work that had brought Menzies back to Prince Rupert. The MLA was a polite, if not completely committed, conversationalist, and it soon became apparent that his evaluation of the research project was not what might be called enthusiastic. Pausing momentarily as he listened to the boarding call, the MLA turned back to Menzies and asked the conversation-ending question: "So, what's in it for industry?"

The central objectives of the Forest for the Future project really has nothing to do with "industry"; at least nothing to do with increasing the short-term profits of the multinational resource extraction corporations that have been dragged kicking and screaming into acceptance, at a minimal level, of the value of Indigenous knowledge.[2] Nor does it offer any magical solutions for community economic development or any other form of get-rich-quick scheme that may inspire those members of our society who, when they look at a tree, only see its value as a commodity. This is not to deny the importance of making a living by working in the woods. It is, however, to highlight the limited vision of those who see value only in activities that generate immediate profits.

Forests for the Future included research and public education activities designed to facilitate the incorporation of core First Nations values into local sustainable forest management (http://www.ecoknow.ca). The project incorporated three central components:

1. applied research into local ecological knowledge
2. policy development and evaluation focused on developing methods for the incorporation of Aboriginal values, rights, and needs into sustainable forest management
3. public education activities designed to facilitate mutual respect, effective communication, and knowledge sharing between First Nations and other natural resource stakeholders.

The research and public education focus of the project was based in the traditional territories of the Tsimshian First Nation, which stretch north–south from the Nass River to Kitasoo/Klemtu, and west–east from the coast to Kitselas Canyon on the Skeena River. Within this territory, the Tsimshian village of Gitxaała was the key focal point of research regarding First Nations knowledge and forestry priorities. Although the project prioritized the development of sustainable Aboriginal communities, it is important to point out that the project results have critical implications beyond First Nations communities.

Following recent court decisions, such as *Delgamuukw v. British Columbia*, it is now clear that effective consultations with and involvement of First Nations is (and will continue to be) of critical importance for the economic and social well-being of all British Columbians, Aboriginal and non-Aboriginal alike. Effective and locally based consultative processes are key ingredients of sustainable forest practices.

Traditional/Indigenous Ecological Knowledge

The relationships between Indigenous peoples and the environment have always been of interest to academics. There is a long history of studying Indigenous land-based practices and traditions. However, during the last few decades, these practices and traditions have become of increasing interest as a source of wisdom about sustainable resource use and environmental conservation. As the disastrous environmental impacts of capitalist industrial development and the shortcomings of contemporary resource management and conservation efforts have become understood, alternative practices and perspectives have been actively sought. The Brundtland Commission report emphasized the potential of Indigenous or traditional knowledges to provide insight for the conservation of biodiversity. Researchers and planners have since focused on the applications of traditional ecological knowledge (TEK) in contemporary environmental and resource management scenarios.

The birth of TEK as a major research focus and resource management tool is related to the attempted shift to an ecosystem-based management approach. Contemporary resource management has, until recent efforts, been guilty of isolating resources and species in both development and conservation planning. Fisheries management, for example, has tended to operate on a species-by-species basis, which has been criticized for overlooking the links between species in terms of habitat and food competition, predatory relationships, and so forth. Initiatives to conserve one type of fish can result in negative impacts on the health of other species. Forestry practices have tended to focus on trees and to ignore impacts on nontimber forest resources, watersheds, and aquatic species.

Recent efforts to conserve biodiversity and to manage based on the health of entire ecosystems have led to the new valuation of TEK. This emphasis on TEK is based on the understanding that traditional Indigenous economies have tended to involve the simultaneous and proximal use of multiple resources on a subsistence basis, rather than the intensive, isolated, single resource use that characterizes industrial capitalist economies. In other words, the way that Indigenous people live off the land often means that they need to understand the way that the different plants and animals interrelate, how the ecosystem works as a whole, and how they can use that system to sustain themselves. This type of small-scale yet system-wide understanding is the approach that resource managers are turning to in order to better manage natural resources and the environment as a whole.

During the last decade, social scientists, biological scientists, and resource managers in Canada have paid more and more attention to what First Nations know about the ecology of their traditional territories. Having lived in these territories for millennia, and having used the local resources into the present time, First Nations communities have a well-developed understanding of the local environment and their own impact on local resources. Traditional ecological knowledge can complement, supplement, and guide biological science and resource management. TEK can provide both the appropriate questions to ask about natural resources and ecosystems and the missing answers to some existing questions. Furthermore, TEK can provide the appropriate structure for sustainable local resource management.

Traditional laws, harvesting patterns, and stewardship roles can provide the most suitable frameworks for territorial resource use.

This being said, it is also imperative that we do not overcompensate and accept unquestioningly the content of TEK. As discussed below (see Butler, Menzies this volume) TEK does not simply accumulate in an unproblematic fashion. As with all systems of knowledge, TEK grows in spits and spurts. It degrades, changes, and transforms, and ultimately its integrity is dynamically linked to wider social and economic processes. The ability to learn from TEK and to apply its lessons in the contemporary world necessitates that we honestly consider the context within which TEK is produced and maintained. To ignore this context benefits neither local resource users nor contemporary resource managers.

Definitions and Attributes of TEK

Traditional ecological knowledge is the term used to describe the knowledge and beliefs that Indigenous peoples hold of their environments that is handed down through the generations. Jameson Brant, a Mohawk, has described Indigenous knowledge as "A body of information about the interconnected elements of the natural environment which traditional Indigenous people have been taught, from generation to generation, to respect and give thanks for" (in Bombay 1996).

Fikret Berkes has broadly defined Indigenous knowledge (IK) as the local knowledge held by Indigenous peoples, and he suggests the TEK is a subset of IK. TEK is the ecological part of IK, the land-based, practical knowledge of species, and the beliefs regarding human interaction with the ecosystem (Berkes 1999).

In resource management scenarios, TEK is often placed in opposition to Western science, particularly biology. Comparing TEK and science in such a way tends to oversimplify and emphasize the differences between these two ways of seeing the world. This can make them appear incompatible and is therefore somewhat unproductive. Such comparisons can also mask over important points of similarity and commonality such as the fact that the underling principles of TEK and science rely upon similar principles of observations.

Drawing upon the previous several decades of TEK-related research, the following attributes can be said to typically describe the central definition of TEK: cumulative and long-term, dynamic, historical, local, holistic, embedded, and moral and spiritual. Each of these attributes is discussed below in greater detail.

Cumulative and long-term: TEK is an ever-growing body of knowledge that has been developed over multiple generations. TEK expands and contracts as each passing generation's experience is compared to the current conditions and past experiences. TEK is often understood as an attribute of communities with long histories of resource use in a particular area.

TEK, as a specifically Indigenous form of knowledge, is often differentiated from what might be thought of as a more inclusive category, local ecological knowledge (LEK; see McGoodwin, Griffith this volume). Many different communities have developed detailed knowledge about the environment around them, such as non-Aboriginal fishing communities in the maritime provinces of Canada. *Traditional* knowledge, however, is generally associated with Indigenous communities or those with several centuries of accumulated knowledge. In this collection TEK is used to refer specifically to Indigenous knowledge and to LEK when we are referring to the more inclusive set of knowledges rooted in local practices.

Dynamic: While the term *traditional* ecological knowledge emphasizes continuity and long-term practices, it is important to note that this does not mean that it is static and unchanging. TEK is rooted in, and informed by, a traditional or customary lifestyle, but it adapts to change and incorporates contemporary information and technology. New information is continually added and old information deleted as the environment is transformed, as weather patterns shift, or as species are wiped out or introduced. One generation may have knowledge of how to hunt with traps; the next generation may translate this knowledge into how to hunt with guns (see Menzies this volume). Non-Indigenous knowledge can be incorporated into TEK, thus expanding its scope (Ruddle 1994).

TEK may be revised daily and seasonally through the annual cycle of activities (Scientific Panel for Sustainable Forest Practices in Clayoquot Sound

1994); thus each season of resource use increases the depth and scope of the knowledge. TEK is not just a knowledge of the past, but also a knowledge of the present.

There are some academic discussions about the loss or "erosion" of TEK as Indigenous communities become more integrated into regional or national economies. It is important to differentiate between situations where a community's TEK is adapting to new environmental and economic conditions, and where TEK is being lost due to a disruption of transmission or population loss. Just because land use activities have changed or decreased does not necessarily mean that a community's TEK is deteriorating.

That said, the emphasis on the importance of elders' knowledge in First Nations communities is valid. Elders often have different knowledge than the younger generations within a community, and 20th-century Canadian Aboriginal policies have disrupted cultural transmission. It is therefore important to many communities to document their elders' TEK, and many First Nations have made this a research priority. It is important to emphasize, however, that younger First Nations people also have TEK that can be extremely important for sustainable resource management.

Historical: It is because TEK is cumulative and dynamic that it provides a historical understanding of environmental change. First Nations knowledge, for example, predates European contact and thus provides a multigenerational perspective on the environmental impacts of colonialism and industrial development. In this sense TEK can be understood as incorporating knowledge of environmental changes since European arrival. However, this is not meant to deny or ignore the reality that just as new information or cultural understanding emerges, some knowledge or information will also be disregarded, lost, or ignored (see Menzies this volume). Nonetheless, Indigenous experiences, as expressed through TEK, have the potential to give us a picture of the rapid transformations of the landscape and natural resources since colonial settlement and also a potential baseline indicator that predates much scientific study.

On the north coast of British Columbia, experience of a precontact environment is only a few generations past. This knowledge is extremely valuable in identifying pre-industrial levels of species abundance, impacts of industrial pollution, and impacts of newly introduced resource-extraction technologies. For example, the difference between an elder's fishing experiences and a young person's fishing experiences can provide insight into environmental change.

Local: TEK is locally developed and provides highly specific and detailed information about areas of traditional resource use. TEK provides an intimate understanding of an area that other forms of research and experimentation cannot match. However, the specificity of TEK has the potential to limit its broad application and requires two basic responses: (1) that in-depth TEK documentation be done for every ecosystem, and, perhaps more importantly, (2) that the ethnographically well-documented motifs of animals as gifts, animal masters, and so on among hunting peoples be understood in their paradigmatic function as an epistemologically rigorous, though alternative, knowledge system to science. All this being said, it is important to also recognize the strong underlying points of similarity between natural science and local ecological knowledge systems in terms of the process of observation, inference, verification, and predication that is common to both modes of apprehending the ecological systems within which human beings live.

Holistic: Traditional knowledge has been described as holistic, meaning that all elements are viewed as interconnected and cannot be understood in isolation. As discussed above, a holistic perspective has been missing from resource management, and efforts are now being made to understand the interrelatedness of species and their environments.

Embedded: TEK is part of a particular cultural context. It is specific not only to an ecosystem, but also to a way of understanding the world. Generalizations about TEK focus on the experience of Aboriginality, the continuity and intimacy of land use, an Indigenous conservationist ethic, and a spiritual connection to the land. It is important to emphasize that there are many traditional knowledges, each one attached to a different Aboriginal culture. A community's TEK is embedded in the matrix of its unique local culture, history, and traditions. It is thus possible to talk about Gitxaała TEK, Tsimshian TEK, and, more generally, Indigenous knowledge.

It is difficult to interpret and use TEK without understanding its cultural context. Practical knowledge of where to find and how to process resources cannot be separated from the traditional structures of territory and resource ownership, cultural rules regarding resource use and waste, and even issues such as the traditional gendered division of labor within a community. Furthermore, most Aboriginal discussions of TEK insist that this practical knowledge derives from and reflects a spiritual relationship with the land and resources.

Moral and spiritual: In many Indigenous cultures, TEK is grounded in a spiritual and reciprocal relationship between the people and their environment. The natural world is often understood as sentient and proactive and infused with spirit. Thus, there are right ways and wrong ways to relate to and interact with the environment (Clayoquot Sound Scientific Panel 1995). Practices are governed by not just a principle of sustainability for survival's sake, but by a moral sanction against waste or greed. Much of the objective knowledge content of Indigenous peoples is framed within these motifs, which, as discussed above under *Local*, can be understood as providing the epistemological (as well as ontological) foundation for Indigenous "science" or knowledge.

TEK Research Issues

Building upon the central attributes of TEK as described above, the following critical issues in terms of the documentation and interpretation of TEK can be noted: cultural triage, decontextualization and distillation of political influences, evaluation of TEK, and differentiation of TEK. Each of these issues plays a critical role in determining the (im)possibility of deploying TEK in contemporary contexts.

Cultural triage: In contemporary contexts, TEK research and more general data regarding subsistence practices are used to identify lands that must be preserved from development in order to protect culturally important resources. This process, however, tends to open up other areas to development and to potential environmental disruption. Although a First Nation may express a holistic conservation position (i.e., all the resources and areas are important), they are often forced to choose between areas of their traditional territory in a way that inevitably results in loss. Stoffle and Evans refer to this process as "cultural triage" (1990). Triage refers to the screening of medical patients to determine their priority for treatments; when not all can be saved, the choice is made to treat those with the greatest chance for survival, and they are ranked according to immediacy of need.

Indigenous communities face cultural triage: "a forced choice situation in which an ethnic group is faced with the decision to rank in importance cultural resources that could be impacted by a proposed development" (Stoffle and Evans 19990:95). This choice preserves some resources but puts others at risk. This form of triage forces an unnatural ranking of species, areas, and heritage sites.

It is crucial that TEK research that contributes to development planning consider both the approaches of holistic conservation and cultural triage. These two positions should be factored into the methodological framework so that participants have the opportunity to emphasize the importance of all resources, while also prioritizing areas and resources if development threatens traditional territory (see Stoffle and Evans for a full discussion of the issues surrounding these two positions).

Decontextualization and distillation: Paul Nadasdy warns that the artifacts of TEK research often possess none of the characteristics that such studies use to define TEK in the first place. During the research process TEK is "distilled" into a product that is easily integrated into the Western resource management system. Although TEK is defined as holistic, oral, qualitative, and intuitive, the research results tend to be categorized, written, quantitative, and analytical (Nadasdy 1999:9; see also Nadasdy this volume). The reports from TEK research are thus often more like scientific reports and remove the traditional knowledge from cultural and ecological context.

Thus a danger of TEK research is that it can simply make TEK a tool of Western science, rather than a complementary approach to resource management. The wisdom of community members is translated into facts and figures that a biologist can use. Furthermore, case studies of several co-management boards suggest that First Nations participants do not feel that their knowledge is contributing to the research agenda (Nadasdy 1999). Community research priorities are not addressed, but community TEK is expected to be provided in order to benefit scientific research projects.

It is critical that TEK research reflect community goals and priorities, and that TEK reports reflect the way that information is transmitted within the community. TEK should not be translated, distilled, or abridged in order to make it fit predetermined, external data requirements.

Political influences: It is critical to understand the political context of TEK expression and use. The expression of TEK is often part of a movement toward political sovereignty and greater control over natural resources. The highly politicized context of the current struggle over Aboriginal rights and title can influence TEK research in a number of ways.

Despite the fact that current TEK research and documentation may contribute positively to a First Nation's land and resource claims, or might increase the community's involvement in resource management, community members might be reluctant to have their knowledge recorded. Some communities have suffered further loss of resource control by participating in research that records their traditional harvest areas and processing methods. Furthermore, traditional structures of resource stewardship and ownership often influence who is able to use and even talk about specific areas. It is extremely important that researchers understand these concerns and these traditional censures when trying to document the area and extent of particular resource utilization. Individuals may not mention the most important areas where they harvest food in order to preserve those areas. Alternately, an individual who is considered a community expert may not give information on certain areas because they personally do not have the right to publicly discuss that territory. A younger person may want to check their contribution with an elder, before having it recorded.

These limitations, if not comprehended by the researcher, can result in areas of prime importance for subsistence being left out of maps and other documents identifying key resource use areas. This is of great concern if the research is expected to prioritize land use patterns and identify areas open for alternative development. Community control of the research combined with the recruitment of community-based researchers will alleviate most of these issues.

Evaluating TEK: Traditional knowledge provides its traditional users with a practical understanding of their environment and the resources that they use. When TEK is being used by a First Nation to inform its conservation and development planning, this body of knowledge has to be gathered from many individuals and sources. Facts about and relationships between species need to be cross-checked between community participants and against other sources. When TEK is used as a basis for contemporary resource management, it must be validated. This validation should be community-based and rigorous.

Information from TEK interviews needs to be considered in light of each individual's personal history and territorial scope of resource use. What areas do they know about; what years did they spend actively using those territories? Information from an elder about salmon fishing at a particular creek is extremely important; however, if the elder has not fished there for two decades, it is necessary to find a younger person who has fished there recently in order understand the health of that run of fish. If the elder fished there seven days a week, but his son was limited to fishing two days a week, their information regarding the fish must be considered in light of these different practices. If one used a beach seine and the other a gillnet, that information must be used to interpret their estimates of salmon abundance. If there is no community member fishing there currently, perhaps commercial fishing records can provide some insight. Similarly, archaeological records might assist in extending the temporal scope of the data about fish in that creek.

Chippewa law professor John Borrows emphasizes that Indigenous knowledge is important, but not perfect, and many sources must be consulted in environmental planning (1997). Borrows and other researchers suggest that the disruption of Aboriginal land use by European colonization and the subsequent disenfranchisement of First Nations from their land have resulted in fragmented TEK that must be pooled with other information sources and evaluated in light of the limitations on Aboriginal resource access since contact.

Differentiation of TEK: Traditional knowledge is not homogeneous even within a small community. People in different positions know different things about resources and the environment. Men and women, elders and young people, have different knowledge. When researching TEK it is important to understand the many ways that knowledge might be differentiated within the community. Researchers will thus have to talk to many different types of people in order to fully document the TEK held in the community.

Putting Words into Action

Over the course of the Forests for the Future project we have attempted to connect local knowledge of the environment and the historical patterns of its use to more appropriate models of resource management in which local peoples take a significant role. As part of our mandate a research workshop was held in Prince Rupert January 31–February 2, 2002. Participants in the workshop included the authors of the chapters included in this collection, community-based researchers from Kitkatla, and members of the general public in Prince Rupert.

The authors of the following chapters and other participants in the workshop bring together a wealth of practical experience in researching, teaching, and applying local-level ecological knowledge in real-time contexts. The research and applied contexts within which these authors have worked include ethnobotany, wildlife management, forestry, and fisheries. The people whose knowledge is drawn upon in the following chapters are from the Indigenous nations of the Tsimshian (Gitxaała and Gitga'at), Nisga'a, Gitsxan, Kluane, and Sto:lo peoples and non-Indigenous communities in the Yukon, northwestern British Columbia, North Carolina, New England, and Newfoundland. In all of these cases the fundamental point of similarity lies in the close connection between local resources users and the environment in which they live and on which they rely for their daily life.

The chapters in this collection are organized in the following manner. The first part of the book consists of case studies that root the discussion of TEK within specific practices of Indigenous peoples of the Northwest Coast. The chapters by Steve J. Langdon and Kimberly Linkous Brown are concerned with the ecological soundness of traditional Indigenous fishing gear. Langdon describes the ingenious traditional methods of the Tlingit for harvesting salmon by use of tidal drift and stone weirs. Here we can see how this approach to harvesting salmon relies upon a local cultural explanatory framework that combines detailed ecological knowledge of specific fishing sites with a cosmological explanation of fish behavior in which the fish turn downstream and "give themselves" to the fishers. Brown's chapter examines how traditional fishing techniques are being adapted by contemporary Indigenous fishers within the context of the modern industrial fishery. In this chapter we can see revealed the manner by which historical practices merge with contemporary socioeconomic conditions. Nancy J. Turner and Helen Clifton's chapter on Gitga'at seaweed harvesting details the practices and knowledge involved in the harvesting and processing of a critically important local food. Charles R. Menzies explores the ways in which wider economic changes interact with local knowledge in ways that underscore the dynamic nature of TEK. In his chapter the argument is made that TEK does not simply accumulate over time but that it is intimately entwined with the subsistence and livelihood practices of a people.

The second part of this collection details the specific obstacles and opportunities involved in attempts to deploy local ecological knowledge in resource management regimes. Caroline Butler reminds us that local Indigenous knowledge must be located within its historical and political economic contexts. Paul Nadasdy argues against TEK researchers' focus on the "technical" problems of integration and instead argues that the political process of integration is as important, if not more important, than the focuses on technical obstacles to integrating local-level knowledge in resource management regimes. The chapters by David Griffith and James R. McGoodwin engage these issues from the vantage point of non-Indigenous coastal communities. Griffith, drawing upon contemporary and historical data from North Carolina, explores the ways in which the economic and political contexts within which live resource-dependent communities are critical in generating local ecological knowledge. McGoodwin's chapter details the specific prospects and problems of deploying local-level knowledge by reference to his and other researchers work in fisheries-dependent communities.

The concluding part of this collection explores the ways in which Indigenous knowledge can be deployed in the education of public school teachers (Gloria Snively) and the ways by which Indigenous knowledge is practiced and transmitted among peoples of the Northwest Coast of North America (Snively, John Corsiglia). Here we are reminded that in our quest to integrate local ecological knowledge and the "science" of natural resource management we must be cognizant of the methods by which local-level knowledge is transmitted and taught.

Underlying and connecting the substantive issues discussed in this collection is a concern with putting words into action. It is not enough to simply describe local ecological knowledge or to dissect it. Rather, the sorry state of K'mksiwah science and its track record over the past two hundred years in this region of North America clearly demonstrates the error of ignoring the Ayaawk and Adaawk of the Gitxaała and other Indigenous peoples. While few—whether First Nations or K'mksiwah—would argue for a complete return to the old ways, it is important to highlight the wisdom of traditional knowledge and its value in contributing to solving our contemporary ecological problems. While the authors gathered here differ in emphasis, theoretical orientation, and substantive case studies, we are united in our desire to integrate local ecological knowledge within contemporary natural resource management as an avenue toward a truly sustainable future.

Notes

1. The Forests for the Future project, as described in the next section, "Forests for the Future: Scope and Objectives," combines research with community extension and public education. As part of our public education mandate a special research workshop was held in Prince Rupert, British Columbia, Canada, in early February 2002. The chapters included in this volume were written expressly for the workshop (Turner and Clifton, Nadasdy, Griffith, McGoodwin, Corsiglia) or by project team members as part of the project research (Brown, Menzies, and Butler), or they were specifically solicited for this volume (Langdon, Snively). The task assigned to each contributor was to draw upon his or her particular expertise in local ecological knowledge research and prepare a chapter that would be useful for community-based researchers and managers whose community futures lay with sustainable relationships with natural resource harvesting. Specifically, contributors were asked to explore the manner by which resource dependent communities (defined broadly) are attempting to organize their survival (or not, as the case may be) in the

present moment. As part of this discussion contributors were invited to reflect on the importance of local forms of ecological and economic knowledge in charting new ways toward community viability by paying particular attention to the appropriateness of integrating traditional or local forms of knowledge with standard resource management models.

2. Over the past several decades a series of Supreme Court of Canada legal decisions has slowly forced large-scale resource companies and the province of British Columbia to come to terms with First Nations' rights and, in so doing, has placed the local ecological knowledge of Indigenous peoples more and more to the forefront of resource management and development. These legal decisions have combined with a growing ecology movement that—rightly or wrongly—has identified Indigenous peoples as a potential "green salvation." Taken together, these two social forces have propelled the issue of tek on to the agenda of multinationals whose primary interest is to maintain their control over and access to precious natural resources by nearly any means necessary.

I

Indigenous Practices and Natural Resources

1. Tidal Pulse Fishing

Selective Traditional Tlingit Salmon Fishing
Techniques on the West Coast of the
Prince of Wales Archipelago

Steve J. Langdon

The French explorer Jean Philippe La Perouse sailed the frigate *Astrolabe* into Lituya Bay on July 3, 1786. Northern southeast Alaska was in the final throes of the Little Ice Age at the time, and the glacial field a mere twenty miles to the east flowed down Sit'eeti G̲eeyi almost completely crossing Icy Strait.[1] La Perouse's arrival coincided with the annual Huna Tlingit sockeye (*Onchorynchus nerka*) salmon harvests from the short, small streams located in their territory on the outer coast from the west coast of Yakobi Island north past Cape Spencer to just beyond Lituya Bay (de Laguna 1972; Goldschmidt and Haas 1998).[2] La Perouse's account provides the first European description (limited as it is) of the weirs, traps, and gaff hooks used by the Tlingit to capture salmon, which his crew observed in operation at the Huagin River, just north of Lituya Bay.

There are several striking aspects to the La Perouse account as it relates to patterns of Tlingit salmon harvesting methods and the abundance of salmon runs they sustained through time. Recent historical experience with salmon productivity indicates that cooler "regimes" of ocean and ambient temperature in the eastern North Pacific Ocean reduce salmonid abundance in southeastern Alaska (Salmon 1997). A notable example of this phenomenon occurred in the late 1960s and early 1970s when southeast Alaskan salmon harvests were at the lowest levels since harvest records of the commercial industry began in the late 1800s. The first striking aspect of La Perouse's experience is that despite the decidedly cooler conditions (although there may have been some warming by the mid-1780s) at the time of his arrival, the French explorer regarded the quantities of salmon available in the streams as "so abundant" that, in addition to eating their fill of fresh fish while in the area, "each ship salted two casks" (de Laguna 1972:387). This is striking because despite the cooler regime, at a minimum there was a healthy return of fish, and the Tlingits apparently were quite comfortable allowing the French to take a sizable number of salmon for their own use.

The second striking aspect of La Perouse's observation is that the Tlingit were using sophisticated mass harvesting techniques on numerous streams in the vicinity, which according to oral traditions had been going on for a minimum of several generations and likely for considerably longer (de Laguna 1972). The upshot of this is that healthy runs of fish were returning to the streams in conjunction with these sophisticated technologies at a time when it is likely that salmon abundance was less than observed at the beginning of the commercial era a century later (Hewes 1973).

A defensible inference from these observations is that Tlingit methods for salmon harvesting were at a minimum not damaging salmon abundance and were likely designed to ensure adequate escapement to the spawning grounds. The premise of this chapter is that Tlingit techniques were selectively harvesting salmon stocks in a manner that ensured the survival of a sufficient number of spawners to assure a continuing supply in the future. The techniques that are described below are based primarily on the observation of the remains of salmon-harvesting structures from the west coast of the Prince of Wales Island along with a limited amount of oral tradition about their functioning. The central premise of the observed technologies is to harvest salmon below high tide in the estuaries located at the entrance to the spawning stream. A further premise of the Tlingit methodologies is to catch salmon using the pulsing flood and ebb of the tide to bring the fish to the harvesting technology. By using these estuarine techniques that harvested on the ebb, the Tlingit ensured that salmon schools moving upstream at full tidal flood had unimpeded access to their spawning grounds.

Background

Fisheries resources were the mainstay of the coastal Alaskan Tlingit at the time of contact with Europeans in the late 18th century. The temperate rainforest of southeast Alaska, which receives well in excess of 100 inches of rain in most years, has thousands of streams and rivers inhabited by salmon that provided the foundation of the Tlingit economy (Langdon 1977). The sophisticated culture the Europeans found in the 1770s included substantial permanent winter houses, stratified social relations, far-ranging trading capabilities, sophisticated artistry, elaborate military equipment and fortifications, and religious beliefs based on mutual respect and reciprocity between human persons and the other nonhuman (fish, animal, bird) persons with whom they co-occupied the environment (Langdon 1997).

This elaborate culture was built on sophisticated systems of salmon harvest, processing, and storage that produced surpluses, in most years, on which the Tlingit subsisted and celebrated during the winter months. A wide variety of techniques for capturing salmon were developed as conditions in different locales required alternative methods. For example, in the rocky shallows of the Chilkoot River, the Chilkoot Tlingit channeled the stream through construction of rock walls running parallel to the river. At the upstream head of these short (less than 20-foot) channels, the Chilkoot men erected small wooden platforms on which a single man stood and used a gaff hook to capture the salmon that traveled up the artificial channel. By contrast, the Yakutat Tlingit of the Lost River collectively constructed a massive weir and large boxlike fish trap that required a substantial labor force to construct and operate them and an authority (the clan head) to distribute the substantial catch that resulted from its operation (de Laguna 1972:387). For the Hutsnuwu (Angoon) Tlingit of Admiralty Island in the central region of southeast Alaska, de Laguna (1960) describes several techniques such as the wooden stake weirs sometimes accompanied by cylindrical basket fish traps (perhaps similar to those described by La Perouse) and stone walls in the intertidal zone.

At the southern extremity of Tlingit territory, on the west coast of Prince of Wales Island, were originally two groups (Klawakkwan and Henyakwan), who utilized a wide variety of techniques noteworthy for their emphasis on estuarine, intertidal harvesting of salmon. Beginning in 1973, I began investigating a related set of questions pertaining to the process whereby the Klawock Tlingit had transitioned from traditional techniques to the contemporary commercial salmon fishery. Initially, my focus was on the historic period from the beginning of the commercial era of salmon salting and canning in 1878 to the current era (Langdon 1977). However, stimulated by de Laguna's (1960:116) description of intertidal semicircular stone walls, I began looking for evidences of these structures, wondering if any had survived into the present century. Finally, one day, traveling south of Klawock in Trocadero Bay, we landed our skiff at low tide near a small stream where my Tlingit friend offhandedly pointed to an intertidal semicircular stone wall, noting in passing that it had been used to catch salmon by his ancestors. The nature of these structures and their use intrigued me, so much so that I determined to return to the area and conduct additional research on their distribution, construction, use, and relationship to villages, clans, and house groups. The question of their antiquity also surfaced.

In the mid-1980s I was able to return to the west coast of Prince of Wales Island and begin a systematic inventory of the central coastline to the north and south of the contemporary village of Klawock. The area surveyed includes a substantial archipelago that separates Prince of Wales Island proper from the North Pacific Ocean. The surveyed area extends from St. Philip's Island to the north to the southeastern point of Suemez Island to the south. A full report of the 1985 survey season accompanied by photos of the various identified sites can be found in Langdon, Reger, and Wooley (1986).

Research has continued since that initial survey, in particular on the site known as Little Salt Lake, where extensive intertidal evidence of weir structures was first identified in 1986 (Langdon, Reger, and Campbell 1993). Finally, the estuary and course of the Klawock River, the most productive river on the west coast of Prince of Wales Island, have been given careful attention due to the river's significance traditionally as a source of salmon and due to its possible vulnerability. The information reported here on the Klawock River has not appeared in previous publications.

Salmon Species and Characteristics

Before we explore the nature of the Prince of Wales Tlingit technologies, a description of the salmon species, their characteristics, and their environments is important to provide the context for relating the harvesting practices to the behaviors and characteristics of the species to which they were oriented.

Salmon species and the riverine systems that support them vary significantly (Schalk 1977; Langdon 1979). The five species of Pacific salmon in southeast Alaska are known colloquially as king (*Oncorhynchus tschawytscha*), coho (silver; *O. kisutch*), sockeye (red; *O. nerka*), pink (humpy; *O. gorbuscha*), and dog (chum; *O. keta*). These species vary in their biological characteristics such as average size, diet, number of eggs per spawner, spawning preferences, amount of time spent in freshwater and salt water, smolt habitat preferences, and age at maturation. These variations are clearly coded in the technologies, preferences, processing practices, and concepts of the Tlingit people of the Prince of Wales Archipelago.

Salmon streams differ in several important ways including 1) species present, 2) number of species, 3) abundance by species, 4) timing of returns of different species, and 5) stability of annual return by species. Larger streams with longer drainage systems and higher volumes of flow support more salmon and more species of salmon. The streams of the Prince of Wales Archipelago can be divided into three tiers based on species and abundance (Langdon 1979). The most numerous are smaller streams in which escapements of pink and dog salmon have averaged 2,000 for each species over a 30-year period. The second tier is composed of moderate-sized streams that support pink, dog, and silver salmon; pink and dog escapements to these streams have averaged between 2,000 and 10,000 fish annually over the 30-year period. The third tier consists of large three or four species systems with average pink salmon escapements in excess of 10,000 and sizable runs of all other species. All of these larger systems are located on Prince of Wales Island proper, where drainages are substantially longer. By contrast, the streams on the smaller islands of the archipelago support much fewer numbers of fish. The Klawock River is the largest system on the island;

escapements of over 1,000,000 salmon to this system were recorded in the 1930s (Langdon 1977).

King salmon, which are found feeding in the saltwater channels and bays, do not spawn in any streams in the Prince of Wales Archipelago so further consideration of their use by the Prince of Wales Tlingit will not be addressed in this chapter. Sockeye salmon are distinctive in that they are found only in stream systems that include a freshwater lake, a critical habitat in the smolt stage of the sockeye lifecycle. Sockeye salmon are the most stable—that is, they show the lowest degree of variability in numbers returning from one year to the next and from one breeding cycle to the next. They also are the first species to return (beginning in late June) and sustain their runs over a longer period of time (through mid-August) than any of the other three species returning to the Prince of Wales Archipelago streams. However, they are found in relatively few streams and in significantly fewer numbers than the other three species. Despite their restricted and limited occurrence, Tlingit clans have almost universally identified sockeye salmon streams as their prime resource property (Goldschmidt and Haas 1946; Olson 1967). It is likely that the characteristics of early return, sustained return, and stability of return in conjunction with taste preference for the higher oil content of sockeye at the time they enter freshwater combined to make sockeye systems of prime value to the Tlingit.

Unlike sockeye, pink salmon and, to a slightly lesser degree, dog salmon are virtually ubiquitous in all freshwater systems, from the tiniest rivulet to the largest rivers, of the west coast of the Prince of Wales Archipelago. By far the most numerous species are pink salmon that are found in over 300 drainages in the Prince of Wales Archipelago. Although information is less comprehensive, coho salmon are also found in a substantial number of streams, but in fewer streams and lesser numbers than pink and dog salmon. The abundance of pink and dog salmon fluctuates enormously (higher degrees of variability year to year and breeding cycle to breeding cycle), they are more concentrated in their availability (fish return in a compressed time period, two to four weeks), and they are lower in nutritional value (caloric value of oil content) when they enter the freshwater streams to spawn.

Dog salmon are important because they are the last species to arrive, and their relatively low oil content makes them easier to dry or smoke for winter supplies. As a final note of possible significance to the discussion below is the fact that approximately 14 percent of pink salmon in southeast Alaska spawn in the gravel beds of the estuarine zone of the freshwater streams (Heard 1991:147). While dog salmon spawn in the intertidal zone of Prince William Sound in the central Gulf of Alaska, the evidence for similar behavior in the Prince of Wales Archipelago is spotty.

Prince of Wales Tlingit Oral Traditions
about Intertidal Rock Fishing Structures

In the 1980s Christine Edenso, a Klawock Tlingit elder of the L'eineidí (dog salmon) clan then in her nineties, described the structure and use of the intertidal stone fish structures as follows:

> I've observed in my younger days that . . . Tlingits used to trap fish at the mouth of the streams. If you go around today by the mouths of the old creek flats, you will see these rocks still piled up as they did in the old days. You will be able to see the outline of where they laid a bunch of rocks to form a wall. In that way, when the tide went out, the fish were trapped behind them and they were easier to catch then. They used to catch all the fish they needed as time went on. Some of the creeks were readily adaptable to this kind of fishing, and that was why they caught their fish by this method. The fish would go up to the mouth of the creeks at high tide. They would get behind the wall and would be trapped then the people would gaff them and pull up all the fish they needed right there.
>
> That was how they used to catch their fish. When you go along the beach . . . low tides, you can still see these places where they made these rock walls and traps and they are quite visible. They are the works of the people a long

> time ago. . . . You can see these rock enclosures all over
> Southeastern Alaska on the west coast, in the tidal flats
> . . . and at any place where there was a good number of peo-
> ple. . . . They used the network of fish traps to corral the
> fish momentarily while the tide was going out. They used
> to gather their fish in that way. (Edenso 1983:36)

In the summer of 2002, when discussing these structures, Tlingit elder Theodore Roberts recalled that in the fall of 1929, as a seven-year-old boy, he
had been taken to the intertidal stone fishing structures inside San Clemente Island and had participated in using them to catch dog salmon. On a
visit to the site in 2002 Roberts described how his grandfather, Fred Williams, had positioned him and the other grandchildren on the outer edge of
the inner trap. As the tide receded, Williams and several other accompanying adults stood in the stream and drove the salmon into the flat where the
trap was located. The children were told to throw small rocks in the water
as the fish approached the wall to keep them back. Roberts also remarked
that the walls were higher than at the time of the recent visit—he indicated they were approximately knee height in 1929.

In the summer of 2003, during interviews concerning traditional ecological knowledge about salmon, Klawock Tlingit elders described the intertidal stone structures as "baskets" and "dishes." The Tlingit term for the
semicircular, intertidal stone trap is *tekshu*.

Members of the Teikweidi (brown bear) clan were early Tlingit occu-
pants of the west coast of the Prince of Wales archipelago. Among their
oral traditions is an account of how they learned to build the intertidal
stone structures from the brown bear, the primary clan crest of the their
clan, by watching the bears fish at natural intertidal pools holding salmon (Salisbury 1962).

Traditional Intertidal Salmon Fishing by
the Prince of Wales Archipelago Tlingit

The field research identified two basic kinds of intertidal fishing structures
based on the materials utilized. The first type is constructed primarily of

1.1. Intertidal bilobed semicircular joined stone fish traps located near San Clemente Island. Tlingit elder Theodore Roberts explained to the author how his grandfather had directed dog and chum salmon fishing activities at this site in 1929. Photo by author.

stone, whereas the others are constructed primarily of wooden stakes. At two sites wood and stone materials were combined in a fishing structure.

These materials are used to construct two basic types of technologies that are here termed *weir* and *trap*. A weir is a linear obstruction or wall constructed to impede or direct the movement of salmon in some fashion. The weir assists in concentrating the salmon so that other devices can be used to catch them. A trap, in contrast, captures the salmon by drawing them into a structure from which they are unlikely to escape.

Stone structures. The intertidal weirs consist typically of a straight stone wall placed across an intertidal section of a stream channel, typically at a right angle to the freshwater flow. The stone weirs were found primarily in the intertidal zone of small streams on the outer islands of the archipelago. These weirs are typically less than 30 meters in length, and most consist of fewer than three layers of stone piled up. Local oral tradition states that tree branches were embedded between the stones of many of these structures to complete their functioning by creating a higher wall. Excavation

1.2. The shallow pools for holding salmon inside intertidal stone fish traps are memorialized by the dish holding three salmon at the bottom of this totem pole. The Kakoshittan clan pole also demonstrates their ownership of Sarkar River and Lake on northern Prince of Wales Island. A descendant replica of this pole was erected in the Klawock totem park in 2003. Courtesy of University of Washington Libraries, Special Collections, UW22306z.

in 1986 of deposited sediments behind one intertidal stone weir located on the east coast of San Fernando Island did indeed reveal a wooden stake that was subsequently dated to approximately A.D. 1050.

In no case did stone weirs of this type extend unbroken across the stream channel above mean high water. In all cases the stone walls extend into the intertidal flat on either side of the stream channel. This pattern of interrupted linearity may be the result of washout due to high volume, conscious gaps left in the weir for trap emplacement or conscious destruction to ensure the passage of salmon. One of the weirs identified was buried beneath approximately two meters of beach sand and gravel (Langdon, Reger, and Wooley 1986). This structure was identifiable only where the stream channel cut through the beach deposits, revealing the larger stone cobbles piled on top of each as is customarily found with intertidal stone weirs. Buried stone cobbles were found on both sides of the stream channel directly opposite each other. This site raises interesting questions about the burial of intertidal stone structures under present beach deposits as well as in upland areas where old beaches are now covered by forest.

Traps are by far the most ubiquitous intertidal stone fishing technology identified. Intertidal stone traps are stone walls constructed in semicircular or arced forms. Although the degree of the arc is normally not large, resulting in a relatively shallow form, several traps were found that had arcs approaching circular or elliptical shape, although all were open on the upland side. All but one was less than 180 degrees from one end of the feature to the other.

The traps identified were of two basic types. The *simple trap* consists of a single-arced stone wall. Approximately two-thirds of the sites in the central region of the archipelago in which a systematic survey was conducted consisted of a single simple trap. In general these traps consist of stone walls made up of two or three layers of irregular stone cobbles from about 6 inches to 24 inches in length stacked on each other. The single trap walls were usually continuous with no gaps as were found in the weirs. They are typically arced constructions, but a variation identified in one location resembles a check mark or the Nike symbol. The maximum circumference (length of trap from one end to the other) was 70 meters, and the minimum circumference was 28 meters. All of the traps except one were constructed so that they were open on the back to the forest, and most were located slightly above half-tide.

While most single traps are found slightly above present half-tide, there are several located near the present mean high-water mark. These constructions appear to be older based on the fact that although their arced form is apparent, there are breaks in the wall. These higher placements may be related to geological uplift in the area, perhaps quite localized, that has raised beaches over the past several thousand years. If this is true, then it is likely that traps high in the upper tidal range are older than those that appear just above present midtide.

All but one of the simple trap sites located in the survey area have been found in the intertidal zone in close proximity to a stream channel. In about two-thirds of the cases the trap does not intersect the stream channel, whereas in the other cases the trap either is bifurcated by the stream or intersects the stream channel at one end. The exception to the general pattern was a single trap located on the west side of Klawock Island that encloses a small cove into which flows a tiny rivulet unsuitable for spawning by salmon. This exceptional structure was found in the vicinity of the prolific Klawock River and likely was used to catch salmon on their way to that system.

The other typical trap configuration identified is the *joined trap*. A joined trap differs from a simple trap in that two (or conceivably more) traps are linked together by a shared section termed the stem. Approximately 10 percent of the fishing structure sites identified are joined traps.

In their basic construction and materials, joined traps are similar to simple traps. They differ from simple traps in that their circumference and area fished is larger. The stone fishing structure inside San Clemente Island described above by Mr. Roberts is dominated by a large joined trap (see figure 1.1). This large bi-lobed structure consists of two traps each approximately 110 meters in length, including the stem portion that bifurcates the joined trap. In the intertidal zone of another stream slightly to the north of San Clemente Island is a joined trap of approximately 80 meters length linked to a simple trap and several other features.

Like simple traps, joined traps are found intertidally in proximity to a stream. The two largest joined traps intersect the stream while a smaller joined trap does not intersect the present stream channel. In terms of their location relative to tidal range, the smallest trap is found completely within the present tidal range but above midtide. The stem of the intermediate trap extends to mean high water, but the two arc ends of the joined trap are only slightly above midtide. On the largest joined trap, the end of one trap and the shared stem extend above mean high water, virtually to tree line such that a small segment of the trap no longer is covered at high tide.

The largest of the joined traps is interesting for several additional reasons. It appears to have been slightly rebuilt at one time in the past to adjust to a change in stream channel. This is evidenced by an abrupt jog in the usually smoothly continuous arc of the segment closest to the stream channel about 10 meters from the stream's present course. The aerial view of the site shows the pattern of a previous stream channel precisely at the point of the jog in the trap. There also appear to be straight extensions for both the old and the new versions of the trap on the opposite side of the present stream channel. Another feature of one of the arced segments is a well-defined gap precisely at the center of the arc where ebbing waters are directed. Since the stream does not flow through this trap, the gap cannot be attributed to flood waters. It appears to have been consciously made by the users of the site to insert a trap to catch fish as they moved back out to the bay on the ebb tide.

An auxiliary feature identified in several traps was a depression, perhaps an excavated area, in the beach behind the wall 1–2 meters in diameter and 20–30 centimeters in depth. As the tide receded below the trap, salt water would be held in this depression, and fish would likely retreat to it, where they would be held live for a period of time. This feature would enhance the quality of the fish as they would remain alive until needed for processing rather than drying up on the exposed tidal flat. In addition, the fish would likely also be protected, to an extent, from predators such as mink and eagles. This feature is memorialized by a wooden dish holding three fish on a pole in the Klawock totem park (Garfield and Forrest 1948—see figure 1.2). An analogue to this feature found in the contemporary world is the Dungeness crab or lobster holding tank found in many seafood markets where the consumer can obtain maximally fresh products.

Four sites in the study area were identified where several stone weirs and traps were combined into a fish-harvesting system termed a *composite*. The most elaborate of these is located at Fern Point (discussed below), a peninsula jutting out off the east coast of San Fernando Island.

Another dramatic example of a composite site is located on the southeastern shore of Lulu Island in proximity to Arrecife Reef. This complex consists of a well-constructed simple trap with a gap at its lowest point. Extending from the north end of the arc is a stone weir that intercepts the intertidal channel of the small stream that empties into the channel at this point. The stone weir extends lineally beyond the stream for another 15 meters. While present at this site at shortly before half tide, I observed the tidal ebb from behind the trap flowing out of the narrow gap; if salmon had been in the ebb tide behind the trap and a wooden trap of some kind had been inserted in the gap, the fish would have been pushed into the structure. The opportunity to view the velocity of the ebb tide exiting from the trap gap demonstrated the operating principle of these structures quite clearly.

A site with multiple weirs, traps, and composites in close proximity is termed a *complex*. The most elaborate of the stone complexes encountered in the survey area is that located at Fern Point on San Fernando Island. A detailed discussion of this site is provided here, and its significance is more fully examined in the conclusion of the chapter. The Fern Point complex is located on the south side of a point that juts out eastward from San Fernando Island; it is located about eight miles southwest of the present Tlingit village of Klawock. For purposes of description, the site can be divided into eastern and western halves, each of which is oriented to an arm of a very small freshwater stream that spills onto the beach inside the point. The components of the eastern portion of the complex consist of a set of three weirs and the three single traps. The weirs are spaced on the intertidal stream arm, with a large (45-meter) trap in the upper tidal area located 80 meters west of a similar sized weir in the lower portion of the tidal range.

1.3. Intertidal semicircular trap located at Arrecife Point (Lulu Island) at half tide. Note the gap in the trap at its lowest point, where a circular basket trap could have been positioned. Photo by author.

In between is a smaller, 20-meter weir located in the lower portion of the tidal range, about 15 meters west of the lowest weir. The intertidal stream arm passes through each weir in turn on its descent to the ocean. Each of the three weirs has the customary opening through which the stream flows, and each creates a small pond behind it even though there is an outlet. These stone weirs displayed the greatest vertical height of any fishing structure identified, with the exception of the Arrecife Reef single trap, measuring 40 centimeters high in certain spots.

Two single traps are located on either side of the western-most weir. The one above it in the tidal range is small, being only 10 meters in circumference, whereas the one below in the lower portion of the tidal range is 30 meters in circumference. The third and largest trap (with a shallow, nearly linear arc) runs from east to west and has one end attached to the shoreward end of the eastern-most weir, creating an awkward, unbalanced complex structure. The western-most weir has a straight stone wall attached perpendicularly to it at its seaward end so it also qualifies as a complex structure. In fact, it might be thought of as two-sided box trap.

To the west on the other arm of the intertidal stream, traps rather than weirs are the prominent technology, with five of them located in proximity to each other. Located well up in the tidal range is the largest single trap found anywhere in the study area; forming nearly a closed circle (approximately 270 degrees—open in the back to the forest), this impressive stone construction measured 120 meters in circumference. Above it and on the west side of the intertidal stream is a small 10-meter trap. Seaward on the eastern side of the largest trap is a 44-meter trap, and immediately below it is another trap 48 meters in circumference. To the west of the latter trap and even lower in the tidal range is a large 105-meter structure, which extends to the west beyond the largest trap above it and completes the Fern Point complex.

Each of the four larger traps contains its own pool of water even at low tide, when they are completely exposed. Each of the larger traps is fed by freshwater from the western arm of the intertidal stream, which first enters the largest trap and then percolates down through the stone wall of the largest trap to subsequently fill the other three before eventually reaching the ocean. These traps have been constructed from the large boulders found in the intertidal area of Fern Point, and some of them may weigh in excess of several hundred pounds, indicating that a substantial, coordinated labor force must have been required for their construction.

The overall east–west extent of the Fern Point intertidal fishing complex is nearly 300 meters, while north–south (from shore to low water) it stretches nearly 100 meters. It is a marvelous accomplishment made even more impressive by an understanding of the intricate knowledge of salmon behavior held by the Tlingit who built it.

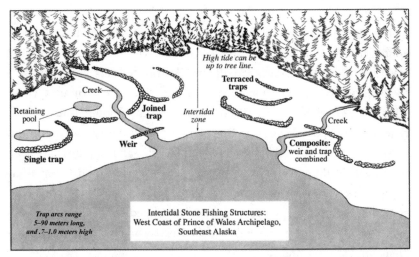

1.4. Forms of intertidal stone fish traps found on the west coast of the Prince of Wales Archipelago in southeast Alaska.

Wood Structures. The remains of a number of wood intertidal fishing structures were also found in the intertidal zone throughout the study area. All of these were found in the estuaries of the streams on Prince of Wales Island proper. Unlike the rocky beaches and intertidal zones of most of the outer island streams, Prince of Wales Island stream estuaries have more permeable substrates ranging from gravel and pebble composition to sand and silty mud. In the best cases, stumps from the wood stakes can be seen rising one or two inches from the surface and their alignments quickly identified. In most cases, stakes generally stick up less than two centimeters above the surface and have a diameter of two to six centimeters. However, in many cases, the entire original section of the stake from above the surface has disappeared and the only portion remaining is a buried section beneath the substrate. In some cases the stakes are extraordinarily well camouflaged and appear to have been precisely cut so as to be virtually undetectable from the estuarine substrate surface. Whether this was the result of human action or natural attrition is not clear. When identified in alignments, extraction of the stake stumps from the intertidal zone invariably revealed that the embedded ends had been carved into some kind of point to allow them to be more easily inserted.

Two sites where the stake remains are extensive are in Little Salt Lake, approximately two miles north of the Klawock River and the Klawock River estuary. Little Salt Lake is actually a well-protected small bay in front of the estuary of two small, short streams that flow into it from the east. These streams are of tier-two size and include small coho populations in addition to their pink and dog runs. Due to the extraordinary preservation and extensive remains found in the estuary, the Little Salt Lake sites have been intensively examined and portions mapped.[3] A variety of different alignments were created in Little Salt Lake by the *Klawakkwan* (or their predecessors) that began over 2,100 years ago and continued until at least 300 years ago. The alignments have been classified as pavements, weir alignments (dense and sparse), and pairs.

A *pavement* is a dense and wide aggregation of wood stakes—from several stakes in width up to two meters. There are three of these structures located in Little Salt Lake. Two of them are essentially linear and appear to act as weirs diverting or funneling salmon movement. One is 80 meters in length and does not intersect the mainstream channel, while the largest, and oldest, one is about 100 meters in length and may have extended across the intertidal stream channel. It is not clear why these alignments are as wide as they are. One hypothesis is that the width represents successive stages of rebuilding as the stakes required replacement. An alternate hypothesis is that is was both a walkway and weir that allowed the Tlingit to have firm footing on a soupy substrate to gaff or dip net incoming salmon.

The third pavement, however, differs from the other two. It is constructed in a semicircular configuration similar to the intertidal semicircular stone traps. One end runs nearly to tree line, while the other intersects and then parallels the intertidal stream channel for approximately 20 meters.

The *weirs* are classified as dense or sparse based on the distance between the stakes. Unlike the pavements, weirs consist of a single linear alignment of stakes. Dense weirs appear to act as diverting or obstructing walls in and of themselves. The sparse weirs are likely to have been the foundation or frame to which the historically observed lattice fences were attached. None of these lattice fences have been identified in Little Salt Lake. In one part of Little Salt Lake two dense weirs were arranged in the shape of a chevron with a gap at the apex, pointing away from the shoreline; it is quite likely that a wooden trap of some kind was placed in the aperture when the weir was in operation.

A final configuration of stakes has been labeled *pairs*. A pair consists of two stakes, typically relatively small in diameter, in close proximity to each other. Sets of these pairs have been spaced to form an alignment. The pairs are found in the silty, soupy mud of Little Salt Lake and usually have a flat stone associated with them. The stone is buried in the mud beside the pair. Pairs are separated by three to five meters typically and appear to have acted like the sparse weir in the firmer areas of Little Salt Lake in providing a framing foundation for lattice fences. One alignment of pairs is in a semi-circular traplike arrangement, while others are linear and act as weirs.

The totality of the alignments in the intertidal areas of Little Salt Lake look like an R and D center for Tlingit intertidal salmon-harvesting technologies. Virtually the entire bay has been brought into the productive process as row upon row of stakes were laid out at various times extending back to over 2,000 years ago. Some extend linearly up into grassy areas now above tidal influence. All of the structures are in the intertidal zone, and surveys of the courses of the two streams that enter into the bay have to date yielded no evidence of structural features associated with salmon harvesting.

The estuary of the Klawock River is also the scene of extensive intertidal wood stake constructions. Along the intertidal river channel are a series of islands whose presence and form are the result of deposition behind stake structures. In addition, there are several evident alignments in the estuary stream channel in which the structure of the stake configurations can still be clearly seen. The visible structure with the greatest integrity consists of over 350 stakes packed tightly together to form an impenetrable wall; they are placed in an asymmetrical V or check mark, with the point directed away from the river. The longer arm of the construction runs parallel to and is closest to the intertidal stream channel, while the shorter arm extends toward the shoreline at approximately a 45-degree angle. This construction has been dated to circa 750 B.P. This appears to be the type of structure that led to the deposition-based islands in areas of the estuary closer to the falls at the mouth of the Klawock River.

Approximately 50 meters south of the estuary is a contiguous lagoon area in which there are other types of stake alignments. In this zone, wood stakes were used to construct semicircular features that appear to have operated on principles similar to the intertidal semicircular traps of the outer islands. They are located in the midtidal range and open to the forest like the intertidal stone traps. Two of these traps, one higher and one lower in the tidal range, are connected by a canal, approximately 2 meters wide and 20 meters in length. The canal is created by two walls of stakes that funnel salmon back and forth between the water-holding traps when the tide is out. A stake from the canal has been dated to approximately 800 B.P. indicating that these wood stake semicircular intertidal traps were likely contemporaneous with the asymmetrical V structures associated with the estuarine stream channel of the Klawock River.

The Significance of Fern Point and Tlingit
Intertidal Salmon-Fishing Technologies

Fern Point is the most dramatic of the sites discussed in this chapter in its demonstration of the detailed understanding of salmon behavior and species requirements on which Tlingit intertidal fishing technologies were based. As described earlier, by far the most numerous species available to the Tlingit of the west coast of Prince of Wales Island are pink salmon that are able to spawn in many streams that in certain years are mere trickles. Dog salmon are the second most abundant species, spawning in nearly as many streams as pink salmon. But pink salmon and, to a lesser extent, dog salmon have a number of limitations for human use. Both species, especially pinks, return in a massive spurt of only two or three weeks duration that severely limits the ability of a Tlingit house group, the core production unit of Tlingit society, to process (smoke and dry) the catch for the winter. Pink salmon also deteriorate very rapidly, losing much of their nutritional value when they hit the freshwater lenses, or interface between salt and fresh water, of the bays and estuaries. It would be highly beneficial to have techniques to catch pinks before they reached their home streams, if possible. Finally, both pinks and dogs return in small quantities to a huge number of streams, which presents a difficult logistical problem since a single small stream cannot support a house group, but several combined probably could. Since the vast majority of the small streams do not provide enough pinks and dogs to provide a winter supply for a Tlingit house group, an efficient way had to be developed to take fish from a number of streams at the same time. Erecting lattice-fence weirs and traps in streams is a time-consuming and costly process, hardly warranted by the return to be obtained from the smaller streams.

Intertidal traps, primarily of the stone variety used in the outer islands, seem particularly well suited to overcome many of these obstacles to the use of pink salmon in the traditional period. First, stone intertidal traps could be used as *passive* fishing techniques that, if well designed, would not require constant monitoring or attention in order to catch fish.[4] The location of the stone semicircular traps in the intertidal zone ensured quick and easy access to them. Fishermen could arrive in canoes and quickly transfer the catch from the trap to the canoe. They could then move onto the next trap and eventually complete the circuit, returning the entire catch from several traps to a central processing camp. This could have provided a solution to the problem of small runs of salmon to many small streams for the traditional Prince of Wales Tlingit.

The Fern Point fishing complex reveals even greater sophistication in the understanding of salmon behavior and putting that knowledge to productive use in two striking ways. As already discussed, there is only a small stream at Fern Point, which is not reported to support salmon in either Forest Service or Alaska Department of Fish and Game records. The question arises, then, why was this elaborate complex constructed at this location?

Pink, dog, and sockeye salmon returning from the Pacific Ocean to their various natal streams form large migratory schools of stocks from many streams. As they proceed from the ocean, up the channels through the islands, stocks gradually separate and leave for their own streams. Thus the further one follows the migration of the fish back to the ocean, the larger the school of salmon that can be fished. This presents the possibility for larger and more efficient harvests if one can take catches from these massive schools rather than wait until each stock has branched off and reached its home stream. Fern Point is located on a major migratory route of salmon returning to approximately twenty-five streams in the vicinity to the east and northeast. The point juts out prominently into the ocean and tidal currents that, in conjunction with prevailing southeast winds, must often sweep large returning schools into the south side cove inside the point. The traditional Tlingit must have observed this pattern and decided to take advantage of it. The benefits of catching fish at Fern Point rather than waiting until they reach the streams include higher-quality fish, earlier harvests, and larger stores for the winter. Support for this thesis is provided by the fact that in the 20th century, a highly productive floating (white man's) fish trap last operated by the Columbia Wards cannery at Craig was located at Point Cuerbo, less than a half a mile south of Fern Point. The former superintendent of that cannery, Carl Aspelund, stated that the Pt. Cuerbo trap was the most productive trap on the west coast of Prince of Wales Island under his jurisdiction.

The second unique element of the Fern Point complex is the fact that the traps and weirs are structured to fish at different tidal ranges. A strong divergent pattern of tidal change characterizes the west coast of the Prince of Wales Island in that one high tide (15–18 feet) is substantially greater than the other high tide (8–12 feet). The traps and weirs are built at different levels in the tidal range, thus increasing the total amount of enclosed fishing area and ensuring that harvests can be made through all tidal conditions. Only certain locations are likely to have been productive enough to warrant this type of investment. Particularly on the western side of the Fern Point complex, water and fish not retained in the highest trap spill over into two additional tiers of traps in which the fish have the possibility of being caught. The visual effect is similar to that of the elegant terraced rice paddies that Southeast Asian people have developed to maximize the agricultural potential of their lands and efficiently use the available water—only at Fern Point the terraces were designed by the traditional Tlingit to optimize the amount of migrating salmon caught in their stone traps.

Conclusion

The traditional salmon-harvesting methods of the Prince of Wales Tlingit were ingenious, efficient, and, perhaps most significantly, selective in providing for sufficient escapement to maintain healthy runs even during the Little Ice Age when salmonid populations were likely at depressed levels. The abundance of pink and dog salmon streams required the development of intertidal and estuarine methods to optimize harvests and make use of multiple small stream systems. However, these same intertidal and estuarine methods were also utilized on the larger systems, such as the Klawock River, that supported more species and greater runs.

Stone and wood materials were combined to produce semicircular traps and weirs to funnel and capture salmon. Three important principles are apparent in the operations of these devices that ensured they would capture only a portion of the salmon presenting themselves at the structures. By capturing only a portion of the run, escapement for spawning purposes was ensured.

The first principle was that the structures were located at approximately half tide in the intertidal zone. Whether constructed of stones or wooden stakes, this positioning ensured that at high tide, the structures were completely below water—that is, no portion of them stuck up above water to obstruct or deflect the salmon. Virtually all of the semicircular traps are located on the tidal flats in immediate proximity to the intertidal stream channels but rarely intersect or cross them. This is important as it is at high tide, on freshets created by new rainfall, that pink and dog salmon schools typically ascend into the streams for spawning purposes. Therefore the intertidal structures would not impede this process.

The second operating principle is that the techniques are designed in virtually all cases to harvest fish only on the ebb tide. That means that the fish are free during incoming tide and at high tide to advance freely up the estuary and into the stream without obstruction or capture. However, on the ebb tide, some of the salmon that did not ascend will be caught in the traps. Thus, the number captured would only be a portion of the number that endeavored to ascend.

FOREST

High water: flood	Salmon pass freely over fish trap structures and ascend streams to spawning grounds	Salmon pass freely over fish trap structures at initial stage of ebb but become trapped toward half tide.	High water: ebb
Stage II			Stage III
Half tide: flood			Half tide: ebb
Stage I	Salmon are below fish trap structures initially and later can go around and over them freely during flood tide	Salmon are trapped behind the trap walls as the tide falls. Initially traps hold water but dry up eventually.	Stage IV
Low water: flood			Low water: ebb

OCEAN

 = Direction of tidal flow

1.5. Tidal stages and salmon capture utilizing tidal pulse fishing practices. Intertidal stone traps constructed according to these principles typically catch salmon during only 25 percent of the tidal range.

The third operating principle was not to block the stream channel above the tidal range. This principle may be specific to the Prince of Wales Tlingit as other Tlingit groups are described as using weir structures that extended from one side of a stream to the other. The Prince of Wales Tlingit, by contrast, did not block the streams.

To provide some quantitative indication of the time these structures were actually in operation catching fish, consider the following. For purposes of discussion and based on the standard positioning of the fish traps at the midpoint of the tidal range, the tidal cycle can be divided into four phases. Two phases occur on the incoming and outgoing tide. On the incoming tide, the six-hour period can be parsed into period 1, from low water to midwater, and period 2, from midwater to high water. Likewise the outgoing tide can be segmented into period 3, from high water to midwater, and period 4, from midwater to low water. As previously discussed, the intertidal semicircular traps do not catch fish on the incoming tide, thus eliminating 50 percent of the available fishing time when fish are present. In most locations where a single trap is located at midwater, the trap will actually be functioning only for a portion of period 3 and not at all during period 4 once the fish and tide have fallen below the nadir point. A standard semicircular stone trap operates only during period 3; thus the actual time of operation is substantially less than 25 percent of the total time in which salmon are in the vicinity. Fern Point represents an example of intensification of the tidal pulse principle by increasing the amount of time the structures are capable of fishing through the construction of interlocking traps both above and below the standard midtidal location. Even with such intensification, the structures still operated less than 50 percent of the tidal cycle.

When the Russians and Euro-Americans entered southeast Alaska and began harvesting salmon for commercial use, they ignored the logic of the Tlingit systems they observed. First the Russians and later the early American cannery workers constructed "zapors" (de Laguna 1972) or barricades, as the Americans called them, that consisted of trees felled across the stream, right at the high-tide line, to prevent the ascent of the salmon and to allow maximum capture of the buildup in the estuary. This clearly violated the Tlingit principle of no obstruction of the salmons' route to the spawning beds. Later, when the pile and floating fish traps were implemented by the Euro-Americans, they were constructed to catch fish no matter what the tidal stage. The webbing and chicken wire leads, wings, and hearts of the white man's traps floated up and down with the tide, acting equally efficiently at all times. The floating fish trap would catch any and all fish that presented themselves to the structure, and only through an act of conscious volition (opening the trap) could some portion of them continue on their route to the spawning grounds. The competition and greed of the capitalist operators led many to circumvent government regulations instituted in the early 20th century requiring them to open the traps for one or two days a week for escapement purposes.

Despite the fact that they had the technical capabilities to radically disrupt and even destroy salmon runs, the operating principles that the traditional Prince of Wales Tlingit used in constructing their harvesting technologies were eminently successful in selectively harvesting in a manner that ensured the continuous replenishment of the runs on which they depended.

Notes

Portions of the information presented here appeared in the following publications: Steve J. Langdon, 1986, "Traditional Tlingit Stone Fishing Technologies," Alaska Native News 4(3):21-26; Steve J. Langdon, 1987, "Traditional Tlingit Fishing Structures in the Prince of Wales Archipelago," in Fisheries in Alaska's Past: A Symposium, Studies in History no. 227 (Anchorage: Alaska Historical Commission). The research reported herein was made possible by grants from the Geist Fund of the University of Alaska Museum, the University of Alaska Anchorage Faculty Development Fund, and Earthwatch. Additional support was provided by the U.S. Forest Service and the Division of Geological and Geophysical Survey of the Alaska Department of Natural Resources.

1. This is the Huna Tlingit name given to the location now known as Glacier Bay following the retreat of the glaciers in the late 18th and 19th centuries. The Tlingit name is translated as "Bay-where-the-glacier-was," demonstrating Tlingit attention to the previous state and the processual quality of their place-naming practices (Thornton 1995: 153).

2. Tlingit society was divided into socioterritorial units known as *kwaans* that consisted of several communities occupying a geographic region in which intermarriage, intercommunity social ceremonies, and truce characterized the relations among the clans and houses of the communities. At least two matrilineal clans from opposite moieties (Raven and Eagle/Wolf) were found in each kwaan due to the Tlingit social rule requiring that a person's spouse must be acquired from a clan of the "opposite" side (moiety) (Dauenhauer and Dauenhauer 1994; de Laguna 1972; Emmons 1991).

3. A preliminary but more complete description of these sites can be found in Langdon, Reger, and Campbell (1995).

4. The author has observed a natural tidal fish trap, a stone depression, holding pink salmon and saltwater in the intertidal zone when the tide was completely out. It was perhaps in such a context that the Tlingit first observed bears taking salmon at low tide and from which comes the Tekwedi clan's legendary account of learning how to build the intertidal semicircular stone traps from the brown bear (Salisbury 1962).

2. As It Was in the Past

A Return to the Use of Live-Capture Technology
in the Aboriginal Riverine Fishery

Kimberly Linkous Brown

> *According to our history it was Coyote himself who introduced selective fishing to First Nations fishermen. Coyote showed the fishermen how to use weirs and traps and other selective methods. One chief was so grateful he offered his daughter for Coyote to take as his wife. These traditional methods provided for an abundant harvest and allowed enough salmon to reach their spawning grounds. Around the turn of the century the salmon canning monopolies persuaded the government to outlaw traditional fishing methods and a new era of fishing had dawned, an era of mixed stock fishing. In those years of abundant harvests nets killed indiscriminately and in the process we lost respect for the salmon and salmon fishermen. Many races of salmon are now extinct. It was the Coho that finally persuaded us to change the way we fish. Now maybe Coyote has returned.*
>
> Philip Covernton and Kim A. Guerin,
> *Restoring Respect*

On May 21, 1998, the Honorable David Anderson, then minister of fisheries and oceans for Canada, announced a fundamental change in the management of British Columbia's Pacific salmon fisheries (DFO news release, May 21, 1998). This announcement came as a result of what the Department of Fisheries and Oceans believed was scientific evidence demonstrating conclusively that wild coho stocks were declining and at extreme risk of biological extinction. A number of actions aimed at restoring, rebuilding, and protecting Pacific salmon stocks were instituted. These actions impacted commercial, recreational, and Aboriginal fishers as the West Coast coho fishery was banned and other salmon fisheries were restricted to reduce the amount of coho by catch.

In 1999 Minister Anderson renewed his call for an emphasis on selective fishing, announcing that "restrictive fishery management measures to conserve threatened stocks would continue for at least the next five to seven years" (DFO news release, January 8, 1999). Alternative fishing plans included gear modifications for gillnet, seine, and troll fisheries in the commercial sector as well as catch and release experiments utilizing a barbless hook in the sport and recreational sector. Alternative gear experiments in the Aboriginal fishery relied on live-capture technologies rooted in traditional practices (DFO news release, May 17, 1999). Federal funds were made available, with the government committing $1 million to help fishermen continue to adjust to the selective fishing requirement, of which $500,000 was allocated to First Nations fishers to purchase selective fishing gear. First Nations fishers used approximately $496,020 to conduct selective fishing experiments utilizing trap and dip net stations, fish wheels, and beach seines (Selective Fisheries Program Weekly Status Report, September 26–October 5, 1999).

But what is selective fishing? How can contemporary selective fishing strategies be reconciled with Coyote's lesson? In this chapter I address these questions and others by discussing the Aboriginal selective fishing experiments conducted in cooperation with DFO's conservation mandate. I begin with a brief discussion of the problems inherent in a mixed-stock fishery before addressing the concept of traditional ecological knowledge. I then briefly discuss the specific customs directing the Aboriginal pre- and post-contact fishery. Finally, I describe the different live-capture technologies employed in the Aboriginal selective fisheries project and discuss some of the various Aboriginal selective fishing experiments conducted by Sto:lo Nation fishers on the Fraser River, Tsimshian fishers on the lower Skeena River, Gitksan/Wet'suwet'en fishers of the Bulkley River drainage, the N'lakapamux of the Thompson River drainage, and the Nat'oot'en fishers of Babine Lake.

Problems of a Mixed-Stock Fishery
and the Need for Selective Fishing

Pacific salmon comprise the genus *Oncorhynchus*, of which six species inhabit the coastal waters of British Columbia. These species include: sockeye (*O. nerka*), pink (*O. gorbuscha*), coho (*O. kisutch*), chinook (*O. tshawytscha*), chum (*O. keta*), and steelhead (*O. mykiss*). As Copes notes, each species incorporate many hundreds of distinct breeding stocks in the Fraser and Skeena River systems alone (1995). As a result several migrating stocks can be found in the rivers at the same time. Some runs are strong enough to withstand commercial, sport, and recreational fishing pressure. Other, weaker runs require careful monitoring and protection from human predation to ensure that they have an adequate escapement to reproduce the run (Copes 1995:7).

The mixed-stock problem is further compounded by the fact that species mix together in their migration to their natal streams. This results in a "bycatch" situation whereby a nontarget species is inadvertently captured with the target species. This is particularly problematic when the bycatch species has been "fished out" or faces biological extinction. This was the specific problem plaguing the Pacific coho. According to the DFO, as a result of this bycatch phenomenon, wild coho stocks in the northwest Pacific faced biological extinction (DFO news release, May 21, 1998). In response to the "Coho crisis," Minister Anderson called for harvest methods that would reduce the coho bycatch mortality. Selective fishing became the ministry's mandate. Fishers were required to adopt technologies that provided for the live release of coho bycatch, thereby selecting for harvest only those species not in crisis. In January 1999 Minister Anderson made it clear that "All Pacific fisheries where by-catch is an issue will become more selective in harvesting fish. In fisheries where selective harvesting standards are not met, and by-catches remain a problem, fishing opportunities will be curtailed" (DFO news release, January 1, 1999).

As reported in the January 1999 Selective Fisheries Review and Evaluation, the Department of Fisheries and Oceans noted that commercial fishers complied with the selective fishing mandate by making changes in how fish were netted, hooked, and collected. Gillnet fishers were required to utilize nets that would allow for the escape of coho bycatch, and seine operators were required to adopt new measures for removing fish from their nets that would allow for faster species identification and the live release of coho bycatch. Troll fishery modifications included the use of crimped barbs and restrictions in fishing depths. First Nations river fishers responded to Minister Anderson's call for the reduction of coho bycatch mortality and submitted numerous selective fishing funding proposals. Aboriginal fishers were granted approval for experimental fisheries that utilized the precontact live-capture technologies that allowed for the selection of noncritical species for harvest while allowing for the live release of coho bycatch.

This is selective fishing—methodologies that allow for the live release on nontarget species and the harvest of only those species not in crisis. However, questions remain—Can the selective fishing plan proposed by the federal government turn back the clock and undo the damage of a century of mixed-stock fishing? Can the knowledge lost by the outlawing of live-capture technologies be regained? How do the live-capture technologies employed in the selective fishing experiments conducted by the First Nations fishers reflect the customs and practices recounted in Coyote's lesson? Before we examine the Aboriginal fishery it is important to arrive at an understanding of traditional ecological knowledge and how it contributes to the Aboriginal selective fishing experiments.

Defining Traditional Ecological Knowledge

Berkes notes that "traditional ecological knowledge (TEK) represents experience acquired over thousands of years of direct human contact with the environment" (1993:1). In his attempt to define TEK, Berkes sifts through what he calls the major works on the subject to arrive at a working definition that underscores the cultural continuity of a set of practices regarding interaction with the natural environment (1993). Berkes highlights the fact that the individual *knowledge systems* of peoples around the world are defined by the specific cultural understandings of the natural landscape (1999:6). For example, Berkes notes that among the Dogrib Dene, the term *nde* is usually translated as "land"; however, its meaning is closer to "ecosystem." The understanding is further complicated by the fact that *nde* is based on the idea that everything in the environment has life and spirit (6). Simply restated, Berkes identifies a number of components comprising the concept of TEK—knowledge, practice, and belief—highlighting the notion that "purely ecological aspects of tradition cannot be divorced from the social and the spiritual" (6).

Hunn (1993) reflects on the tradition of Coyote stories among the peoples of the Northwest and the Columbia Plateau. The traditions conveyed in these stories include ideas of religion, patterns of artistic expression, and familial relationships in addition to knowledge of economically valuable resources (Hunn 1993:14). Examination of these stories reveals the interconnectedness of the ecological aspects of a tradition with the religious, aesthetic, and social aspects of that tradition. Cruikshank (1998) emphasizes the interconnectedness among the physical, social, and spiritual aspects of tradition in her discussion of Indigenous oral narratives as reflections of "lived" local knowledge.

Among the Aboriginal peoples of British Columbia, this interconnectedness or "lived" local knowledge is reflected in such practices as the *first salmon ceremony* among the Sto:lo. As part of this ceremony, the first salmon caught for the year is shared with the entire community. The bones of the salmon are then ceremoniously returned to the river to ensure the continued return of the salmon resource (Amoss 1987). The present-day practice of this ceremony among such groups as the Sto:lo reflects the continuity of customs that serve to remind future generations not only of the importance of the salmon resource but also the importance of preserving knowledge and customs.[1]

The archaeological, ethnographic, and historic data regarding the coastal and river Aboriginal fishers of British Columbia bear out not only the importance of salmon in the diets of these peoples but also the components of "culture" and social order that relate to the procurement of salmon. Essential to procurement is knowledge—knowledge regarding the construction and placement of weirs and traps as well as the knowledge of migration patterns including the bays and eddies where fish collect as they make their way to their natal streams. But this knowledge includes more than just the *how* and *where*. It also encompasses the relationship between that *how* and *where* and the spiritual and social components of the individual First Nation—knowledge that is reflected in the social customs that direct fishing practices. It is this system of interconnected knowledge that forms the basis of the strategy underlying the experiments conducted by First Nations fishers as part of the federal government's selective fishing plan.

The Aboriginal Fishery

The complex relationship between the salmon resource and the first peoples of the Bulkley, Fraser, and Skeena River watersheds and Babine Lake has been observed and described by ethnographers, archaeologists, and historians. The importance of salmon as a primary food source is borne out in studies revealing high concentrations of Pacific salmon protein in the diet of Northwest Coast and Coast Salish Aboriginal peoples (Chisholm et al. 1983; Hewes 1947). Myths, legends, and ceremonies illustrate the role of salmon in First Nations cosmology (e.g., Amoss 1987; Boas 1891, 1895; Drucker 1965; Duff 1952; Hill-Tout 1902; Jenness 1934, 1943; Lerman 1950, 1976; Miller 1997; Seguin 1984). Salmon as a commodity of exchange in affinal relationships and formal trade arrangements is illustrated in the ethnographic and historic accounts and is supported to some extent by the archaeology of the area (e.g., Copes 1993; Duff 1952; Kew and Griggs 1991; Meggs 1991; Morrell 1989; Taylor 1993).

Traditionally, Aboriginal fishers utilized a number of highly successful fishing technologies. Live-capture technologies such as trap and weir systems were used in the Skeena and Bulkley drainage by the Tsimshian, Gitksan, and Wet'suwet'en fishers as well as the Nat'oot'en fishers on Babine Lake (Berringer 1982; Copes 1991, 1993, 1995; Drucker 1965; Meggs 1991; Morrell 1989; Newell 1993; Souther 1993; Taylor 1993). Sto:lo fishers of the Fraser watershed utilized weirs and traps on the Sumas, Chehalis, and Chilliwack Rivers (Berringer 1982; Copes 1995; Duff 1952; Hill-Tout 1902; Jenness 1934; Newell 1993; Souther 1993). Another live-capture method, dip netting, was employed by groups of the Skeena and Fraser Rivers, of the Bulkley River drainage, and on Babine Lake (Berringer 1982; Kew 1989). For all of these groups, knowledge, access to salmon fishing sites, and technologies were regulated by customs specific to each group (Drucker 1965; Duff 1952; Mills 1994; Morrell 1989; Richardson 1982; Taylor 1993). In some groups, such as those located in the Skeena and Bulkley River drainages and on Babine Lake, the distribution of the harvested salmon resource was also controlled (Drucker 1965; Mills 1994; Morrell 1989; Richardson 1982; Taylor 1993). Beginning with the Sto:lo peoples of the upper Fraser River, traditional fisheries customs and technologies are described in more detail.

Exclusive tribal or village ownership of resource areas was practically unknown to the Upper Sto:lo except for the case of salmon dip-net stations. Though dip-net stations were "owned," use was extended to anyone who could claim the right through kinship as designated by "names." For the most part, the stations in the lower canyon were owned by families in the nearby villages; however, kinship webs would bring fishers claiming rights to the station from as far away as Musqueam and Vancouver Island. These kinship webs were formed through intervillage marriage alliances, thereby expanding hereditary access to the canyon fishing sites. Contemporary Sto:lo fishers continue to acknowledge family fishing sites; however, the years of intense fisheries regulations have caused somewhat of a breakdown in the governance of fishing practices. Former Sto:lo Nation fisheries director Ernie Crey notes that in the wake of over a century of regulation, fishing times, sites, and techniques are no longer decided upon by Siya:m (community leaders) as in the past, but by fisheries officers (1998, personal communication with author).[2]

Traditionally, Tsimshian fishers harvested all five species of Pacific salmon. Fishing technologies included trolling in the tidal pools for spring salmon among coastal villages as well as drag seines, gillnets, spears and harpoons, and dip nets. Selective technologies included traps, weirs, tidal traps, and dip nets (McDonald 1985:135). McDonald notes that technologies were specialized to particular environments and species. In Kitsumkalum, at the northern reach of the territory, fish traps and dip nets were only used at canyon sites (135).

Among the Tsimshian peoples of the middle and lower Skeena, traditional fishing sites were controlled by corporate matrilineages and managed by the House chiefs, with each House controlling several fishing stations (Halpin and Seguin 1990; Miller 1997; Newell 1993; Richardson 1982; Taylor 1993). Taylor notes that hereditary chiefs still control the allocation and management of the traditional areas (43).

Among the Gitksan fish resources were controlled. Fishing grounds were treated as property of a particular kinship group (Morrell 1989:233). Access to fishing grounds was held by matrilineal Houses, with the head chief of each House having ultimate authority and responsibility for each House's fishing grounds. Distribution of the resource was also controlled by the House chief (Morrell 1989; Taylor 1993). Morrell (1989) and Taylor (1993) report that this system of House control over fishing grounds has remained intact to present.

Fishing technologies included trap and weir systems on the Skeena and its tributaries. Dip nets, gaffs, and baskets were used to harvest fish from the traps. The Gitksan trap systems were so highly efficient that about two months of work provided sufficient stores for subsistence as well as a surplus production that constituted a major commodity in the trade with interior neighbors (Copes 1993:11). Surplus harvests were traded with interior peoples, as the Gitksan established a thriving precontact "commercial" fishery (Morrell 1989; Taylor 1993). As in the past, the Gitksan pilot sale or "commercial fishery" is a surplus fishery. Salmon were harvested first for food, social, and ceremonial purposes, with surplus salmon harvests making up their "commercial fishery."

The Wet'suwet'en of Bulkley River drainage are an Athabaskan-speaking people with a long history of interaction with the Gitksan peoples of the region. Mills notes that although the Wet'suwet'en pattern of summer gathering and winter dispersal is typical of that of Aboriginal peoples in the interior of Canada, the Wet'suwet'en differed from the interior Natives in that the abundance of salmon in the Bulkley River in summer made it possible for them to live in a large village with cedar-plank houses during the summer (1994:39–40).

Much the same as with their Gitksan neighbors, among the Wet'suwet'en ownership of the principal salmon fishing grounds was controlled by Clans consisting of a grouping of Houses (Copes 1993; Morrell 1989). Each hereditary chief was responsible for regulating access to his group's fishing grounds (Morrell 1989:234). Distribution of the fish processed by each House was also controlled by the House chief, and as with the Gitksan, this practice continues in the Wet'suwet'en fishery today. As noted by Morrell, the current Gitksan and Wet'suwet'en fishery management systems give the hereditary chiefs all of the power for allocation of the harvest (1989:234).

The primary fishing technology was that of a system of traps. As with the Gitksan, dip nets, gaffs, and baskets were used to harvest fish from the traps (Jenness 1943). Taylor notes that in the postcontact commercial fishery Wet'suwet'en fishers continued to rely on the inland fishery as an important source of food, unlike their Gitksan neighbors who participated early on in the commercial fishery (1993:13).

Jenness (1934) notes that the social organization of the Babine Lake Carriers differed depending on their proximity to their down-river Gitksan or Nuxalk (Bella Coola) neighbors. Those inhabiting the Bulkley River, Stuart Lake, and Babine Lake region adhered to the matrilineal organization of their Gitksan neighbors. But the Carrier around Fraser Lake and Stoney Creek, who had frequent contact with the Bella Coola, placed more emphasis on the father's rank than the mother's. Though not stated explicitly in the ethnographic literature reviewed for this discussion, it can be inferred from the readings that there was some control over the access to the salmon resource. Meggs (1991), in his discussion of the vanishing salmon resource, refers to control as coming from (perhaps hereditary) village chiefs.

The bulk of the Nat'oot'en salmon harvest was taken in traps and weirs near the entrance to Babine Lake, a huge sockeye nursery at the headwaters of the Babine River (Meggs 1991:74). So rich was the Babine Lake salmon resource and so efficient was the Nat'oot'en system of traps and weirs that coastal canners referred to the system as the Babine Barricades. The trap system was operated under the direction of the chief and provided harvest not only for subsistence purposes but also as stores for trade with interior neighbors. At the end of the fishing season, the system was dismantled and a new system constructed the following year.

Selective Fishing Methods—Live-Capture Technologies

Aboriginal selective fishing projects relied on alternative methods such as dip nets, fish traps, trap nets, and beach seines—these methods representing a revival of precontact fishing technologies. Additionally some projects employed fish wheels—postcontact, selective technology based on the underlying concepts of precontact, live-capture technologies (Robbins 1996; von Brandt 1964). Beginning with the dip-net operation used by all groups in this discussion, the following overview of live-capture fishing technologies illustrates how these methods work to minimize nontarget species mortality by selectively targeting only those species not at risk. The ethnographic record reflects the use of dip nets by the Aboriginal population, particularly in the fast-flowing canyon waters of both the Fraser and the Skeena River watersheds (Barnett 1955; Berringer 1982; Drucker 1965; Hill-Tout 1902; Jenness 1934; Kew 1989; McDonald 1985, 1994; Morrell 1989; Newell 1993; Souther 1993; Stewart 1977; Suttles 1951, 1987; Taylor 1993; Underhill 1945).

Dip netting is highly selective as fish are removed from the water one at a time and may be released quickly. Canyon dip-net operations were mounted from the shore or suspended platform, and the fisher used a small net at the end of a long pole to catch passing salmon one by one. The fish were removed from the water as they pass, one by one. Dip nets were also used in connection with fish traps as a means of harvesting the enclosed fish.

Fish traps are passive fishing devices utilized by virtually all upriver Aboriginal peoples (Berringer 1982; Coupland 1988; Drucker 1965; Hill-Tout 1902; Jenness 1937; Kew 1989; McDonald 1985, 1994; Morrell 1989; Newell 1993; Souther 1993; Stewart 1977; Suttles 1951, 1989; Taylor 1993; Underhill 1945).

Evidence of intensive weir and trap fishing on the central coast of British Columbia is found in the archaeological record (Matson and Coupland 1995). Traps are placed in the path of migrating fish whereby the fish are funneled into the trap. Once in the trap, fish are guided through a series of smaller and smaller chambers toward a holding area. Weirs worked similarly as traps, blocking passage and causing live salmon to be collected for harvest by net or gaff (Stewart 1977). Traps and weirs such as those employed by the Babine Lake Carrier were highly selective in that only those species targeted would be removed from the collection of trapped fish. Nontarget species would be released live.

Trap nets were also used in some of the Aboriginal selective fishing experiments. Trap nets were placed in the path of the fish and then lifted from the water by hand or other means. This technology resembled the reef net technology described by Suttles (1951) and Stewart (1977) as employed by Aboriginal peoples of western Washington and British Columbia in that lead lines were utilized to guide fish toward chambers in the net system. Similar to reef-net systems, trap nets are considered an active rather than passive fishing technology because of the use of the lead lines. Rather than the fish passing into the net at their own pace, lead lines guided the fish toward the net (Stewart 1977; Suttles 1951). The trap consisted of a 60-fathom lead net with eight-inch mesh that guided passing fish toward a small opening in a single suspended chamber (the spiller). The lead and spiller were anchored to the ocean floor in 8 fathoms of water. The trap was tended by a 26-foot modified herring skiff and a 12-foot aluminum skiff. Again as with the reef net, the net meshes are not large enough to gill the fish, merely to hold them. As with other selective methods, the plan was to harvest the target species and for nontarget species to be released live.

Fish wheels were used in Alaska, in the Yukon, and on the Columbia River system many years ago (Robbins 1996; von Brandt 1964). In his discussion of fishing technologies, von Brandt describes the fish wheel technology as dating back to the 14th century and employed on rivers throughout the western Mediterranean (1964:156–57). He suggests that with the migration of peoples from Europe to North America, the technology spread to the West Coast, especially the rivers of British Columbia and eventually as far as Alaska (156–57). Robbins notes that fish wheels were first used on the Columbia in 1879 as part of the non-Aboriginal commercial fishery (1996:11). He also notes that because competitors thought the owners of fish wheels enjoyed an unfair monopoly advantage in the taking of fish, pressure was brought to bear in the state legislatures to outlaw the devices first in Oregon in 1926 and finally in Washington in 1934 (11).

A fish wheel consists of a series of baskets mounted on a wheel. The wheel is suspended on an axle over a river at the height that permits the water flow to catch the baskets and turn the wheel. This structure sits on a foundation anchored in a suitable spot in the river. As the fish swim upstream, they encounter a series of leads that direct them toward the fish wheel. When the fish swim under the wheel, the baskets sweep through the water and scoop them up into a collection box where they can be sorted. Again the target species is harvested and the nontarget species released live.

Finally, the beach seine is a modification of the prevalent commercial practice of purse seining and is typically used in river settings. According to Stewart, this technology was employed by Aboriginal peoples of Western Washington and British Columbia (1977:87). Precontact application required the use of rocks to fix the net to the shore, and canoes were used to lay out the lines (87). As part of the contemporary experiment, operators work from the beach with the help of motorboats, which lay the net in a semicircle leading away from the beach, downstream for some distance, and then back to shore. When the beach seine net is fixed at both ends to shore, it is drawn in along the bottom instead of being pursed as with the conventional seine gear. As the net is pulled toward the beach, the fish are captured in a smaller and smaller enclosure from which they may be dip-netted and sorted so that the target species is harvested and the nontarget species is released live.

Coyote's Lesson—Selective Fishing Experiments

In connection with Minister Anderson's coho recovery plan a number of successful experimental selective fishing techniques were conducted on the Fraser, Skeena, Bulkley, and Babine watersheds in 1998. Many of the projects had been in operation prior to the coho alert. The technologies employed in these experiments include those technologies described in the previous section—dip nets, fish traps, trap nets, fish wheels, and beach seines. Dip-net operations have been carried out by the Gitksan-Wet'suwet'en at the Morristown Canyon fish ladder—targeting pink salmon. Dip-netting was also used by the Babine Lake Nation (Nat'oot'en peoples) at the Babine fence, which is a Department of Fisheries and Oceans counting facility.

In 1998 the Tsimshian Tribal Council proposed a project for an in-river fish trap on the lower Skeen River. The 1998 proposal never advanced past the stage of site selection (Todd Johansson, personal communication with author, 1999). However, this project was approved under a food, social, and ceremonial designation (Section 35 fishery as described by DFO) for the upcoming 1999 season. The Metlakatla Development Corporation received approval for a trap net in the Skeena River. This project was a commercial venture on the part of the Metlakatla Development Corporation and is similar to the trap-net operation proposed by the T'sou-ke Band in 1998. The T'sou-ke Band experiment, however, was not successful in that the design of the trap resulted in very little catch with three salmon in the trap and five salmon gilled in the lead. Funding was made available in 1999 for expanding the trap-net experiment. The objective of the 1999 experiment was to test the operation and effectiveness of an aquatic sorting tray. Testing took place over a 33-day period from August to October, and all species were targeted. The trap net caught 900 fish, and all were released with the exception of 42 mortalities resulting from seal predation (Third Selective Fisheries Multi-Stakeholder Workshop, Richmond BC, November 22–24, 1999).

The Kitsumkalum Commercial Fishermen submitted three projects for consideration: a trap net in the mainstream Skeena adjacent to Kwinitsa targeting sockeye, pink, chum, and chinook; three fish wheels spanning the Skeena at China Bar targeting sockeye and pink salmon; and a large beach seine on the Skeena at China Bar, again targeting sockeye and pink salmon. All three of these projects were submitted as commercial ventures. The fish wheel and beach seine proposals were not approved (DFO Selective Fishing

Project List, January 1999). The proposal for a trap in the mainstream Skeena was approved—not, however, as a commercial venture. A prior agreement as part of the Aboriginal Fisheries Strategy precluded the sale of fish caught under this proposal.

In 1998 the Cooks Ferry Band (N'lakapamux or Thompson) and the Nicola Watershed Stewardship and Fisheries Authority built a traditional weir in the Nicola River just upstream from Spences Bridge. By referring to a photograph from 1889 and after consulting with elders about its location, the N'lakapamux or Thompson built a weir using traditional materials and knowledge. This weir consisted of a wall of wooden poles lashed to together, the fence tapered to funnel fish toward a catching basket. According to the manager of the Nicola Watershed Stewardship and Fisheries Authority, one purpose of the weir was to incorporate the traditional knowledge of elders into the modern fisheries management. The weir was built to count chinook and to provide a controlled food catch.

According to the Department of Fisheries and Oceans selective fisheries reports, fishwheels have been in operation in British Columbia for the past five years and have been an important component in the development of selective fishery strategies. The Gitksan placed a fishwheel in the Babine River targeting sockeye and pink salmon. In addition, the Skeena Fisheries Commission had two fish wheels operating in the Kitselas Canyon. In 1999 testing was conducted on the mainstream of the Skeena River in Kitselas Canyon during the last week of July to the first week of October using the Kitselas-fish wheel and fish trap. Chum, sockeye, chinook, and pink salmon were targeted while all coho and steelhead were released. As noted in the reports to DFO regarding the selective fishing experiments, the fish wheel and fish trap proved to be effective in the strong currents of the Skeena River.

On the Fraser River, the Skway Band of the Sto:lo Nation, working together with the University of British Columbia and the British Columbia Ministry of Environment Lands and Parks, applied to set up a fish wheel in Skway territory (about three kilometers upstream from the confluence of the Chilliwack River). The project was operated under the authority of a communal license for food, social, and ceremonial purposes with the target species being sockeye and chum. The Skway Band project was again approved for the 1999 season along with a proposal from the Sumas Band of the Sto: lo Nation. They received funding for a fish wheel modification and beach seine project.

Conclusion

This overview of the various selective fishing experiments conducted by the First Nations groups of the Fraser, Skeena, Bulkley, and Babine watersheds focuses on one segment of the fisheries and oceans minister's $400 million salmon recovery plan—a plan consisting of salmon enhancement projects, vessel tie-up programs, license buy-backs, fishing bans on select stocks, and the creation of a "rainbow" of fishing zones along the coast and river systems.[3]

Fisheries Minister Anderson called selective fishing the cornerstone of his salmon recovery plan, defining selective fishing as a conservation-oriented management approach that allows for the harvest of surplus target species or stocks while avoiding or minimizing the harvest of less productive species or stocks. Toward that end, Minister Anderson has called for the continuation of selective fishing measures through the year 2005 (DFO news release, June 18, 1999). But is the minister's call to action a case of too little, too late? Has a century of regulation brought about a loss of knowledge of the old fishing ways and the lessons of Coyote?

When British Columbia joined Canada in 1871 and the first salmon canneries appeared, changes in the Pacific Coast fishery were imminent. Beginning in 1878, regulations were implemented with the expressed goal of eliminating the live-capture fishing technologies utilized by First Nations peoples. By 1894, First Nations peoples were prohibited in any place from taking fish by spear, trap, or pen—dip nets were allowed only with permission (Gifford 1989). In 1904 fish weirs were banned on the Skeena River, and by 1919 beach seines were outlawed (Souther 1993). These regulations forced the replacement of selective live-capture technologies with mixed-stock net fisheries. As the number of canneries grew, so did the number of fishers and nets in the water. A century of mixed-stock fishing contributed to the Coho crisis of the late 20th century.

As the story goes, Coyote's lesson was lost when the salmon-canning monopolies ushered in an era of mixed-stock fishing that killed indiscriminately and in the process contributed to a loss of respect for the salmon resource. And as the story goes, it was coho that finally brought about the need for a change in the wild salmon fishery. The ability to selectively harvest a target species is vital to the success of Fisheries and Oceans' plan to restore coho stocks. Live-capture technologies offer the most effective means of harvesting target species while allowing the live release of nontarget species. The use of live-capture technologies such as traps, weirs, dip nets, and beach seines by the Aboriginal peoples of western British Columbia has long been documented in the ethnographic, archaeological, and historic records (Barnett 1955; Berringer 1982; Copes 1991, 1993, 1995; Drucker 1965; Duff 1952; Jenness, 1934, 1937; Kew 1989; Matson and Coupland 1995; Meggs 1991; Morrell 1989; Newell 1993; Souther 1993; Stewart 1977; Suttles 1951, 1989; Taylor 1993). These live-capture technologies formed the basis of the selective fishing plans submitted by First Nations fishers.

In 1999 14 fish trap projects, 20 beach seine projects, and 8 fish wheel projects were funded as part of the Aboriginal selective fishing program (including the Sumas and Skway projects). All the projects were considered experimental and were conducted, for the most part, in an effort to determine the effectiveness of selective fishing. The experiments conducted by the First Nations fishers in 1998 and 1999 have shown that target species can be harvested by means of live-capture technologies without harm to nontarget species. The preliminary summary of selective fisheries projects released by DFO in October 1999 indicated a high level of success in the live release of coho in the Aboriginal experiments (DFO 1999a). Because of this success, some of the First Nations selective fisheries projects continued through 2002. For example, in November of 2001 and 2002, Sto:lo fishers conducted beach seine operations in conjunction with a sale agreement. Fishers were able to target chum salmon with the live release of coho bycatch (Ken Malloway, personal communication with author, 2002).

The knowledge of the past has been brought to bear on the future. The traditions conveyed in Coyote's lesson demonstrate the need to focus on the interconnectedness of the physical, social, and spiritual elements of lived local knowledge. The experiments conducted by the First Nation fishers as part of the DFO minister's selective fishery mandate represent a return to a reliance on the lesson of Coyote—a lesson rooted in knowledge, practice, and belief.

Notes

1. Among the Sto:lo this practice has continued. Individual families, bands, and the collective Sto:lo Nation hold first salmon ceremonies each year.

2. In the years 1878, 1888, and 1894 fisheries regulations were enacted that served to eliminate live-capture fishing technologies as part of the up-river Aboriginal fishery. Under these regulations obstructions such as traps and weirs were outlawed as well as the use of spears. Dip nets could be used only with permission. Additional regulations outlawed the sale or trade of Native-caught fish and mandated the time, place, and method of Aboriginal fishing (Gifford 1989).

3. Zones are designed by colors such as red and yellow. Red zones are those areas where critical Thompson and upper Skeena coho are prevalent. In these zones, fishing plans targeted zero coho mortality. Yellow zones are those areas where these critical stocks are found in lesser numbers. In these areas, coho were to be avoided and released when caught by commercial, sport, and Native fishermen (Selective Fisheries Review and Evaluation, January, 1999).

3. The Forest and the Seaweed

Gitga'at Seaweed, Traditional Ecological
Knowledge, and Community Survival

Nancy J. Turner and Helen Clifton

Traditional food systems are an integral part of people's culture and lifeways. Foods provide far more than calories and nutrients; they help define
the identity and heritage of a people. Gathering and obtaining food is a primary occupation in land-based societies, and the knowledge required for
food procurement is an essential component of people's traditional ecological knowledge and wisdom. As such, it is embedded in people's philosophy
and worldview, in a vast and complex array of strategies they use to sustain
themselves within their territory over many generations, and in the many
ways by which they acquire and communicate knowledge to other members of the society and to future generations (Turner et al. 2000; see Figure
3.1—schematic diagram of TEKW).

For the Gitga'at of Hartley Bay and surrounding territory on the north
coast of British Columbia, red laver seaweed (*Porphyra abbottiae*), called
ła'ask, is a traditional food that represents all of these components of Traditional Ecological Knowledge and Wisdom. The harvesting, processing,
and use of this seaweed, undertaken for many centuries by the Gitga'at
and their ancestors and still practiced today, is infused within all facets of
Gitga'at culture and lifeways and is vital to their identity, health, and well-
being as a people. The continued use of this seaweed by the Gitga'at, in the
face of economic restructuring and accelerating cultural change, since the
time of European contact is remarkable. In a sense the use of the seaweed

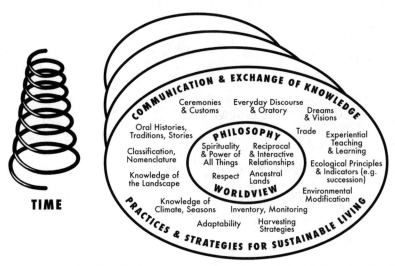

3.1. Components of traditional ecological knowledge and wisdom of Aboriginal peoples of northwestern North America.

represents the resiliency of a people. The adaptations that have been made by the Gitga'at to enable and facilitate its continued harvest and use reflect people's abilities to adjust to changing conditions and still retain the essence of their culture and traditions. In terms of community survival under new and changing economic and cultural regimes, the Gitga'at seaweed harvest represents hope and inspiration for maintenance of cultural integrity and provides a model for sustainable resource use based on principles of respect, reciprocity, and cooperation.

In this chapter we present some of the details, particularly the cultural aspects, of the harvesting, processing, and use of this valuable marine alga and describe how they serve to define and strengthen the Gitga'at community and provide continuity and resilience for the Gitga'at people. From a scientific perspective there is still much to be learned about the taxonomy, life cycles, and ecological aspects of ḷa'ask, but the depth of Gitga'at traditional knowledge about these topics indicates the tremendous value and potential for Indigenous knowledge to inform scientists and others about the life cycles and interrelationships of the natural world. The reason we use the title "The Forest and the Seaweed" is that in the holistic perspective of the Gitga'at and other First Nations, the two are integrally related, a fact we demonstrate in our discussions here.

Our collaborative research on Gitga'at traditional ecological knowledge relating to plants and the environment is part of an ongoing major research project, Coasts Under Stress. Its goal is to identify the important ways in which changes in society and the environment in coastal British Columbia and coastal Newfoundland and Labrador have affected, or will affect, the health of people, their communities, and the environment over the long run. The Gitga'at community at Hartley Bay, like many other communities of coastal British Columbia, has been subjected to severe economic restructuring, resulting from loss of commercial fishing revenues. Their territory has been encroached upon and their resources depleted from logging, commercial fishing and shellfish harvesting, and even tourism. Their efforts to maintain their cultural integrity, community values, health, and well-being in the face of these changes are exemplary. Their continued harvesting and use of traditional resources like seaweed contribute to these efforts.

Seaweed Use Worldwide
Seaweeds—or, more technically, macroscopic marine algae—are used by humans all over the world as sources of food, medicine, and materials. In countries such as Japan, seaweed accounts for some 10 percent of the diet; in 1973 Japanese seaweed consumption reached an average of 3.5 kilograms per household (Indergaard 1983). Seaweeds are widely eaten in other regions of the world as well, particularly in China, Korea, parts of Ireland and Scotland, and Polynesia and Hawaii (Aaronson 1986; Abbott 1974; Druehl 2000; Guiry and Blunden 1991; Guiry and Hession 1998; Indergaard 1983; Madlener 1977; Milliken and Bridgewater 2001; Ostraff 2003). Seaweeds also have many industrial uses, especially in food, cosmetics, and agricultural industries (Guiry 2002). Seaweeds are known to be highly nutritious. In mainstream North American society they are considered a "health food"; their health and nutritional benefits have long been known and appreciated by the Gitga'at and other Northwest Coast Indigenous peoples.

Interest in seaweed products is growing, and there have been a few "cottage industries" that have developed on the Northwest Coast for harvesting seaweeds for the marketplace, notably at Barkley Sound and in the vicinity of Sooke, both on the west coast of Vancouver Island. A commercial kelp-harvesting plant at Masset, Haida Gwaii (Queen Charlotte Islands), for the purpose of developing industrial kelp and fertilizer products, proved not to be economically viable and existed only for a few years in the 1980s. There are rumored efforts to develop industrial production for red laver on the British Columbia coast as well, but this has yet to be confirmed. A small red laver–growing industry has been established in Puget Sound, Washington State (Druehl 2000), and there are efforts to start cultivating Porphyra in the vicinity of Prince Rupert, with Louis Druehl as an adviser to the project.

In contrast, in Japan, seaweed production is a multibillion-dollar industry, and many kinds of seaweeds are cultivated, especially for the domestic food market. The most important types are nori (Porphyra species), kombu (Laminaria spp.), and wakame (Undaria spp.). As of January 2002 about 350,000 tonnes of wet nori alone are produced annually in Japan with a retail value in excess of US$1 billion. The Japanese nori industry is a highly mechanized, efficient operation that employs some 60,000 people on a part-time basis. Nearly 70,000 hectares of Japanese waters are occupied by Porphyra-growing nets (Guiry 2002).

In British Columbia, Coastal First Peoples, especially those of the northern Coast Salish, Kwakwaka'wakw, and peoples of the central and northern coast, all include red laver (Porphyra abbottiae and other Porphyra spp.) in their diets (Turner 1995, 2003). The Nuu-Chah-Nulth and Ditidaht of the west coast of Vancouver Island evidently did not themselves eat this seaweed, but within the early 20th century many of these people harvested it for sale to local Asian communities in Victoria and elsewhere (M. D. Williams 1979; Turner et al. 1983). Peoples of the central and northern coast, including the Heiltsuk, Haida, and Coast Tsimshian, have also harvested a variety of seaweeds with herring roe deposited on them, especially the fronds of giant kelp (Macrocystis integrifolia), which are eaten by these people and also exported to Japan in large quantities today. Traditionally, seaweeds also had many technological and medicinal uses among British Columbia First Peoples. For example, bull kelp (Nereocystis luetkeana) stipes were cured and used all up and down the coast for fishing lines (Turner 1998).

The gelatinous substance from the receptacles of sea wrack (*Fucus* spp.) was, and still is, used as a medicine for burns and sores, as well as to strengthen the limbs and as an eye medicine.

Seaweeds can be indicators of environmental health. They are dependent on the ocean for their reproduction, growth, and dispersal, and they can vary in their growth rates, seasonality, and reproductive capacity depending on the ocean currents and tides, temperature, and other factors such as pollution (Druehl 2000). Humans, too, can impact the growth and reproduction of seaweeds, including the *ła'ask* of the Gitga'at. In the following section, we describe the use of this alga by the Gitga'at, and the multifaceted knowledge system that has supported its use.

Gitga'at Seaweed Use

The Gitga'at are a Sm'algyax- (Tsimshian-) speaking people whose main village is Hartley Bay, situated at the confluence of Greenville and Douglas Channels about 140 kilometers (90 miles) south of Prince Rupert, where a large number of Gitga'at people also reside. Their territory encompasses a vast number of islands, as well as a substantial portion of the British Columbia mainland. The larger islands within Tsimshian territory include Gil, Gribbell, and Princess Royal islands.

Like other coastal peoples, the Gitga'at rely on the bounty of the forests and oceans combined to provide them with the foods, materials, and medicines they need for sustenance. They enjoy a diet of plenty of salmon, halibut, and other fish, together with marine mammals like seal, shellfish such as sea urchin and chitons, land mammals like deer and bear, game birds including ducks and geese, and a variety of plant foods, including berries, root vegetables, green shoots, inner bark of hemlock, and edible seaweed (Port Simpson 1983). Although elders of the Gitga'at community still enjoy many of the traditional foods, many of the younger people prefer store-bought foods, and some of the traditional foods, especially the wild greens, roots, and inner bark, are scarcely known to the younger people. One elder commented, "The more you eat the [old] foods, the more you like it." This statement reflects a common catch-22 facing those trying to maintain cultural traditions. People like what they are familiar with, and dietary preferences are no different in this regard (Kuhnlein 1990). Nevertheless, ła'ask is one food enjoyed by virtually everyone.

Every year, for most of the month of May, the elders of the community, including Helen Clifton, and until 2004, Johnny Clifton, go to the seaweed camp at Kiel (K'yel) on Princess Royal Island (Lax'a'lit'aa Koo), to harvest the seaweed and to fish for halibut and other traditional activities.[1] Whenever they are able, the younger adults and school-age children generally come to Kiel during the Victoria Day long weekend in May. Previously, before children were required to be in school at this time, the entire families stayed down at Kiel while the seaweed harvest and halibut fishing took place. Much else has changed in terms of harvesting practices, transportation, and living conditions at the seaweed camp, but the seaweed harvest remains a time-honored tradition that brings cohesion to families and communities, provides important opportunities for knowledge acquisition and communication, and promotes health and well-being both through providing a nutritious food and through requiring a healthy outdoor lifestyle and promoting cultural values.

Ła'ask: The Seaweed

The main species of red laver harvested by the Gitga'at is Porphyra abbottiae. Other species are known to have been harvested and used by coastal peoples, including P. torta and P. lanceolata (samples identified by phycologist Sandra Lindstrom). Likely there were others as well, since there are approximately 21 different Porphyra species growing along the Pacific Coast of British Columbia and Alaska, Washington, and Oregon (Lindstrom and Cole 1991; Turner 2003), all of which would be edible. As noted, Porphyra species are eaten in other parts of the world, including Japan, Korea, China, Scotland, and Ireland.

The life history of Porphyra is complex. Porphyra species, like other algae, reproduce by spores but also undergo sexual reproduction. They have two main, different mature forms, one with a single complement of chromosomes, the haploid phase, and one with two sets of chromosomes, the diploid phase; this is known as an "alternation of generations" in a life cycle. The best-known, edible phase is haploid.[2] The haploid plants are thin, membranous, and dark greenish purple. Both the haploid and diploid plants produce spores that are released into the water, and depending upon the type of spores and the means of their production—by mitosis or meiosis, they will grow into plants of the same or the alternate generation. This reproductive strategy thus provides various means for the plants to grow, depending on particular environmental conditions. The male and female reproductive parts or gametes, called "spermatia" and "carpogonia," respectively, are produced at the margins of the mature seaweed blades in the case of the spermatia, or inside the margins in the case of carpogonia. The spores produced that result from fertilization are released with the dissolution of the tissues along the margins. These might appear to be "rotting," but in fact they are just undergoing another stage in a rather amazing life cycle.

This scientific understanding of the life cycle of *ƚa'ask* was obviously not known to Gitga'at or other First Nations harvesters, having required microscopic examination of the seaweed through its life cycle stages. However, the manifestation of this life cycle—in particular, the growth and development of the young haploid phase (the edible seaweed phase) on the intertidal rocks of the shores of the islands where the Gitga'at have ventured to harvest them for generations—was well known. So, too, was the seaweed's capacity to regenerate itself. The growth rate of the seaweed varies up and down the coast and also from site to site even within Gitga'at territory. On May 18, 2001, Helen Clifton explained that people in other communities generally picked seaweed earlier than the Gitga'at: "It's picked earlier than us. We're the last ones to pick seaweed. So, Gitxaała, Metlakatla, Kitasoo way, they will have picked seaweed . . . at Klemtu they picked 18 sacks of seaweed!" She said that her husband, Johnny Clifton, who was born at Kiel, knew all the different places around there where the early seaweed grew, as well as the places where the last seaweed was picked, just before they returned home. She said, "So there's places around here, like the island in front of us is one of the first places to pick. . . . There's certain places down here that's the early seaweed . . . Johnny knows, all these years." Helen calls the places where the seaweed grows "seaweed fields" or "seaweed beds" because of the great density of seaweeds grown there. In past decades, people camped out in family groups near the different picking grounds. For example, Johnny's aunt had a place at Fly Bay out at the point; this was the first place they would go and pick, the first seaweed that was mature enough. At other sites, it matured later, even though "It's all the same seaweed. It's just, their growth is slower than the ones at first" (Helen Clifton, personal communication, May 18, 2001).

There are other types of seaweed, and the pickers have to learn to differentiate these from the edible type: "You have seal seaweed that grows in between good seaweed, we call it 'seal seaweed.' They're wide, and they look like they've got a rainbow [iridescent seaweed, Iridea]. . . but it's very colourful, and so I've learned to pick through that seaweed, if there's good seaweed on that rock."

Helen described how traditionally the women would systematically pick the seaweed:

> They wouldn't spot-pick seaweed. The whole group would go out
> and clean out one place. . . . And the next time they'd go for seaweed
> they would start at the place where they stopped the day before,
> or the tide before. And, so then the island was picked clean, either
> side, the Campania [Island] side or down here, Princess Royal side.
> And so you wouldn't have to go searching for seaweed. You knew
> exactly where the group stopped, and you would start from that
> point on until you were all finished.

In discussing how sustainable the seaweed harvest is, Helen confirms what many Aboriginal harvesters understand about the plants they use routinely:

> It's better when it's picked every year. It's just like any plant that
> has been trimmed, it will grow stronger and better . . . for sea-
> weed, it's just like any garden, it has to be tended. So if you pick
> it every year then it grows strong the next year, it keeps coming
> back. So if it isn't picked for a few years, then it just has rotted
> away on the rocks there.

One of the concerns Helen has is that people are not picking the seaweed routinely and systematically any more, and she fears that the seaweed beds and the seaweed produced are deteriorating because they are not being tended. Another major concern of hers is the prospect of climate change, which was manifested for her in the continuous, uncharacteristic rains they have experienced through the month of May for four consecutive years (2000–2003). This not only makes predicting the growth of the seaweed problematic; it also prevents people from harvesting the seaweed, since one of the important taboos people observe is not to pick seaweed when it is raining. Helen commented, "It's hard to say [about whether they'll be able to pick seaweed] because the weather has changed so much, it's hard to say what's happening to the natural growth of whatever. . . . We work with the tides. Whatever we're getting here depends on the tides, and the weather." Another taboo, Helen explained, is that you do not pick seaweed when it is floating in the water, but only when it is attached to the rocks, exposed by the low tide. This means that people should not be "greedy" with the seaweed. Limiting the harvest to the time of the lowest tides, when the seaweed is exposed, is both a safety measure, in which the risk of being washed away by the waves is lessened, and a conservation measure: at least some of the seaweed plants are inevitably left to grow and reproduce when there is such a narrow window for harvesting.

In order to pick the seaweed safely and process it effectively, it is necessary to have the right combination of sunny days and low tides first thing in the morning. As noted, the seaweed can only be picked at low tide from the rocks where it grows, and it can only be picked in dry weather. Picking seaweed in the rain is dangerous because it becomes so slippery, especially on the almost vertical rock faces where some of the best seaweed grows. In any case, seaweed picked in the rain does not taste as good. The seaweed is piled up and packed into large bags, and then it is taken to special locations on sunny rocky headlands to be laid out to dry. It is formed into squares or into shapes that conform to the shape and pattern of the rocks and is allowed to dry from about eleven o'clock or noon to about three o'clock, when the squares are turned over to dry on the other side through the late afternoon sun and into the early evening when the rocks start to cool off. Drying occurs both from above and from below, since the rocks are warmed by the sun and in turn help to dry the seaweed on the bottom, while the sun dries it directly from above. The dried squares are stacked up, about twenty-five together, and placed into cotton seaweed sheets, made by sewing together nine opened-up flour sacks into a large sheet. The seaweed is then packed on people's backs or taken by speedboat back to the camp at Kiel, to be stored in a dry place, usually in a special "seaweed house," until they can be taken back to homes in Hartley Bay for further processing. Instead of the rocky bluffs, some women have used square cedar trays for drying their seaweed. Annetta Robinson, who is originally from Gitxaała, inherited about a hundred such trays from her mother; she remembers helping her mother make them. She kept some of these for drying her own seaweed and gave some to her cousins. Helen explained that these trays are used in places where there are not good rocks for drying seaweed, and they are especially useful for older women who cannot easily climb around over the rocks to dry their seaweed.

Helen's goal is for herself and her family members to pick at least seven large (100-pound) sacks full of the seaweed during the course of their stay at Kiel. This is the minimum amount that she and her family process and use for their personal consumption, for trading, and for gifts. When this amount is multiplied through all the Gitga'at families (perhaps ten or more) who have harvested seaweed, at least in the past, it translates into about seventy 100-pound sacks or more: perhaps 3000 kilograms of fresh seaweed or more.

The seaweed grows quickly; Helen gauges the rate of growth and predicts the stage of readiness of the seaweed by watching the growth of the stinging nettles (Urtica dioica) at Kiel; as the stalks of the stinging nettles mature and elongate, so too do the seaweed fronds. Helen explained that people could harvest two pickings of the seaweed from the same site in the same year. It regenerates itself quickly. It is pulled off with the fingers, and the small ends remaining attached to the rocks will continue to grow so that, in about a month's time, one can return and pick the next growth.

Formerly the Gitga'at would pick and dry one harvest of seaweed and take
it up Douglas Channel to Kitamaat village to trade with the Haisla people
there for eulachen grease, a nutritious fat rendered from a small smelt that
comes in large numbers up the rivers to spawn in the spring. They also traded their seaweed with the upriver people for soapberries, 7is, and other valued products from the Skeena, and with the Nisga'a of the Nass Valley for a
different type of eulachen grease. Then they would return to Kiel and harvest another crop of seaweed for their own use. This second crop was preferable to the Gitga'at, because it was said to be more tender and to have a
finer taste, as noted by Helen:

> I've heard. . . . The women from long ago said that they would . . .
> do the first picking of seaweed and then it would be a month, not
> even a month, that the second growth would be ready to pick again.
> And they liked to keep the second growth for themselves because it
> was a finer seaweed . . . , as compared to the first growth.

Helen also noted that the second-growth fronds were narrower than the
first growth. One Gitxaała man said that the Gitxaała still routinely harvest two crops of seaweed, one at the morning low tide at the beginning of
May and one at the low tides at the end of May.

Obviously, people had to be finely attuned to the tides and the currents,
as well as to winds and weather conditions. Any ocean-based activities on
the north coast can be treacherous, and this is especially so when people
are harvesting from the rocks right at the tide line. They are vulnerable to
being swept away by rogue waves or to being caught by unexpected storms.
Helen warned that people have to always be alert and to follow the lead of
the most knowledgeable ones when it comes to knowing when to stop harvesting because of rising tides or incoming storms. This type of knowledge comes only with experience and careful attention, and it is one of the
concerns of elders that younger people no longer understand these imper-
atives and may put themselves and others in danger. In the winter of 2000
a young man drowned, and the reason was in part that he did not understand the power of the currents and tides, or the ferocity and bitter cold of

the north wind, and tried to swim out to retrieve his boat that had drifted away from the beach.

Formerly, seaweed harvesting was women's work only. The men would venture out to fish for halibut or to hunt or trap, and it was the women who went out in groups in their canoes to get seaweed and bring it home to process. Helen recalled that long ago they used to have sails fixed to their canoes, as well as using paddles. One of the women would steer and would guard the canoe while the others picked seaweed, making sure to keep it from the rocks. She would also watch the tides and weather and warn the others if it was time to stop. Several canoe loads of women might cross the channel from Princess Royal Island (Lax'a'lit'aa Koo) to Campania Island (Kagaas) together, to camp out and spend the days picking seaweed. Children usually stayed behind at Kiel or other camps, to be cared for by older siblings or young mothers who stayed behind. Older children might be taken along to help look after the canoes or boats. The entire seaweed-picking endeavor was—and still is—one of cooperation and teamwork. Nowadays men also help out, especially with running the boats and transporting the seaweed. Seaweed harvesting is very much a family activity.

The Forest and the Seaweed

Where does the forest come together with seaweed harvesting? In many ways, the interconnection between forest and seaweed is epitomized in the large dugout canoes of western red cedar (Thuja plicata) that the women used to travel to and from their seaweed grounds. It is also in the situation of the seaweed camp itself, nestled at the edge of the towering forest of Sitka spruce (Picea sitchensis), western hemlock (Tsuga heterophylla), and red cedar, with the cabins intermingled with dense salal (Gaultheria shallon) and huckleberry bushes (Vaccinium parvifolium), which provide additional food and materials for the Gitga'at people. The trees provide much needed firewood and construction materials. Helen explained the importance of wood for fuel, some of which is obtained as driftwood: "There's certain little bays and little places where all the driftwood is at. And so, because we use a lot of wood, if you don't have the sun, you're using a lot of wood to try to dry your halibut, your fish."

All of the plants around the camp are useful for one purpose or another. Although the salal in the area does not bear fruit at the time the seaweed harvesters are there, its leaves are important for the later seaweed curing process. Helen always gathers dozens of large salal leaves, or has her grand-daughters and the other girls staying at the camp gather them for her. The salal leaves are also made into decorative headbands by these girls. In fact, there are over ninety species of plants in Gitga'at territory, most of them from the forests and their associated bogs, marshes, and riverbanks that are named by the Gitga'at and have direct cultural significance.

Another connection between seaweed harvesting and the forest is reflected in one of the Gitga'at taboos associated with picking seaweed: people were warned never to harvest cedar bark (used for clothing, basketry, mats, and even roofing) during the time that people were picking seaweed. Harvest-ing and working with cedar bark is said to cause rain, and as already noted, one should not pick seaweed when it is raining. Helen explained that pull-ing the bark from the cedar tree exposes the wood and can "burn" the tree if it is then exposed to the hot sun. Nature therefore always seems to make a protective blanket for the newly harvested cedar tree by producing a fog, mist, or rain, thus giving the tree time to heal itself and allowing it to con-tinue to live and grow. This is why it inevitably rains when people are har-vesting cedar bark, and why these two activities are incompatible. Tradi-tion therefore dictates that women should wait until after the seaweed has been harvested and dried before they go to peel cedar bark.

Back Home in Hartley Bay

The squares of seaweed, if they are thoroughly dry, will keep well for sever-al weeks. Once the people have returned from Kiel, in the fine, sunny days of June, they will undertake the next phase of the seaweed processing. Hel-en has two bentwood cedar boxes, one of which is probably well over a hun-dred years old, as indicated by the wooden pegs that hold the joined cor-ner ends together and the bottom onto the sides. These are what she uses to shape and cure the seaweed. The square shape of these boxes produces squares of seaweed of a standard, time-honored size, a size that has served as a form of currency in trading; similar squares of dried soapberries and Saskatoon berries are produced by the Gitxsan, and these squares become an equivalent for exchange. The women moisten the sun-dried squares of dried seaweed, sprinkling them with salt water; then the squares are formed and packed down into the cedar boxes in layers.

Helen explains the whole process:

> You form a square something the way you form an envelope—in a triangle. I'm making a square. And so I will put little patches of seaweed where it's thin, until I've got the thickness. I would make it about, maybe about an inch and a half thick, this square. And so I will put it into the box. And . . . I have dish towels and I put it on top of that square, and then I'll get somebody that's got clean feet and clean socks. And they will step on it and kick—it's called kicking—stepping on the seaweed, flattening it out, and it's gluing together by the pressure of the foot. And so, women that really know how to stamp on the seaweed would specifically do the corners . . . after they're finished, . . . you take the cloth off and you put the salal leaves, face down, . . . The light side down. And on the seaweed you'd have about nine big leaves across the square. . . .
>
> Then . . . you'd lay the cedar bark, . . . And you've got long cedar bark [ribbon], let's say you've got about a ten-foot [thin strip] piece of cedar bark. (I'm exaggerating a little. I don't think it's quite that long.) But you'd lay it diagonally along on top of the salal leaves, and then you'd put the next cake of seaweed on. Sometimes you have a woman that's pretty strong; she can do two cakes at once. And so you would . . . do the same thing, salal leaves down, the diagonal cross with the bark, until you get the box completely filled. And you would fill it overflowing. And so you have a board that fits right on the top of that box. And so you put the board on. You put the cloth on top of the seaweed, put the board on, and then you put big heavy rocks. And so, . . . I leave that [seaweed] in the box

for three days. So, we say, there's an expression that it "gets its flavor." It takes three days to absorb that . . . salt water [and] . . . to adhere together. So then you'd smell real good seaweed.

So then it's time to get the women that come to chop the seaweed. So now we use axes. We use the yew wood block . . . they're sawed-off yew [Taxus brevifolia], a hard wood. They put something around it. Sometimes they use cardboard; you nail the cardboard around the top of the block [projecting up about four inches high]. When they're chopping seaweed on the block, [then] it doesn't fall off the block because the cardboard outer covering keeps the seaweed in. . . . And so they put that chopped seaweed in big, big containers and then . . . , as soon as the sun shines, that seaweed's going out. And so I'd take a tarp, put a seaweed sheet on there, and sprinkle that seaweed on the seaweed sheet again. . . .

And so you need to dry it in June. This is because of the long daylight hours, hours of sunshine you get in June. Also, you HAVE to dry it in June, before the grasses really grow long. If the grasses grow long then they retain the dew of the evening. You see, and so the evaporation of that dew is coming . . . and you're putting your seaweed close to the ground. So, because right in the village we don't have rocks and things there; we're using boardwalks, and so the top will be the rock. Because the top would warm up the same as a rock. You're putting your white seaweed sheets, . . . white . . . retains the heat of the sun. . . . And so then you're sprinkling it in a fine [layer], about half an inch, around all over with seaweed.

So that takes all day to dry. And . . . you're moving that seaweed. About every two hours . . . —you'd have a flat stick, like a yardstick. And you would move the seaweed so that it's turning over. It's turning over and drying so that it all dries. . . . After the sun starts to set, the seaweed is cooling off now, and before that dew

starts again, you gather the seaweed. You pull up the four corners
of the sheets and shake the seaweed down to the center, and pack it
inside this way, holding onto the drawn-up corners. . . . You have
to let it cool right down, in a dry place. [Helen puts it in her living
room]. You open up the corners so it doesn't steam or sweat and it
dries completely. So overnight you'll let it cool and . . . then you're
putting it into tight containers. . . . What we usually do is take a
certain amount out of the big containers—just enough seaweed
that you're going to eat—and put it into a smaller sealed container;
the less you expose the seaweed to the air, the better. Because every
time the air hits that seaweed, it changes it. Eventually the sea-
weed will turn a different color. And it has a different taste. So if
you keep the large container closed, and just take out what you're
going to eat for that meal, . . . it will retain its original flavor from
when it was put into there.

Helen explained that some women use green cedar branches instead of salal leaves to place between the seaweed layers. Also, women today may use a length of twine laid diagonally across the seaweed layers instead of a strip of cedar bark.

As in the harvesting of the seaweed, the chopping and drying process-es are undertaken with cooperation and reciprocity. Helen described how women all through the village would come to help her when it is time to chop the seaweed:

Somebody will say, "When are you going to chop your seaweed?"
And I have to send somebody out: "Well, granny's going to be chop-
ping seaweed on such and such a day." I send word throughout the
community, and so they drift up. Some people have an hour or so,
[but] they'll come out. And so, they all help each other, the wom-
en. Some of them have enough daughters or granddaughters to go
and help. It works that way in every house, [when] they're chop-
ping seaweed. If you've got an hour to spare, two hours to spare,
whatever time you have, you go and help chop seaweed. Especial-

ly if you don't have seaweed. You will earn some seaweed; they'll
give you some seaweed. You earn it.

Thus, the work of seaweed production is one that brings people—especially women—together, to socialize, to learn from each other, and to share the products of their labors. In this way, it is a constructive and healthful activity that contributes to the well-being of the whole community.

Nutritional and Health Contributions

Louis Druehl (2000:155) wrote that "Nori (*Porphyra*) is probably one of the healthiest foods on our planet. . . . It is rich in carbohydrates, proteins and vitamins." *Porphyras*, like other marine algae, have a high protein content, said to be 25–35 percent of dry weight for Japanese nori (*Porphyra* spp.). They also contain significant quantities of vitamins and mineral salts, especially iodine. The vitamin C content of the Japanese species is about 1.5 times that of oranges. What is particularly significant is that up to 75 percent of the protein and carbohydrates, at least of the Japanese nori, are digestible by humans, which is very high for seaweeds (Guiry 2002).

We suspect—although this remains to be demonstrated empirically—that the complex process of drying, rehydrating, curing so it "gets its flavor," and redrying the seaweed also helps to break down the complex proteins and carbohydrates and enhances the digestibility of the seaweed. Other peoples along the Northwest Coast also had intricate procedures for curing edible seaweed, including packing them in boxes interspersed with cedar boughs, sometimes even saturating them with juice from chewed rock chitons or clams, presumably to enhance the flavor or digestibility of the seaweed (Boas 1921).

Ła'ask is also used directly as a medicine. Johnny Clifton explained that eating seaweed will alleviate heartburn and indigestion, just like Tums or Rolaids. It is also used as an antiseptic poultice for a deep cut or swelling; according to Helen, it will take the swelling right down and will keep a cut from becoming infected.

When eaten as a component of a traditional diet, together with seafood like halibut and salmon, crabs, game, berries, and wild greens and root vegetables, there is no doubt that seaweed helps to promote good nutrition and health. Additionally, the lifestyle associated with the seaweed harvest—being physically active and working outdoors, with safety a prime consideration—would also promote good health and well-being. Culturally and socially, too, the family and community closeness and cooperation, the opportunities for learning and teaching, and the closer understanding of history and traditions of people's heritage that comes with harvesting and using traditional food all promote emotional and mental health. Environmental health is also a consideration. The seaweed is harvested sustainably, maintaining its capacity for regeneration and renewal. Furthermore, people who are out on the lands and waters on a continuous basis have the opportunity to observe closely any changes or impacts that might be occurring in the environment, including changes in populations and health of other life forms. Ultimately, this close monitoring can result in adaptive behavior and can enhance a society's resilience and capacity to maintain cultural integrity in the face of change (Berkes and Folke 1998).

Changes and Adaptations in Seaweed Harvesting and Use

Many changes have occurred over the years relating to the Gitga'at seaweed harvest; some of these have already been mentioned. Fewer people harvest the seaweed today than in the past, at least in part because the younger people have wage jobs and because children have to be in school and cannot take an entire month to be away from the village. Some Gitga'at people live away from Hartley Bay, in Prince Rupert or Vancouver, and this makes Kiel even less accessible. Men now do participate in what was once entirely a women's occupation. Speedboats and skiffs today replace the cedarwood dugouts of bygone years. Nylon onion sacks are used in preference to hemp gunnysacks, which had, in turn, replaced the original cedar bark containers. The gunnysacks tend to accumulate and hold water instead of allowing it to drain away, thus causing the seaweed kept in sacks to sweat, retain its heat, deteriorate, and rot more quickly. This is why mesh onion bags are preferred today. Fewer of the traditional seaweed beds are used in harvesting, and, undoubtedly, less seaweed is picked than in the past, when, according to Helen and Johnny, all the seaweed-producing shorelines of Campania and Princess Royal islands were cleaned off each season. Methods of processing and cooking the seaweed have changed as well. Nowadays, some of the seaweed is dried in thin sheets or left in squares without chopping it; the younger people enjoy just frying these squares up in lard, like potato chips, and eating them as a snack. Few people have the chance to make halibut-head soup and some of the other dishes that were commonly prepared and eaten with the seaweed traditionally.

People are also concerned about environmental pollution and its impacts on their traditional foods. Seaweeds, for example, can absorb heavy metals (Sirota and Uthe 1979), but the actual risks of such contamination are little studied or understood.

The changes in the weather have resulted in attempts to adapt by freezing the seaweed so that it could be dried at a later date, when the weather improved. Helen commented:

> For years you could depend on "April showers will bring May flowers." You need that for . . . [predicting] the weather. Worldwide, the weather is so different now, you can't depend on those old sayings. You're lucky if you get one day of sun. And if you're not at the right tide, even if you pick that seaweed for that [day], you might be picking late afternoon, and you can't dry it on those rocks. Some of our people have tried to experiment right now, and tried to put some into the deep freeze to see [how it does]. And yet, some of our older people will taste it, and there's a difference. There's a difference to that seaweed that has been frozen. And so they will taste it. Even though we try to save it, . . . they'll try many ways because we haven't had the sun that we used to depend so much on.

Helen and other Gitga'at elders are concerned that the younger people cannot easily participate in seaweed picking. In part this is also due to the uncertainties of the weather:

> And so our young people that can help us—because they're working, they come down here on weekends—and so they get stuck because

they're weatherbound.[3] *They can't make it down here; they can't help us. They get the wood, they get the water, they do many things for us. We need their help, us elders that live here.*

The elders are looked after in other ways, too. Helen noted that there are special seaweed-picking places that are reserved especially for the older women, who are not as nimble and cannot leap from rock to rock or climb down steep rock faces to seek out the best seaweed. The flatter, more even places where the seaweed grows, therefore, are kept for the elders.

Helen also recognizes that the young people are missing out on much of the traditional education that they would have received in the past during stays at Kiel and other places out on the land and waters in Gitga'at territory. Because they are not able to experience firsthand the effects of tides, currents, and weather, or how to harvest and process their traditional foods, they may not be able to carry on these traditions or pass them on to the next generations.

The seaweed, too, is affected by the weather. Helen explains:

> Sometimes . . . there's a difference of seaweed. With the weather conditions that we've had now—we're having hail, we're having snow—and if the seaweed is just starting to grow on the rocks. They're just like any plant: if they've been hit by frost and it's real cold—we did have some really cold north wind in April, it was beautiful weather once the sun came out, but really frosty, icy conditions. So we could tell, all the seaweed, if there was snow, the tide was down, a big snowstorm came in, or hit by hail. And we'd have to break the ends off of the seaweed there. The seaweed is a beautiful greenish color, and the ends will all start to have curly heads . . . seaweed is smooth, when you feel it. You get to the curly parts [at the ends of the seaweed], they're rotten, they're tough, they're kinky. That seaweed is not good. You learn that with experience.

Conclusion

Times are certainly changing, and the Gitga'at, like people of other coastal communities, have had to face the changes and adapt to them. Cultural traditions like harvesting and eating *ła'ask* are at risk of being lost if a certain threshold of practice and passing on the associated knowledge is not reached. Helen Clifton has thought a great deal about these changes and worries about the future of the young people in her community and about the environmental changes as well:

> I just wonder if [the old people] were alive what they'd say about this weather that we're having now, what they would have to say. They would say somebody did something. . . . [That's] why the weather is the way it is. And of course, we know who that is! But those are some of the things that happened here, that's changed over time. It's the Mickey Mouse [CB radio], VHS, and TV. Yes, you see kids today, you would find a rare kid that would know whose speedboat that is coming, whose boat that is!

In many ways it is the small details of cultural and environmental knowledge that are the most important, and they are the most in danger of slipping away in the society-wide rush toward globalization and cultural homogenization. If the details of how to harvest and how to cure seaweed pass out of people's knowledge and experience, more would disappear than just one food source. The Gitga'at, and all humanity, would be poorer for this loss. It is thanks to the Gitga'at elders, who work hard to keep their cultural traditions alive, that seaweed and other traditional foods are likely to be harvested and enjoyed far into the future.

Notes

We would like to thank all the members of the Gitga'at Nation, Hartley Bay, especially Chief Johnny Clifton, Chief Pat Sterritt and Art Sterritt, Annette Robinson, Jimmy Robinson, Marven Robinson, Ernie Hill, Lynne Hill and Cam Hill. We are also grateful to Dan Cardinall, Irma Beltgens, Michael Roth, Anne Marshall, Robin June Hood, Sandra Lindstrom, Barbara Wilson (Kii7iljuus), and Judy Thompson (Edosti) for their contributions to this chapter. Our research was supported by the Coasts Under Stress Research Project (Rosemary Ommer, PI), and by the Local Knowledge, Natural Resources and Community Survival workshop organized by Charles Menzies. This chapter has also been published in Eating and Healing: Traditional Food as Medicine, ed. Andrea Pieroni and Lisa Leimar Price (Binghamton NY: Haworth Press, 2005). We would like to dedicate this chapter to the children of the Gitga'at Nation and to the memory of Chief Johnny Clifton, who passed away in the spring of 2004.

1. Other food that people have traditionally gathered from Kiel include halibut, red snapper, seagull eggs, small and large chitons (China slippers), abalone, and giant mussels ("all the seafood you could get"). However, according to Helen Clifton, the latter were harvested only after the seaweed had been picked and dried because harvesting the mussels is said to cause rain.

2. The life cycle of Porphyra is described in full by Michael D. Guiry, a phycologist, on his Web site, "Welcome to the Seaweed Site," http://seaweed.ucg.ie/ (1999). The haploid plants grow from spores that were produced from the diploid phase through meiosis. The diploid phase, called the Conchocelis phase, was discovered only in 1949 by the British phycologist K. M. Drew-Baker. Before this time, it was not recognized that it was the same plant as the membranous haploid form. The Conchocelis-phase organisms produce two types of spores from the ends of their branchlets. Under some conditions, they produce diploid spores, which will grow into other individuals. However, under other, specific conditions of light quantity, light quality, length of day, and temperature (the permissive conditions differ between species and sometimes between strains of a species), the filaments form swollen branches (called "conchosporangia") in which the cells, still diploid, develop into branches that protrude from the substrate and eventually release their contents as individual wall-less cells called "conchospores." It is these cells that eventually undergo meiosis—which is a complex process, with secretion of cell walls and splitting of the chromosome pairs. There are usually four haploid cells surviving. Hence, the blades, unlike the plants they are derived from, are haploid.

The haploid plants, again under specific conditions of light quality and quantity, length of day and temperature, will eventually produce gametes. Male gametes (called "spermatia") are produced in packets at the blade margins and are released by disintegration of the margin. The female gametes, or "carpogonia," are produced back from the margin. Each carpogonium develops a special receptive surface, to which the spermatia attach, allowing fertilization to occur. The fertilized cell, the zygote, now diploid (with a double complement of chromosomes) divides to form a structure called a "carposporangium," which releases diploid spores, or "carpospores," as the blade margin disintegrates. The carpospores germinate to form new diploid Conchocelis-phase filaments, which germinate on, and frequently penetrate, a shell substrate. Although calcium carbonate is not absolutely required for their growth, apparently, it is only within this substrate that the filaments can survive in nature without being browsed by herbivorous snails and other marine grazers.

3. Note: on our way down to Kiel with Marven Robinson in May 2001, we had to go to the outside of Campania Island because the waves and currents were too strong on the inside of the island. Marven kept in close radio contact with Johnny Clifton, who advised him how the weather was at Kiel.

4. Ecological Knowledge, Subsistence, and Livelihood Practices

The Case of the Pine Mushroom Harvest
in Northwestern British Columbia

Charles R. Menzies

Traditional ecological knowledge (TEK), the local understandings of plant, animal, and habitat relations held by Indigenous peoples, is emerging as an important focus of applied social research (Sillitoe 1998). In a world in which ecological concerns are accelerating and faith in technological fixes is collapsing, TEK is held up as a beacon of hope. TEK is said to offer the promise of ancient, culturally relevant, and environmentally friendly ways and means of reintegrating alienated industrial women and men with our natural world. From new age environmentalists to "hard" science natural resource managers, TEK is being put forward as the solution to a myriad of problems created by industrial resource extraction and intensive factory-style agriculture. Widespread interest in Indigenous knowledge systems has been spurred on by spectacular scientist-led resource collapses, such as the collapse of the North Atlantic cod fishery in the 1990s (Rogers 1995; Berrill 1997). In the face of such ecological crises researchers and lay people alike have turned to alternative knowledge sources such as TEK to find solutions where scientific knowledge has failed.

The application of TEK is not unproblematic (see, for example, Cruikshank 1998:44–70; Nadasdy 1999). The extent of the difficulties of applying TEK to contemporary ecological problems or in integrating it with natural science models ranges from the technical (a focus on the obstacles to integration) to the epistemological (a focus on mutually exclusive cultural ways of knowing). While the jury is still out on the possibility for real-time applications of TEK on a wide scale, this stream of writing clearly identifies important areas of difficulty in any rapprochement between TEK and scientific knowledge.

TEK is often described as an enduring, culturally unique, and habitat-specific set of knowledges that have enabled Indigenous peoples to live within their territories for millennia without noticeable ecological degradation. While some concede that some knowledge has been "lost," most accounts of TEK focus on the ecologically and culturally specific accumulation of knowledge over time.[1] The key point in these analyses is a focus on cultural values as existing independently from a people's real-time subsistence and livelihood practices (be they hunter-gatherers, agriculturalists, or wage laborers). Thus, Indigenous peoples are understood to have an intrinsic cultural value of respect and are therefore "natural ecologists." However, the weight of evidence would appear to support a somewhat more complicated picture in which cultural values create particular pathways locked within limits set by how a people organizes its subsistence and livelihood practices (Brody 2000; Wolf 1999).

While everyday subsistence and livelihood practices are situated within broadly defined cultural frames, TEK proper is best understood as experiential knowledge resulting from human/environment interactions. It is also important to highlight that TEK is not simply the product of a blind process of knowledge accumulation. Nor is it tied to sets of abstract, timeless cultural values disarticulated from material practices or everyday processes of subsistence. Rather, traditional ecological knowledge is tied directly to the material conditions under which individuals and communities organize their subsistence and make their living. As such, TEK shifts and changes in accordance with transformation in economic activities. There are jumps and breaks, fragmentations, and coalescences.

In this chapter I argue that TEK is an embodied practice directly rooted in everyday livelihood activities. This argument is developed through an exploration of the case of the pine mushroom industry and the local ecological knowledge of Nisga'a and Gitksan peoples in the Nass Valley and Upper Skeena watershed. This task is accomplished by first situating contemporary livelihood practices within their ethnographic context. I then discuss the customary use and knowledge of pine mushrooms among Tsimshianic peoples. This customary knowledge is then juxtaposed with the TEK of pine mushrooms as it has emerged within the context of a newly commoditized transglobal market for exotic food products. I close by considering the dynamic and material aspects of TEK within their Tsimshianic cultural framework.

Ethnographic Context

The ethnographic data discussed and analyzed in this chapter emerges from my ongoing research relationship with First Nations and non-Aboriginal communities in north coastal British Columbia.[2] This region is simultaneously an ethnographic exemplar (popularized by "salvage" ethnographers such as Franz Boas, Maurice Barbeau, John Swanton, and Edward Sapir, among others) and a key site of industrial capitalist resource extraction. While ethnographers like Boas scrambled to collect all manner of cultural artifacts in order to freeze the region's Indigenous cultures in an ethnographic amber, Boas's field site was becoming fully integrated into a world capitalist system in such a way that had profound effects upon these Indigenous societies (Wolf 1982:182–192; 1999:69–131).

The three northern nations that have occupied north coastal British Columbia since time immemorial, Tsimshian, Nisga'a, and Gitksan, share a common political structure, family of languages, and history. Among these Indigenous peoples effective political organization is vested at the level of extended, matrilineal family or household groups. Until the late 1800s, household groups were essentially synonymous with residential units (though individuals who married out maintained their membership in their house of birth). The house groups maintain and manage the use of and access to a patchwork quilt of resource-gathering territories (see, for example, Cove 1982).

Each of these north coast nations maintains a set of rules of use and access regulated by kinship. Thus, a husband has certain rights to use his wife's hunting, fishing, or gathering territories, but only as long as he is married to her. Men and women have access to their mother's house group's territories. With these rights of use and access come clearly defined responsibilities concerning the sharing of foods and resources harvested from within the territory.

The histories of the house groups of the Tsimshian, Nisga'a, and Gitksan document their origins and important ancestors and record the key events of their past. These stories describe cataclysmic natural events, the expansion and retreat of peoples, and impressive moments of technological and socioeconomic innovation and transformation. The most recent cycle of change began with the arrival of Europeans—K'mksiwah—within the territories of Sabaan and of Tsibasa of the Gitxaała people in 1777 (Hutchinson and Marsden 1992).

From their first trips to the territories of the Tsimshian, K'mksiwah were primarily interested in extracting resources—fur, fish, timber, and minerals—for use within the developing international capitalist economy. However, during the fur trade period (maritime trade, 1770s–1830s; land-based trade, 1830s–1880s) the actual extraction of resources and production of commodities was controlled directly by Tsimshian, Nisga'a, and Gitksan peoples according to customary practices and corresponded to already existing regional trade networks and alliances (see, for example, Marsden and Galois 1995; Fisher 1977[3]). Not until the beginning of the period of industrial capitalist resource extraction did the K'mksiwah attempt to grasp direct control over the process of production and the organization of social labor.

The impact on Tsimshian, Nisga'a, and Gitksan societies was direct and ultimately destructive (in an economic sense), in that industrial capitalism is premised on direct control over labor power and the process of production (see McDonald 1994, for a case study of the Tsimshian community of Kitsumkalum).[4] Thus, the previous situation during the fur trade, in which control over labor and production remained under the command of First Nations kin groups, was directly attacked through the imposition—at times by force—of a colonial legal system that criminalized customary harvesting techniques and trade relations, banned key social institutions, and intruded into customary laws regarding the inheritance of property (see, for example, Harris 2001). However, the legal and regulatory gaze of the colonial state in British Columbia has only looked on those resources that were commoditized within the capitalist economy, leaving other resources to exist within the context of customary use rights of the Tsimshian, Nisga'a, and Gitksan peoples. Thus pine mushrooms remained outside of the capitalist economy until the late 20th century. They entered into the commodity circuit within the context of a changed legal climate in which Aboriginal rights have finally begun to be recognized (at least within law, if not always in practice) and the context of the negotiation and ultimate enactment of a treaty between the Nisga'a and the colonial states of British Columbia and Canada. This changed legal and political context has had important implications for the development and subsequent regulation of the pine mushroom industry. In the balance of the chapter we turn to the cultural context of Tsimshian ecological knowledge and the specifics of pine mushroom ecological knowledge held by Tsimshianic peoples.

Customary Use and Knowledge of Pine Mushrooms

The customary use of salmon, berries, and a variety of roots, tubers, and other plants are well documented in the ethnographic literature (Kuhnlein and Turner 1991; Compton 1993; L. M. Johnson 1999; Johnson Gottesfeld 1994; McDonald n.d.). The use of mushrooms by Tsimshian, Nisga'a, and Gitksan is less well documented. Community members generally accept that pine mushrooms were a minor food or medicine—if used at all—in their traditional practices.

Pine Mushrooms are capped mushrooms that grow 10 to 15 centimeters high.[5] The cap is white when young. It turns gradually brown as the mushroom ages. These mushrooms are often found growing in groups or clumps in coniferous forests of pine, fir, hemlock, and red cedar that range from 35 to 200 years of age. The mushrooms are normally hidden under the forest litter, with only a slight bump or mound to give away their location. Ethnobotanical data collected by others and recorded in interviews with

Nisga'a and Gitskan pine mushroom pickers suggest that this association between mushrooms and particular tree species was noted by Nisga'a and neighboring peoples.

Two general comments concerning local ecological knowledge of pine mushrooms prior to the development of the commercial harvest can be made: there were very limited observations on the use of mushrooms as either a food or a medicine and observations on local awareness of mushrooms garnered while gathering other plant materials or during hunting trips.

Research into local Tsimshian ecological knowledge has been relatively limited in scope. Earlier ethnographers have focused on oral history (such as William Beynon, Franz Boas, and Maurice Barbeau). The subsequent generations of ethnographers expanded this focus to include social structure and organization (Garfield 1939; Cove 1982; Adams 1973), linguistics (Dunn 1978; Rigsby 1967; Seguin 1985; Tarpent 1983, 1997) and political economic issues (McDonald 1994; Marsden and Galois 1995).

Although there has been some ethnobotanical work in the region (Compton 1993; L. M. Johnson 1999; Johnson Gottesfeld 1994; McDonald n.d.; H. I. Smith et al. 1997), this remains a relatively understudied area. What can be gleaned from the previously published materials are scant hints and suggestions of how mushrooms have been used in customary Tsimshian, Nisga'a, and Gitksan societies. None of the published accounts provide direct evidence that Tsimshian, Nisga'a, or Gitksan people actually consumed mushrooms as a food, though McDonald does list mushrooms as a food plant in a paper otherwise dedicated to horticulture and berry crops within Kitsumkalum territory.[6]

There is clear evidence that other forms of fungi were recognized, named, and used by coastal peoples (Blanchette et al. 1992; Compton 1995; Compton et al. 1995), though not as a food source. However, current research underway in the Tsimshian territories strongly suggests that even though K'mksiwah science group such things as puff balls, bracket fungi, and capped mushrooms together, Tsimshian categories do not.[7] This is an important ethnographic detail that cannot be overlooked. Thus, it might make sense, from within a Western botanical framework, to group such varied items as shelf, bracket, or other types of fungi, puffballs, and mushrooms. But from within the context of a Tsimshianic understanding of the environment, these fungi belong to conceptually different categories of things that do not necessarily share features with each other.

Various types of tree fungi, for example, are called *adagan* ("ghost bread" in English, but it contains in its root the word *gan*, or tree). The generic word for mushrooms, *gaayda baa'lax*, is a compound word that, loosely translated, means "ghost hat."[8] However, the similarities in English belie the Indigenous differences in *sm'algyax*. The word for fungus contains an embedded reference to something on a tree, whereas the word for mushroom refers specifically to a functional similarity to an item of clothing, a hat.[9] Although this does not conclusively prove whether or not Tsimshian peoples consumed mushrooms as food or if they recognized all fungi as belonging to similar categories of things, it does demonstrate that mushrooms and other fungi were sufficiently recognized as to be named.

Mushroom use is markedly different among interior and southern Aboriginal peoples in British Columbia where mushrooms were extensively used as food and in medicinal and ritual practices. For example, peoples of the interior plateau used as many as six different species of mushrooms as food or medicines (Kuhnlein and Turner 1991). In terms of the food use by Tsimshianic peoples, it may well be that the diversity and density of food resources in their regions were such that mushrooms were not worth the investment of time to harvest and process when compared to other animal and plant food resources available.

Compton's extensive study of northern Wakashan and southern Tsimshian ethnobotany clearly demonstrates that mushrooms were recognized and named, even if they were not a food item of any importance. According to Compton, "the Hanaksiala and Haisla did not typically use mushrooms, however, one type of mushroom . . . said to treat sore throats" (1993:140). Compton speculates that it was the pine mushroom that was used as a minor medicine. However, beyond a brief discussion of puffballs (they were thought to be harmful to eyesight) and shelf fungi (used in shamanic rituals and winter dances), no other discussions of mushrooms are included in his otherwise extensive report.[10]

Prior to commercialization, customary knowledge of pine mushrooms among Tsimshianic peoples was not particularly extensive. The mushrooms had little apparent use as either a food or as a medicine. However, interview data do suggest that local people understood elements of the mushrooms' ecology, particularly as it related to the distribution of particular game animals and other forest resources. It was this knowledge upon which contemporary pine mushroom pickers built when they entered the pine mushroom industry in the late 20th century.

The Pine Mushroom Industry
and Local Harvesting Knowledge

Changing attitudes toward industrial logging have created a space for non-timber forest products such as pine mushrooms to become a more appealing commercial target of exploitation in British Columbia's forestlands. Over the course of the last several decades, pine mushrooms have been transformed from a minor plant item (noted but rarely consumed by Tsimshianic peoples) to a major cash harvest. Starting in the early 1970s firms such as Betty's Best Mushrooms, Matsumara Enterprises, and Mo-Na Food Enterprises began experimenting with the commercial harvest of mushrooms. In the ensuing years a highly flexible, though tightly controlled, industry emerged that is for the most part outside of the regulatory gaze of government agencies.

During this process a pine mushroom TEK has emerged that is simultaneously "traditional" and "contemporary." The example of the pine mushroom harvest is used to demonstrate how local knowledge has altered and adapted to new conditions and how this is simultaneously connected to customary land-use patterns and to the contemporary processes of the global capitalist economy in which the pine mushroom is a luxury commodity in Japan.

As government agencies became aware of the growing economic importance of nontimber forest products, they tried to define a social and economic space within which the governance of the pine mushroom harvest would default to the government and would, therefore, remain out of First

Nations control and, technically, open to non-Aboriginal economic development. However, the pine mushroom picking areas fall within so-called Crown lands, that is, unceded First Nations traditional territories in places such as the Nass River Valley.

The Nisga'a Treaty, for example, explicitly mentions mushroom picking areas, and the Nisga'a Tribal Council has been engaged in establishing management policies governing Nisga'a Treaty Lands and surrounding territories (most recently a $250 access fee has been implemented for non-Nisga'a pickers). As a result, government attempts to regulate this recently commoditized natural resource have not been as successful as government attempts to control commoditized natural resources in the late 1880s. It is important to point out that despite the Nisga'a's ability to regulate harvesting practices within their Treaty Lands, the effective economic control of the pine mushroom industry is maintained by a small group of industrial resource-processing firms.

The export of pine mushrooms is tightly controlled by four or five major firms, all but one of which is tied to the fish-processing industry. It appears that the emergence of the mushroom-buying firms is closely linked to the expansion of Japanese-financed fish-buying companies that began entering the British Columbia fishing industry in the late 1960s and early 1970s. Although these firms are big players in the mushroom industry, they are relatively small compared with their competitors in the fishing industry. Arrayed below these major firms is a hierarchical system of smaller firms, brokers, and field agents (again, there is a close parallel with the fishing industry in which independent brokers and field buyers work on contract for larger firms while maintaining some modicum of independence).

The purchase and export structure of the pine mushroom industry has all the appearances of an elaborate pyramid scheme. The pickers, situated at the bottom of the pyramid, earn anywhere between a few hundred dollars to a few thousand dollars per year. The median income of Nass River pickers is estimated to be approximately $3,500. At the next level of the pyramid, field buyers earn between $35,000 and $60,000 per season. The revenues of the big five processors sitting at the apex of the pyramid ranges between a low of $3.75 million and $16 million in pretax income annually.

The large British Columbia exporters of pine mushrooms have a relatively flexible supply system that allows them to concentrate buying efforts in the production areas of most abundance in any given year. For example, 1997 was a poor year in the Nass Valley (Nisga'a and Gitksan territories), but the Powell River area harvests in south coastal British Columbia were considerable. The larger operations shift their buying efforts by moving their mobile agents and capital to productive areas. International access is also a significant advantage. The 1998 season in British Columbia was very weak, but Hi-To Fisheries was able to maintain its supply to Japan by increasing its U.S. purchases to 80 percent of the total, up from the usual 20 percent. The smaller, locally based buyers are limited to the yearly productive variations of their areas.

The critical level for exerting economic control is effectively at the level of processing and exports, as opposed to harvesting. The large processing firms have the knowledge, established contacts, and economic resources to maintain their control over the industry. Given this situation, the Nisga'a have started to explore how they might effectively increase their economic control over the industry and thus retain a greater economic benefit to their nation while simultaneously exerting regulatory control over mushroom harvesting.

Contemporary pine mushroom ecological knowledge can, in a general sense, be understood as including specific ecological knowledge (relating to the location of pine mushrooms and appropriate harvesting methods) and economic knowledge (concerning local and global market prices, selling techniques, and the behavior and attributes of local field buyers and brokers). In field interviews conducted during the mushroom seasons of 1999 and 2000, Nisga'a and Gitksan mushroom pickers and brokers describe how they have drawn upon their local knowledge of lands near their villages and within their traditional hunting and food-gathering territories in order to locate prime mushroom-picking areas. Observations of potential mushroom habitat was accumulated during hunting and other food-gathering and foraging trips. As the mushroom industry grew, Nisga'a and Gitksan community members were able to apply their knowledge of the land and move into mushroom picking in a highly effective manner.

One Gitksan community member explained what he saw as a relationship between bears and his ability to find pine mushrooms. The following example was given: "Before anyone ever thought about picking pine mushrooms, I spent a lot of time in the fall hunting. As I worked through my house territory I would see bear signs. You could tell a bear had been there by the claw marks on the trees or by the ripped up ground. The bears eat mushrooms, just like the Japanese! I didn't think much about this until these guys started turning up on my house territory, about fifteen to twenty years ago, looking for mushrooms. Then I thought about the bears and realized that if I knew where to find the bears, I also knew where to find mushrooms."

Another community member explained that red squirrels eat pine mushrooms: "You know that a really good spot of mushrooms is nearby when the squirrels started telling you to go away. They're really territorial, those squirrels. They eat the mushrooms and don't want anyone coming by. If they see you coming, they'll let loose. I've even seen a squirrel try to chase a guy off. I think they must really like the mushrooms."

In these and other interviews Gitksan and Nisga'a mushroom pickers described various indicators that helped them find mushrooms. These indicators include such items as the presence of certain types of animals, combinations of different tree species, variations in ground cover, and moisture content of ground and soils.[11] This TEK had been gleaned in the course of regular subsistence activities during which Nisga'a and Gitksan peoples moved through their territories, actively observing, recording (in oral stories), and reflecting on the structure of the landscape. Younger male mushroom pickers (under 40) recalled hunting trips with their fathers and uncles during which mushrooms were observed but not harvested or otherwise interfered with. Younger female pickers had similar stories of encountering mushrooms while berry picking with their grandmothers, mothers, and aunts.

All of the Nisga'a and Gitksan mushroom pickers interviewed emphasized the potential fragility of mushroom patches and the need to treat them with care and respect. There was a clear recognition of the conflict between logging practices and the preservation of mushroom patches. On a number of occasions interviewees described the destruction of prime mushroom patches by non-Aboriginal firms logging in their house territories. The harvesting practices of itinerant, non-Aboriginal pickers were also criticized. Nisga'a pickers in particular were critical of outside pickers who harvested mushrooms by clear-cutting; that is, they raked up the thick moss to uncover mushrooms, thereby destroying the productivity of the entire mushroom patch for subsequent years.

Many Nisga'a and Gitksan mushroom pickers (especially older interviewees over 40) described the maintenance and ownership of mushroom patches in a manner strikingly similar to descriptions of berry patch maintenance.[12] Mushroom patches were described as owned property of villages (by Nisga'a pickers) and house groups (by Gitksan pickers). The Nisga'a tended to highlight village commons (areas adjoining villages or understood to be within the traditional territory of village members) as being restricted to village members only. Gitksan community members were more likely to identify house group membership and ownership as the key criteria limiting access to mushroom-picking areas.

Both Nisaga'a and Gitksan mushroom pickers emphasized the importance of respectful harvesting practices. Although methods differed among individual pickers, there was a general consensus that appropriate harvesting practices were limited to hand picking mushrooms. It was also emphasized that larger mushrooms should be left behind. Pickers strenuously objected to raking and other destructive practices. In all field interviews Nisga'a and Gitksan pickers talked about the importance of preserving mushroom areas as a living store of wealth that required their husbandry to ensure sustainability over the long term.

This contemporary knowledge parallels, but is not the same as, the customary ecological knowledge of pine mushrooms previously held by Indigenous peoples in northwestern British Columbia. As described above, the customary use and knowledge of pine mushrooms was limited to a generic understanding of mushrooms within the landscape and a limited use of mushrooms as a food or medicine. The customary knowledge of mushrooms provided the basis upon which contemporary ecological knowledge emerged.

Contemporary knowledge parallels customary knowledge through a similar relationship to customary land use and governance systems. For example, Nisga'a pickers preferentially harvest mushrooms from their village and house-group territories from which they also harvest other plant products and in which they hunt for game.

Contemporary knowledge of mushrooms differs from customary knowledge with respect to the different socioeconomic context within which mushroom harvesting occurs. That is, mushrooms previously had no significant economic or social value. This is represented linguistically by what seems to be a single generic term for all capped mushrooms. Within the context of the mushroom industry, common English names have emerged that identify different commercially valuable mushroom species, and within the species, specific names are used to identify differing stages of growth that are related to different commercial grades and values as well as a series of terms linked to specific mushroom habitats.

The commoditization of pine mushrooms within the global capitalist economy has created a new context within which First Nations people now operate. During the initial states of the resource extraction industries (fishing, forestry, and mining) Indigenous peoples were excluded from active control over harvesting (see discussion above). However, the emergence of new forest resource commodities, such as pine mushrooms, has occurred within a very different socioeconomic context that opens up the possibility of a return to more direct control over natural resources and land by First Nations in their home territories. In this context, new forms of ecological knowledge have also emerged.

Discussion

Contemporary discussions of TEK tend to focus on the antiquity of ecological knowledge and invariably make reference to rather broad, abstract value statements derived from oral histories. Among the Tsimshianic peoples the history of the downfall of Temlaxham is, among other things, a central account of the dangers of disrespecting one's animal cousins. In this historical account the people have lost their sense of respect for the animals and the world within which they live.

"While people lived at Temlaxham, some hunters found a hillside filled with mountain goats and killed them all except for a young kid which they brought back home and abused by shoving it repeatedly into a fire. A kind-hearted boy took the goat home and rubbed vermilion paint over its burns. Then he let it go. Other people were not as respectful. It was the custom, after goats were killed, for children to dance with goat skulls on their heads, mocking these animals. No one thought anything of these incidents because the people of Temlaxham had grown wasteful and had lost pride in themselves" (Miller 1997:62).

The story continues with the arrival several days later of two strange men wearing white blankets. These men invite the inhabitants of Temlaxham to a feast. The people, assuming that the strange men are messengers from new neighbors accept the invitation. However, the strange men were really mountain goats come to take vengeance on the wasteful people of Temlaxham. All of the people who attended the feast, except the boy who comforted the tortured young goat, were killed in a massive landslide caused by the chief of the mountain goat people. The boy returned to Temlaxham, "where a few of the old and young had stayed. He told them the story of the revenge of the Mountain Goats and, for a time, people were again respectful, but it did not last" (Miller 1997:63).

The story of Temlaxham continues. The people prosper. They have no enemies, and there is no end of food. The town grows and grows. "Soon there were so many people that they could not keep track of each other. The elders ignored the children, who did many things which were forbidden. Everyone did as he or she pleased. Great chiefs would give feasts and kill many slaves. They wasted food. The people had become wicked" (Miller 1997:63).

This time disaster is precipitated by a group of young children torturing and mocking the spawning trout. The children capture the trout when they have no need of food. Then they torment the spawning fish, killing them simply for the pleasure of watching the pain and anguish of the trout as they die. These thoughtless acts bring on a flood that drowns the children and ultimately floods the town of Temlaxham. The people who survive are forced to disperse to the far ends of what are now the territories of the Nisga'a, Gitksan, and Tsimshian peoples.[13]

Historical accounts of such events as the downfall of Temlaxham are to be found among most Indigenous people's histories. As in the Tsimshian history of Temlaxham, these accounts typically describe how a particular people's ancestors grew tired of showing proper respect to their animal brothers and sisters who gave their bodies as food. The ancestors would either engage in indiscriminant hunting or fishing, waste food, or use only a particularly favored portion of the animal they killed. Eventually the animals would grow tired of this disrespect and would withdraw. Or they would take vengeance on their tormentors. The ancestors either starve or are killed outright by the angered animals. Salvation and reconciliation occurs through the realization of a child who, through his or her epiphany, comes to understand why the animals have withdrawn and who then makes restitution to the animals and commits to teaching her or his people the necessity of respect.

These histories provide a clear cultural framework for Indigenous ecological knowledge. They are not, however, ecological knowledge in and of themselves. Ecological knowledge emerges through direct interaction with the environment: through fishing, hunting, and gathering (Berkes 1999). Knowledge emerges in the active use of the landscape. The histories, stories, and myths that are often highlighted as examples of ecological knowledge are in actual fact simply the cultural framework within which knowledge of the environment is transmitted. To understand actual ecological knowledge one must participate in the real processes of hunting, fishing, and gathering. This is a form of pragmatic, tactile knowledge that ultimately is dynamic and responsive to change within the material environment (which includes both the natural and the social).

The pine mushroom industry provides an example of how ecological knowledge is transformed in the context of changing socioeconomic practices. The important point is that ecological knowledge is dynamic. It is responsive to changes in subsistence and livelihood practices. Overlooked in more romantic accounts is the pragmatic utility of local knowledge systems in hunting, fishing, and gathering economies. This is the real knowledge that hunters, fishers, and gatherers use to locate and collect and— when markets and exchange networks exist—use to sell, trade, or barter their products. If TEK is to be understood as anything more than cultural-ly specific stories, it is imperative to recognize that ecological knowledge is dynamic and emerges from locally specific interactions between people and their surrounding environment in the context of their everyday subsistence and livelihood practices. Understood as such, local ecological knowledge should not be presented as a straightforward process of accumulated facts waiting to be mined and translated by trained scientific specialists.

Knowledge emerges in bursts and goes through periods of slow advance-ment. Knowledge can stagnate, degrade, or even disappear. The key point is that ecological knowledge is ultimately the product of a dynamic process linked to the economic and subsistence practices of hunting and gathering peoples. Mushroom TEK has thus developed in ways that are simultaneous-ly linked to customary, precontact knowledge and uses and that also reflect new uses and applications. In the pursuit of mushrooms Nisga'a harvest-ers employ knowledge of likely sites gleaned during other food-gathering and hunting journeys through their territories. Their knowledge of mush-rooms and harvesting also includes knowledge of the market for mush-rooms and the capitalist market economy in general that has been collect-ed by virtue of their existence within a global capitalist resource extraction economy for more than a century. To ignore the dynamic nature of ecolog-ical knowledge and its link to wider socioeconomic processes is to main-tain a colonial ideology that locks Indigenous peoples outside of history and ultimately denies them their humanity.

Notes

I recognize the chiefs, elders, and people of Gitxaała who have opened their box of wisdom in a way that that has allowed me to reflect on the knowledge that is required to fish, hunt, gather, and process foods and materi-als from the land and water. Although the research from which this particular chapter draws is more concerned with the experience of Nisga'a and Gitksan mushroom pickers than with Gitxaała, my time in Lach Klan has been a pivotal influence in the writing of this essay. Caroline Butler and Linda Matson, co-researchers on the original mushroom project, are to be thanked for their meticulous and creative approach to short-term, high-intensity research. My thanks and appreciation also to members of the Nisga'a and Gitksan nations who shared their knowledge with me over the past several years. Thanks also to my colleagues at UBC, especially Bruce Miller, Julie Cruikshank, and Pat Moore, with whom I have discussed these issues at length. Time for research-ing and writing this chapter was made available by the good graces of my family and through the timely contributions from a Social Sciences and Humanities Research Council of Canada research grant and the Wenner Gren Foundation for anthropological research.

1. There is also an important debate regarding the nature of Indigenous or folk classification systems (see Berlin 1992 and Ellen 1993). While this debate over the nature of taxonomic systems is critical, the central issue in this essay concerns the interaction between Indigenous ecological knowledge and the economic context within which it exists. Thus my concern here is more with the ways in which ecological knowledge changes and adapts to transformations in livelihood practices shaped by the economy in general.

2. My research in this region has focused on the industrial resource extraction economy (Menzies 1990, 1992, 1993; Butler and Menzies 2000) and relations between Aboriginal and non-Aboriginal peoples (Menzies 1994, 1996). More recently, this work has been extended to include community-based ecological knowledge research with Kitkatla First Nation (Menzies et al. 2002).

3. Daniel Clayton (2000) urges caution in accepting Fisher's thesis that First Nations and non-Aboriginals formed mutually beneficial relations that encouraged an efflorescence of Aboriginal cultures without revision, given the many advances in scholarship since the publication of *Contact and Conflict* in 1977 (xvii–xix).

4. In addition to the economic effects of industrial capitalist resource extraction, European businessmen and other newcomers brought diseases, such as small pox, measles, and flu, to the Americas. This "microbial" colonialism had a direct and devastating impact on peoples never before exposed to European diseases (Boyd 1999; C. Harris 1997; Brody 2000).

5. The Ḵ'mksiwah botanical name for pine mushrooms is *Tricholoma magnivel*.

6. Even in the absence of mushrooms as a traditional food source, Tsimshian, Nisga'a, and Gitksan knowledge holders understand the distribution and general ecology of mushrooms within their territories. That this is so can be inferred from interview data with contemporary elders and mushroom pickers.

7. One aspect of our Forests and Oceans for the Future project involves collating Indigenous taxonomies for plants and animals. One of our objectives has been to determine to what extent previous taxonomies more accurately reflect the researchers' understandings of taxonomies or that of Indigenous knowledge holders. In some cases it seems as though the principles of Ḵ'mksiwah botanical classification have had more of an impact than they should.

8. "The word for mushroom literally translates as 'ghost hat.' The morphology is: gaayt = hat (noun used here as modifier; the final –t changes to a –d before the connective that follows). –m = connective used to link modifiers to head words. –baa'lax = reincarnate/ghost/spirit(noun)" (Margaret Seguin Anderson, personal communication with author, 2002). Linguistically, the word for *mushroom* is very different from that for *fungus* and reflects contemporary ecological knowledge among the Tsimshian as reflected in interviews with Kitkatla community members in 2002.

9. Dunn (1995:17) also lists a word, *gaaydi ts'u'uts*, whose primary translation is glans (penis) and is secondarily listed as mushroom. In the more recent Tsimshian Language Authority dictionary, it is *gaayda baa'lax* that is given as the word for mushroom.

10. It is not possible to determine if the absence of data on mushrooms and other fungi actually represents Aboriginal knowledge or the particular topical focus of the investigator. It is likely, however, given the fact that mushrooms have been an important food in European diets and are the object of much subsistence activity among European settlers in North America, that the lack

of information in the ethnographic literature accurately reflects the state of Indigenous awareness of mushrooms in north coastal British Columbia.

11. Although more ethnographic detail relating to the specific details of the indicators that Indigenous pickers employ might satisfy our intellectual curiosity, to reveal such information in this form raises critical ethical issues relating to intellectual property rights and the ability of Indigenous peoples to control access over their own knowledge (see Menzies 2001). Given the highly competitive nature of mushroom picking and the incursions of K'mksiwah pickers and researchers in this region, it would not be ethically appropriate to reveal details of mushroom picking that do not directly advance the intellectual argument of this chapter, namely that the economic context within which knowledge emerges plays a critical role in shaping such knowledge.

12. For comparisons with the ownership and maintenance of berry patches, see McDonald (n.d.) for a discussion of Kitsumkalum-Tsimshian practices and Thorton (1999) for a discussion of neighboring Tlingit berry patches in Glacier Bay, Alaska.

13. The history of Temlaxham is also an important account of the dispersal of the Tsimshianic peoples that underwrites social connections between house groups from Kispiox to Kitkatla.

II

Local Knowledge and
Contemporary Resource Management

5. Historicizing Indigenous Knowledge

Practical and Political Issues

Caroline Butler

As the crises in the world's fisheries become increasingly harder to ignore, mainstream fisheries management has come under increasing pressure to change. In the search for alternatives to the dominant models of fisheries management, Indigenous knowledge has been championed as a potential substitute for, or supplement to, scientific knowledge about resources and as a basis for Indigenous or co-management systems. Scholars, activists, resource managers, and users are looking to those ways of knowing marginalized by colonial or state domination to inform the fisheries structures of the future. Indigenous knowledge and its place in the management of fisheries and other natural resources is increasingly a topic of discussion in policymaking forums.

Yet, somehow in this discussion, which is premised upon colonial domination, that very domination is being effectively eclipsed. The massive disruption of Indigenous resource use that these failing structures have perpetrated is forgotten in the efforts to promote Indigenous knowledge and management systems as the solution to the global crisis. In this chapter I argue that a critical recognition of the impacts of colonialism on Indigenous knowledges is crucial if there is to be any successful integration into resource management. An uncomplicated and uncritical promotion of Indigenous knowledge as the solution to the global crisis in natural resource use is both practically and politically dangerous. Placing the burden of sustainability and responsible resource management on the shoulders of Indigenous knowledges dooms them to failure. And failing to recognize and highlight the impact of colonial domination on Indigenous systems of knowledge and management effaces the culpability of colonial states.

Complicating Indigenous Knowledge

I have chosen to discuss these issues using the label of "Indigenous knowledge" (IK), but this is only one of many types of knowledge discussed in the growing literature on alternative resource management systems. Traditional ecological knowledge seems to be the most popular term used—this is used to refer to both Aboriginal and non-Aboriginal knowledge of the local environment. I have chosen IK as a referent because I am focusing on issues of colonial domination, and because I am using a case study of a First Nation within the Canadian state to illustrate my points. However, many of the issues that I broach may be just as relevant regarding non-Indigenous knowledges (see, for example: McGoodwin and Griffith this volume). My discussion of the current literature will touch on discussions of traditional knowledge (TK), traditional ecological knowledge (TEK), Indigenous knowledge (IK), and local knowledge (LK) because these are essentially related in their marginalized position relative to and as proposed alternatives to mainstream fisheries knowledge.

Berkes suggests that the term "local knowledge" is useful for referring to more recent knowledge (1999:8) and is utilized when discussing non-Indigenous artisanal fisheries (Ruddle 1994). Kuhn and Duerden suggest that TEK is essentially local knowledge because it is based on experience (1996:74). So all traditional knowledge is local, but not all local knowledge is traditional.

A cursory survey of the literature on traditional knowledge suggests an emphasis on continuity and cumulative acquisition over long periods of time. Inglis specifies a knowledge base developed over many hundreds of years (1993:vi). Berkes describes a cultural transmission of information down through generations (1993:2), as does Martha Johnson (1992:4). Legat does not specify a temporal framework but relates TK to a "traditional way of life" (1991:1). A great deal of the Canadian work on TK has developed in northern communities and has focused on the ecological knowledge of Aboriginal peoples. TK is thus generally associated with communities with long histories of resource use, specifically Indigenous or "non-industrial" societies (Berkes 1993:3).

It is perhaps the primacy of northern examples and case studies that has encouraged a somewhat uncomplicated understanding of traditional knowledge and its potential integration into resource management. The concentration of most of the key studies of TK in fairly remote communities seems to have resulted in a failure to adequately flesh out the complexities of alternative knowledges and their interconnection with dominant knowledges and structures. Although I am sure that few scholars of northern life would suggest that Indigenous resource use has been untouched by non-Indigenous forces, their discussions of Indigenous knowledge and Indigenous resource management are premised on a continuity of access and lack of external interference. There are serious limitations to the relevance of these studies to resource issues in the more densely settled parts of North America.

The emphasis on long-term use and continuity has, however, been tempered by a recognition of the dynamic nature of TK. Berkes recognizes that TEK "builds on experience and adapts to change" (1999:8). Ruddle suggests that local knowledge often becomes "hybridized" with nonlocal knowledge, and that new knowledge is constantly added in response to change (1994:163, 176; see also Menzies this volume). Johnson criticizes the tendency for TK to be associated with a static image of the past (1992:4).

Although the necessarily dynamic nature of traditional knowledge has been indicated, a somewhat uncritical emphasis on the temporal aspect of this knowledge persists. Most descriptions of TK refer to long-term resource use, to knowledge developed from cumulative practical experience (for a parallel discussion, see both Snively and Corsiglia in this volume). This emphasis may reflect the circumstances of TK's current use in resource management spheres. TK is constructed as the opposite of mainstream management structures, which are relatively new, externally formulated, and rarely site specific, and therefore its worth is seen to lie in its historical and local nature. One of the major failures of "modern" resource use has been the lack of attention to long-term effects, and the reaction to this is a search for long-term perspectives and solutions. The valorization of TK's temporal characteristics is extremely problematic because the assumption of continuity fails to recognize historical change, cultural interaction, and power relations.

Pálsson suggests that a focus on "practical knowledge" resolves the issues of Indigenous versus traditional versus local, by avoiding both cultural and temporal boundaries (1997:52). It is the practical knowledge that fishers gain from daily resource use that is of interest and use to fisheries management. This focus on practical knowledge and experience, however, reveals the inadequacies of many discussions of TK—they do not interrogate the practical knowledge of resource users. The literature on TK assumes the generation of knowledge through experience but does not problematize that experience. Colonial force, for example, has significantly impacted the resource-use experience of Indigenous peoples; in some places, this interference has occurred for four centuries.

We have reached a moment when fisheries managers are realizing that their knowledge of the ocean resources is inadequate, and they are looking to resource users for information about particular resources. Practical knowledge is being recognized as a necessary supplement to scientific knowledge. Therefore when we ask about a resource, we have to ask about resource use—knowledge must be related to experience. I contend that external forces of change have in many cases seriously impacted traditional knowledge because Indigenous practices have been interrupted or inhibited by these forces (see Menzies's discussion of pine mushroom knowledge in this volume and its relation to changes in the wider political economy). Indigenous knowledge can be valuable only when one has a detailed understanding of the processes resulting in the production of that knowledge and, specifically, the practical experience of resource use that generates it.

The experiences of the fishers of the Sto:lo First Nation in southern British Columbia provide a valuable case study of the forces acting upon indigenous knowledge. Sto:lo territory stretches along the Fraser River valley, the most densely populated area of the province. Massive non-Native settlement and industrial development have occurred on Sto:lo land, significantly impacting Sto:lo fishing activities. Sto:lo fishers have valuable and important knowledge to contribute to the management of the Fraser salmon stocks; however, the utilization of the knowledge must be related to a detailed examination of the history of Sto:lo fishing since contact.

In the following pages I provide a discussion of the context of Sto:lo fisheries knowledge production. This discussion draws heavily on the work of Lawrence Felt, who has cogently argued for the understanding of fisheries knowledge as a social construction (1994:253). According to Felt, fishers' knowledge must be examined in light of the context of its production, use, and articulation—the forces that influence both the practical experience of fishing and the assertion that knowledge must be identified. Felt's argument has both practical and political implications—the experience of fishing that generates the knowledge and the political situation that shapes its expression must be illuminated. I therefore identify the forces of change influencing Sto:lo fishing since contact and locate Sto:lo fishing knowledge in local and national political struggles.

Changing Practices, Changing Knowledge

The incorporation of Indigenous knowledge into contemporary resource management structures requires an evaluation of the forces impacting that knowledge. The colonization of Sto:lo territory and the alienation of Sto:lo resources by non-Natives has had significant impact on their relationship with the land and resources. The fishing practices of the Sto:lo peoples have been transformed during the one-hundred-and-fifty years since contact, and, therefore, the knowledge generated by fishing and about fishing has necessarily been impacted. In the following sections I consider the forces of change—social, environmental, and regulatory—engendered by colonization and their implications for Sto:lo practical knowledge of the river resources.

Social Change

The Sto:lo First Nation has a population of approximately five thousand, most of whom now live on 23 reserves along the Fraser River between Mission and Hope, British Columbia. The word Sto:lo is the name of the river in the nation's traditional language, Halkomelem (Carlson and Eustace 1997:140); they are thus the people of the river. Since time immemorial the Sto:lo and other First Nations of southern British Columbia have relied on the Fraser salmon stocks to provide them with food and trade products. Until the latter half of the 19th century Sto:lo fishing activities continued to follow established patterns of participation, and the river continued to provide the bulk of Sto:lo food and trade products. The establishment of Fort Langley in 1827 as an inland trading post for the Hudson Bay Company does not appear to have significantly inhibited Sto:lo fishing and, in fact, provided a market for surplus salmon. However, as non-Native settlement increased in Sto:lo territory, Aboriginal access to the river was compromised, and fishing participation decreased. As Duff points out, during the gold rush of 1858, some of the most gold-rich stretches of the Fraser were found between Hope and Fort Yale (1952:41). Along this part of the river were found a huge concentration of Sto:lo fishing sites and drying racks for the processing of salmon. The influx of settlers during the gold rush accelerated the movement of Sto:lo villages to reserves downriver in the Fraser valley. Sto:lo fishers then had to make a seasonal migration to their canyon fishing sites.

The movement downriver and away from the richest fishing sites resulted in smaller harvests. Legal restrictions of the sale of the Indian catch (see below) further limited the Sto:lo people's ability to continue to make a living from the river. Many people were motivated to turn to wage labor for income. Sto:lo men and women were employed in the salmon canneries that were established at the end of the 19th century, in the hop yards in the valley, and in logging, berry picking, and other enterprises. Employment in the industrial or agricultural economy rarely accommodated seasonal harvesting activities; this reinforced the alienation of wageworkers from fishing. One Sto:lo elder suggests that it was in the hop yards in the 1930s that Sto:lo people first began to buy dried salmon with cash because they were no longer producing it themselves.

Elders also point to the residential school experience as a significant force in separating the Sto:lo people from their fishing traditions. Sto:lo children were removed from their communities and placed in boarding institutions where they were prohibited from speaking their language and were taught "civilized" skills. Mrs. Lena Moran, an elder in her seventies, believes that the children of her generation who were sent to residential school lost a great deal of their culture through the assimilationist policy of the schools. As she commented: "Over the generation we never thought to teach the kids Native things. We were whitewashed, brainwashed."

After the move downriver, many families relied on the Canadian National Railways (CNR) as a means of traveling to their canyon fishing sites. Throughout the middle part of the 20th century, they often rode on the cargo trains to the seasonal fishery and were dependent on the trains to transport their harvest home. However, during the 1970s the weigh freight stopped running on the CNR, and the people who fished on that side of the river no longer had access to their sites, unless they could acquire a boat.

Social and economic shifts during the last century and a half have resulted in major changes in the relationship between the Sto:lo and the Fraser River resources. Non-Native intrusion forced the Sto:lo people to move from their canyon villages downriver, away from their primary fishing sites. Fishers then had to migrate seasonally to canyon fisheries, impacting the regularity of their fishing activities and shifting the site of daily production. Decreased participation led people to look for other means of making a living; employment in industry and agriculture further inhibited regular involvement in fishing. Colonial policies promoting the assimilation of Aboriginal peoples to white society resulted in the residential school system and the discouragement of fishing as a livelihood.

Environmental Change
The history of the Fraser River and Sto:lo fishing territory in particular is a story of environmental degradation and disruption. In the mid-19th century the gold-panners came and went; their disruption was intense but short-lived. The most physically destructive force was the railroads constructed in the late 1800s and early 1900s. The construction of the Canadian Pacific Railway (CPR) line on the west bank of the river resulted in landslides that

buried many fishing sites and shifted the flow of the river, destroying the eddies that attracted the salmon. The Canadian National Railways (CNR) line was even more devastating. The track was built only a few meters from the water, leaving little space for the erection of drying racks or campsites to replace those lost during construction. The damage to the salmon fishery in general caused by the CNR was staggering. In 1914, blasts from the railroad construction caused a huge landslide at what is known as Hell's Gate (upriver from Sto:lo territory). The slide resulted in a significant narrowing of the river and, consequently, a quickening of the current. Salmon were unable to swim past the slide and died en masse before reaching their spawning grounds. The stocks from that cycle are still recovering.

The railroads resulted in major changes to both the river and to Sto:lo fishing. The landslides changed the flow of the river, thereby shifting the productive fishing spots. Many Sto:lo fishing sites were lost completely, and others were significantly altered. Some families were forced to move their fishing activities downriver, which severely inhibited harvest success. The establishment of drying racks was curtailed by the lack of shore area available after the CNR construction; there are hardly any permanent fishing sites left on the east side of the river.

The Fraser River valley has also been transformed by development initiatives. In the 1920s Sumas Lake, in the lower part of Sto:lo territory, was drained to create farmland for non-Native settlers. The lake had been a prime sturgeon-fishing area for the Sto:lo people.

During the 20th century, increasing settlement and development along the banks of the Fraser River has resulted in pollution and spawning habitat destruction. As early as 1889, boat traffic on the Fraser River was identified as a possible risk to fish stocks. Industrial logging practices and the use of the Fraser to transport enormous log booms have been criticized as destroying fish habitat and water quality. The bottom of the Fraser River is regularly dredged, which disrupts the river bottom and muddies the water. The most densely populated area of British Columbia lies along the Fraser River; residential and industrial sewage has poured into the river untreated for many decades. While fishers have noticed an improvement in the river water quality over the last 30 years, environmental degradation has been significant.

Non-Native settlement, industry, and resource extraction have effected serious environmental change along the Fraser River. The river flow has been altered, the banks degraded, the bottom disrupted, and the water quality polluted. The density of settlement in the lower mainland of British Columbia has resulted in rapid environmental change and disruption that has necessarily impacted Sto:lo knowledge of the river.

Regulation

The strongest force pulling Sto:lo fishers from the river has been the increasing regulation of the fisheries by the Canadian state. The governments of Canada and British Columbia supported the growth of capitalist industry and the British Columbia economy through regulations that aided the industrial salmon fishery, specifically the large canneries. The regulatory system thus worked to shrink Native harvests in favor of the non-Native commercial fishery, to severely limit Native salmon sales, and to channel Native labor into the canneries.

Government regulation began to impact Sto:lo fishing in the late 19th century. In 1878 weekly fishing closures and gear restrictions were first introduced on the Fraser when British Columbia was brought under the jurisdiction of the Canadian Fisheries Act. Although the Native population was unofficially exempt from these regulations, a distinction was made between "Indian fishing" and "modern fishing," so that Indians fishing with "modern appliances" came under the general law (Ware 1983:18).

In 1888 this distinction became fully legislated with the creation of the Indian food fishery. A proviso to the Fisheries Act initiated the licensing of the industrial fishery and restricted Indian fishing rights just to salmon caught only for the purpose of feeding themselves (see Newell 1993:47). This legislation created an artificial economic distinction for Aboriginal fishing activities, making subsistence an Indian activity and situating the sale of fish as a White enterprise. Basically, by prohibiting the sale of Indian-caught salmon, the government prevented Aboriginal people from continuing to draw their livelihood from fishing.

In 1894 a permit system was adopted for the management of the invented food fishery, adding seasonal closures and gear restrictions (Ware 1983:22). In 1909 weekly closures were imposed (Newell 1993:94), and Indians were required to report their catches (McKay 1977:44).

The increasing curtailment of Aboriginal harvesting is reflected in the changing language used to describe fishing periods. In the early part of the 20th century, access was discussed in terms of "closures." Today Sto:lo fishers talk about short "openings." Elder Fred Prentiss describes how Sto:lo fishing has been inhibited by non-Native regulation: "My white son-in-law told me I should be happy—We've given you three days to fish, he told me. I said, no you didn't. He said, yes we did. I said, no—you've taken four days away. Before you came here we fished everyday."

The regulations worked to transfer the bulk of the salmon harvest from First Nations to the industrial fishery and to transform Aboriginal people from independent producers to wage laborers for the canneries.

More recently, the environmental degradation and industrial harvest pressures have resulted in conservation concerns regarding the Fraser River's salmon stocks. Conservation initiatives have impacted heavily on Aboriginal catches in the last several decades as run-specific closures have coincided with Sto:lo food fisheries.

Although the Sto:lo and other Fraser River First Nations have acquired the right to sell salmon through the Aboriginal Fishing Strategy established in 1992, AFS commercial openings have been few, and short, and have failed to provide Sto:lo fishers with their desired access to the salmon resources. The sales allocation has been unreliable, and Sto:lo participants remain unable to make a living from fishing.

During the last hundred and fifty years, external regulation has completely changed Sto:lo fishing practices. Traditional fishing methods were outlawed, and fishers were restricted to using set gillnets rather than traps, fish wheels, or mobile nets. Whereas Sto:lo families used to fish when they wanted to, and according to need, fishing became restricted to short openings, and harvest limits were imposed. Sto:lo fishing used to be an integrated activity, providing food and products for trade and sale, according to need. The intrusion of government regulation resulted in the separation of the salmon fishery into different categories—food and commercial—dislocating the interconnected aspects of the Sto:lo economy.

The Department of Fisheries and Oceans (DFO) now determines the timing and practice of Sto:lo fishing and regulates the disposal of the harvest. Although recent shifts in fisheries management have resulted in greater salmon harvest allocations to First Nations along the Fraser, and the inclusion of First Nations in the management structure, the Sto:lo have little real self-determination regarding their fisheries.

Implications

Traditional knowledge is promoted as a valuable addition or supplement to scientific knowledge about resources because of its association with long-term resource use, management, and adaptation. However, such a characterization of traditional knowledge assumes regular, uninterrupted, uninhibited, self-determined resource use. I suggest that the history of Canada precludes the existence of a system of resource use unchanged by the forces of colonialism, and that a consideration of traditional knowledge in resource management necessitates a consideration of these forces. The Sto:lo experience provides an extreme experience of disruption and external interference in the practice of Aboriginal resource use.

Non-Native settlement and government policy have completely changed both the circumstances and practice of Sto:lo fishing. The river environment and the salmon resource itself have been impacted, and Sto:lo fishing methods and use of the harvest have changed. Sto:lo families no longer all live on the banks of the river; they don't fish everyday. Salmon is no longer a staple in the Sto:lo diet, and fishing is not the livelihood of most of the population. The Department of Fisheries and Oceans dictates where the Sto:lo fish, what they fish, how they fish, and when they fish. But where, what, how, and when are precisely the questions that traditional knowledge is supposed to answer. Not only have the where, what, how, and when of fishing changed during the last century, but they have been determined by external forces. Fishing practice and the decision-making (and knowledge-making) processes have been alienated from the Aboriginal resource users.

Sto:lo fishers know a great deal about the Fraser River and about salmon, and this knowledge could contribute to the sustainable management of the Fraser stocks. However, documentation of Sto:lo fisheries' knowledge must also document the practical experience of the contributors. Elders, whose knowledge of fishing may include the experiences of their parents and grandparents in the 19th century, know different things than young Sto:lo fishers whose participation has been shaped by the Aboriginal Fisheries Strategy. An understanding of fishing in the Fraser canyon is strengthened by information on the old fishing sites and the newer ones established after railroad construction. Fishers who fish every year and therefore harvested from each of the four runs have a different understanding than those whose participation has been irregular. The segregation of commercial and food fisheries have created two different kinds of fishing experience and thus two different kinds of knowledge. Some fishers make a seasonal trip to a family site in the canyon; others fish regularly at more recently established sites closer to their reserves. When asking what Sto:lo fishers know, it is also important to ask how they know it—what are the circumstances of their fishing experience, how have these circumstances changed over time? Sto:lo knowledge needs to be directly related to the variants of Sto:lo fishing experience.

Ideological Issues

As I discuss above, the history of resource use and access has major relevance regarding the generation and preservation of traditional knowledge. However, Lawrence Felt points out that the utilization of traditional knowledge requires consideration of not only the circumstances of knowledge production (i.e., fishing practice) but also the context of its use and articulation (1994:253). Felt suggests that knowledge claims are influenced by factors such as competition for the resource and participation in unions and other organizations. Fishers often assert conclusions about the salmon resources that reflect their economic interests or the perspective of their organization. Thus, in considering Sto:lo traditional knowledge, it is crucial to pay attention not only to its production, but also to its *construction*, the highly politicized circumstances of its assertion, and implementation.

Mark Nuttall, commenting on the use of Indigenous knowledge in the Arctic, indicates that such knowledge is increasingly becoming a "political resource" used by Aboriginal leaders and communities (1998:27). Similarly, Frank Sejersen describes Indigenous knowledge as a "political crowbar" (1998:46) that can be used to Indigenous groups' advantage in a colonial context. The use of Indigenous knowledge is a political act—it is a claim of Aboriginality, an assertion of land and resource rights, and a demand for management power.

Sto:lo traditional knowledge claims operate within a highly politicized context and against several different levels of opposing claims. At the national level, Sto:lo Indigenous knowledge is framed by the broader struggle for Aboriginal rights. Since the utilization of Indigenous knowledge in the Berger inquiry regarding the impact of the Mackenzie Oil Pipeline, such knowledge has found increasing power and generated growing interest in the spheres of Canadian politics and resource management. Alliances of Aboriginal and environmental concerns have emphasized the value of Indigenous knowledge and have drawn public attention to the need for its "preservation." Resource degradation and environmental crises have precipitated the search for alternatives to dominant management systems, and Indigenous knowledge is promoted as a key to such alternatives. This valorization necessarily influences the rhetoric of Aboriginal claims and frames discussions of co-management.

At the provincial level, Indigenous knowledge has become wrapped up in the treaty process; the landmark Delgamuukw decision in the Supreme Court (Delgamuukw v. British Columbia [1997] 3 S.C.R. 1010) reinforced the relevance of Aboriginal oral tradition in the settlement of land claims. This ruling has significant implications for the use of Indigenous knowledge in the assertion of sovereignty and resource ownership. Such knowledge has a newfound weight in the non-Native system—which will mean new uses and new applications.

At the local level, on the Fraser River, Sto:lo ecological knowledge is embedded in highly politicized and competitive circumstances. The historical construction of Aboriginal fishing as a noncommercial enterprise has pitted Sto:lo fishers against the non-Native commercial fishers in the struggle for salmon allocations and quotas. Non-Native fishers protested the Aboriginal Fisheries Strategy and pilot sales program as a race-based fishery that afforded Native fishers an unfair advantage. Fisheries regulations have thus created a situation where Native and non-Native fishing interests are considered as opposing each other. The salmon sports fishery constitutes another discrete resource claim, and these three categories—Native, commercial and sports—have been constructed as a triangle of competing interests.

The structure of the Aboriginal Fishery Strategy also places different First Nations along the Fraser in competition with each other. The Aboriginal salmon allocation must be divided among several nations, and the struggle often plays out in an upriver versus downriver opposition.

Thus Sto:lo claims are articulated in opposition to these competing claims and are made against a government that has curtailed Aboriginal fishing and other Indigenous traditions for over a century. These claims are made in the context of a growing revival of Aboriginal cultural practices and increasing assertions of political sovereignty and self-determination. Sto:lo traditional knowledge or Indigenous knowledge is part of larger claims and is a premise of these claims. DFO conservation initiatives are resisted with an assertion of the superiority and priority of Indigenous conservation knowledge and practices. Management structures are challenged on the basis of Aboriginal tradition and expertise.

Indigenous knowledge is thus a tool in the Aboriginal struggle for access to resources. The claim of prior rights and prior knowledge grounds the Sto:lo fight for a portion of a disappearing resource because it is a rhetoric unique to First Nations fishers, a group who have been historically disadvantaged and dispossessed. Just as Indigenous knowledge has been impacted by the forces of colonialism that have dislocated First Nations from their resource base, it has also been impacted by a political situation in which IK is a key tool in the assertion of sovereignty. IK has been constructed as an epistemological opposite to Western knowledge, specifically to science. It has been promoted as an alternative in situations where science has "failed."

It has been situated as a basis of rights to resource access and management and is the foundation of Aboriginal claims against competing resource users. As such, IK has been inextricably wrapped up in ideas of Aboriginal culture, sovereignty, difference. IK is not simply a body of knowledge, but a political discourse.

This entanglement with political struggles and cultural claims complicates IK's successful incorporation into management strategies. I am not suggesting that IK assertions are false attempts to claim resource access, or that the content of IK is necessarily "polluted" by resource competition. Interrogating the "integrity" of IK is an unproductive project, because it implies an immutability that is neither possible nor desirable. IK is valuable precisely because it is dynamic and adaptive. What I am suggesting is that when considering IK, it is crucial to understand the context of its articulation (see again Felt 1994)—the political and ideological forces that influence its construction. Above I argue that one must have a critical understanding of the practical circumstances of resource use and access that shapes Indigenous ecological knowledge. One must also have a detailed understanding of the political circumstances of resource use and access that shape assertions of Indigenous ecological knowledge.

Evaluating Change

The history of Sto:lo fishing on the Fraser points to successive changes in the circumstances of resource use over the last hundred and fifty years, resulting in multiple and varied experiences of salmon harvesting. Sto:lo fisheries knowledge must be documented, therefore, by talking to many different fishers: old and young, subsistence and commercial, and so on. Their understandings of the salmon resource must be read against the backdrop of their practical experience of harvesting (how often they do, how they do it, what external restrictions dictate fish harvesting) and the political circumstances of their expressions of that experience.

Joyce Lui has identified some necessary questions in the evaluation of local knowledge for resource planning. They include queries regarding whether the information can be proved or compared with another report, how detailed the information is and how many observations it is based on, to what scale it is accurate and whether it can be mapped, and, finally, how this information affects the individual who provides it (1995:27). These questions help to establish the validity and applicability of the information provided by resource users. They are premised on an evaluation of the qualifications of the contributor.

Such an evaluation is a necessary starting place for the implementation of alternative knowledge in resource management. Information about a resource must be located within the context of its generation—an understanding of how the information was gained, when it was gained, how it was transmitted. One of the criticisms of resource management systems has been their failure to look at the big picture—the multiple and interrelated forces impacting the health of resources and their sustainable harvest. Therefore, the information or knowledge that informs new management methods must be evaluated in terms of its relation to the big picture—facts must be contextualized, connections fleshed out, and influencing factors identified.

The issue of "evaluating" knowledge that is intended to complement mainstream scientific data becomes somewhat more complicated when dealing with Indigenous knowledge. The "evaluation" of Indigenous knowledge according to non-Indigenous measures and standards could easily become an act of colonization. The necessary contextualization of data and the necessary recognition of Aboriginal sovereignty and rights of resource management require close collaboration in data collection, assessment, and implementation. The growing recognition of First Nations' rights to manage the natural resources within their traditional territories is working to transform natural resource management structures and to expand the data that inform this management. The contemporary context of multiple user groups and stakeholders has resulted in structures of co-management, which, although not reflecting complete Aboriginal self-determination in resource use and management, have made some progress toward power sharing. Increasing efforts toward the integration of Indigenous knowledge and Western resource management reflect an affirmation of Aboriginal rights and title. It is therefore crucial that the way in which Indigenous knowledge is made available for co-management of natural resources reflects community protocols and priorities.

The utilization of Indigenous knowledge in resource management is itself inevitably a transformative act. Kuhn and Duerden point out that the abstraction of TEK is a problem inherent to its integration into mainstream resource management (1996:78). When empirically based knowledge is removed from its local and specific context, it is necessarily changed. First Nations and other Indigenous groups are rightfully concerned about the current interest in their knowledge and the desire to translate it into resource management and other external structures. However, Indigenous knowledge can be respectfully and appropriately used to inform resource management structures that shape the harvest of resources by Indigenous peoples. The incorporation of Indigenous understandings can establish better management practices and enhance Indigenous control of resources. IK can be evaluated and utilized in a noncolonizing, nontotalizing way when its documentation, evaluation, and use is done in close collaboration with the contributing community. The harvesters themselves know best the circumstances of their resource use and can best formulate questions to differentiate their experiences. Furthermore, issues of intellectual property and the protection of sacred knowledge can best be dealt with through collaborative research and management partnerships.

Menzies (2001) has outlined the necessary structures for collaborative research with First Nations communities. Documenting, evaluating, and implementing Indigenous knowledge for resource co-management requires a research structure that is developed and implemented by the community. Menzies recommends a long process of community consultation, team interviews, and several levels of data review. This type of structure would enable community members to define relevant data, identify local experts, evaluate data appropriately, and define the ways in which their Indigenous knowledge may best be integrated with scientific data for co-management needs.

Historicizing Indigenous Knowledge

Indigenous knowledge has not developed, and does not exist, in a vacuum. The forces of change generated since contact have influenced Indigenous understandings of natural resources and the environment. These forces have been different and of varying strength in different parts of Canada, but they have been in effect in every community. Indigenous knowledge is inextricably related to the experience of colonial domination because it is this experience that has constructed it as a separate way of knowing. IK is a discrete category of knowledge because of its opposition to Western knowledge—it is IK's history of marginalization and neglect by the dominant society that makes it a novel and innovative approach to resource management at the beginning of the 21st century.

However, as Agrawal points out, there are pitfalls to this opposition of knowledge types. Promoters of IK remain trapped in the dichotomy of Indigenous versus Western, and this acts to reproduce the distinction that underpinned IK's denigration by scientists and dominant societies (1995:420). Agrawal emphasizes that the dichotomization of these knowledge systems assumes that they have had completely segregated evolutions and neglects the realities of contact and exchange (422). Furthermore, the vast variations within the knowledges diminishes the significance of the differences between them (421).

A more productive approach is recognizing the many different types of knowledges with "differing logics and epistemologies" (Agrawal 1995:433). And it is necessary to emphasize the diversity within knowledge systems, so that the varied knowledge of Indigenous peoples is not glossed over. The rigid dichotomy of Indigenous versus Western keeps Indigenous knowledge trapped in history—Western knowledge is thereby modern and dynamic, Indigenous knowledge is related to the past and to precontact resource use experience.

Much of the current literature on TK or IK identifies the value of this knowledge as lying in information about precontact resource management. However, there are limits to the worth of precontact understandings and structures in such complicated resource use situations as the Fraser River salmon fisheries, with multiple user groups and a high degree of competition and external regulation. Rather, what can be truly valuable and relevant to the pressing resource management issues of today is Indigenous knowledge's cumulative and dynamic aspects. Indigenous knowledge is necessarily a knowledge of change; through considering Indigenous experiences and resource knowledge, we are given a picture of the rapid transformations that have been wrought on the landscape and natural resources during the centuries of colonial settlement. Indigenous knowledge's spanning of the precontact past, the processes of colonization, and contemporary circumstances is the key to understanding the problems of current management strategies. For example, the differing perspectives of Sto:lo elders and young fishers can provide an understanding of the impacts of regulatory change during the last fifty years of the Fraser River fisheries. Indigenous knowledge is uniquely positioned to reveal the shortcomings of resource management structures by highlighting the impacts of these structures over time. A detailed, historicized explication of Indigenous resource use and Indigenous knowledge in a colonial context thus has applications beyond the construction of an opposite or alternative to Western scientific knowledge.

In addition to its practical value in revealing the impacts of settlement, development, and regulation and the complexities of environmental change during the last few centuries, a historicized IK has important political implications. This approach brings to the fore issues of power, control, and sovereignty in resource use and management. Emphasizing the colonial domination of Indigenous resource activities does not undermine the value or integrity of IK; rather, such emphasis engages its history of disruption and oppression and in doing so can contribute to the project of enhancing Indigenous self-determination in resource use. Berkes points out that "the use of traditional knowledge provides a mechanism, a point of entry, to implement co-management and self-government and to integrate local values into decision-making" (1999:181). A historicized IK highlights the disruption of Indigenous systems and makes a cogent argument for the aggrandizement of Indigenous resource control.

The Sto:lo Nation case study suggests the multiple and constantly changing experiences of salmon harvesters on the Fraser River. These experiences have generated multiple and dynamic knowledges of the salmon resources. A successful management system will integrate these knowledges. The case study indicates that the development of an industrial fishery and the marginalization of Aboriginal fishers have created competing user groups with different experiences and different understandings. The experiences and knowledges of non-Aboriginal fishers must be examined as well as those of Aboriginal fishers. A historicized understanding of Sto:lo fisheries knowledge thus highlights the need to break down oppositions between user groups to create a management structure that reflects various knowledges, interests, and values to meet the needs of all salmon harvesters.

What resource management has been lacking and what it is currently searching for is usable practical knowledge about resources. Indigenous knowledge is one type of knowledge system that can inform management structures. However, practical, experience-based information must be related to the experience and practice of resource use. Indigenous knowledge must thus be historicized—it must be understood in light of the forces of change acting upon Indigenous resource activities since contact. This historicized perspective, which evaluates knowledge against experience, can provide an understanding of resource and environmental change over the last few centuries—the critical period of resource extraction. Furthermore, a perspective attentive to the power relations of colonialism and the history of Indigenous dispossession provides a valuable tool in Indigenous political struggles for sovereignty and land claims. Engaging critically with the practical and political issues of Indigenous knowledge production thus provides both practical and political benefits.

6. The Case of the Missing Sheep

Time, Space, and the Politics of "Trust"
in Co-management Practice

Paul Nadasdy

In July of 1996 Yukon government biologists conducting an aerial survey of the Ruby Range in the southwest Yukon counted 147 fewer Dall sheep than they had just the year before—an apparent decline of almost 26 percent in the course of a single year. This drop in the population was potentially of serious concern to the members of the Ruby Range Sheep Steering Committee (RRSSC), a multi-stakeholder co-management body established in 1995 specifically to address concerns about perceived declines in the Ruby Range Dall sheep population. When biologists presented the results of their sheep survey to the RRSSC on January 28, 1997, however, no alarms were sounded. Indeed, by the time they presented their survey data to the committee, they were confident that the sheep population had not, in fact, declined at all. Significantly, the biologists had not come to this conclusion on their own; instead, they had come to their current knowledge of the sheep population by integrating their own knowledge (the product of aerial surveys and other techniques of scientific wildlife management) with the very different knowledge of another member of the RRSSC.

Any attempt to understand why the biologists were not worried about the sheep population must begin with a look at the unusual circumstances surrounding the aerial survey itself. For one thing, biologists had performed the 1996 annual survey in July rather than in June, when it was normally carried out. The second unusual thing about the survey was that there had still been significant snow cover in the mountains when it was carried out, making it harder to spot the white Dall sheep from the air. The biologists confessed that these factors had caused them to mistrust the results of their survey and suspect they were not comparable to the survey data from previous years. Fortunately, the big game outfitter in the area, also a member of the RRSSC, had conducted his own sheep count during the autumn 1996 hunting season. Eight hunting guides working for him had counted the sheep in his outfitting area and had obtained results very similar to the Yukon government's aerial survey—except in one game management subzone in his area,[1] where they counted approximately 100 more sheep than had been counted in the helicopter survey. Further, they counted all of those 100 sheep in an area where the aerial survey had found no sheep at all. After the hunting season, the biologists and outfitter had gotten together to compare data. Together they had decided that those 100 sheep must have been missed by the helicopter survey because they had been outside of the study area in July, but that they had then returned to it by the start of the hunting season a few weeks later. They came to the joint conclusion that the drop in the sheep count represented problems with the survey (different time of year, snow cover, and 100 moving sheep) rather than a drop in the actual number of sheep. So by the time they presented the results of the survey to other members of the RRSSC in January 1997, biologists felt confident that it was their survey data—rather than the sheep population—that had a problem.

This tale of the 100 missing sheep should be heartwarming to proponents of co-management. It is a perfect example of the kind of "knowledge-integration" that is supposed to be the centerpiece of co-management practice. By integrating the outfitter's local land-based knowledge with the scientific knowledge generated by biologists, these RRSSC members had improved everyone's overall knowledge of the sheep; by working together in this way, biologists and the outfitter had helped to build trust and a cooperative relationship among (at least certain) members of the RRSSC. This new integrated knowledge of the 1996 Dall sheep population combined and reflected both the outfitter's and biologists' knowledge of the sheep. That this occurred should not be particularly surprising. After all, knowledge-integration of this sort is integral to the very idea of co-management. Aware of the limitations of wildlife biology and other management sciences, biologists and scientific resource managers have increasingly come to recognize the value of local knowledge (knowledge held by First Nation people as well as those Euro-Americans who spend considerable time out on the land, such as hunters, trappers, and outfitters) not only as a corrective to the knowledge they generate, but also because it can fill in the temporal and geographical "gaps" in that knowledge. This was certainly one of the goals underlying the creation of the RRSSC in the first place.

As it turns out, there were numerous other instances over the nearly three-year life of the RRSSC in which committee members might profitably have worked together to integrate their different ways of knowing about Dall sheep. Unfortunately, however, the case of the missing sheep described above was virtually the only significant instance of knowledge-integration that occurred during the entire RRSSC process, a process that involved not only Yukon biologists and outfitters, but also First Nation people, federal government officials, and members of interested environmental organizations. The question that I address in this chapter is the following: Why, if everyone involved in the RRSSC process endorsed the idea of knowledge-integration (and they did), was there only a single instance in which they actually succeeded in doing so?

Much of the literature on co-management and traditional ecological knowledge (TEK) addresses precisely this issue when it focuses on the many technical and methodological obstacles to knowledge integration (see, for example, Usher 2000). The prevailing view is that the integration of science and TEK is hampered by the difficulty of collecting TEK and by qualitative differences in the form of scientific versus traditional or local knowledge—which supposedly make them at least somewhat incommensurable. Elsewhere (Nadasdy 1999) I have criticized this view, arguing that TEK researchers' preoccupation with technological and methodological obstacles to knowledge integration have obscured the power relations that underlie the whole process of knowledge integration and co-management. I argued that the supposedly "technical" process of translating First Nation elders and hunters' lived experiences into a form compatible with the institutions and practices of state wildlife management (e.g., numbers and lines on maps) takes those very institutions and practices as a given. Because of this, the practice of knowledge integration and co-management ends up taking for granted existing Aboriginal-state relations and perpetuating—rather than transforming—unequal power relations. In this chapter, however, I examine a different aspect of the co-management process.

Despite all that is lost and transformed in the process of translating First Nation people's lived experiences into numbers and lines on maps, *something* survives. After all, the numerical or graphic understandings sought by biologists are not completely foreign to the experiences of First Nation people. Elders and hunters often possess detailed knowledge about sheep (how many, when, and where) that can be expressed in forms that are entirely compatible with those regularly used by biologists. These numbers and lines on maps—however decontextualized they may be—are nevertheless rooted in First Nation elders' and hunters' experiences on the land. Thus, some would argue that integrating these numbers with the knowledge of biologists should still be of some benefit—despite all the problems inherent in the translation process. And precisely *because* these numbers and lines on maps have been decontextualized, this integration should be fairly straightforward. Yet, even after First Nation people and biologists have agreed on the numbers and what they mean, knowledge integration remains fraught with difficulties. Many of these difficulties—again—appear to be technical or methodological in nature. Just as in the case of gathering and translating TEK, however, it would be a mistake to focus solely on the technical dimensions of this stage of knowledge integration. To do so would ignore the political context in which it takes place and take for granted existing political inequalities.

In this essay I explore the political dimensions of this "second stage" of knowledge integration by looking at the case of the Ruby Range Sheep Steering Committee in the southwest Yukon. Committee members did indeed face technical and methodological obstacles in their attempts to gather and integrate different ways of knowing about sheep. Over the course of nearly three years, however, they intentionally worked to overcome these obstacles. They gathered information about Dall sheep from various sources—from First Nation elders and hunters to outfitters to biologists—and successfully managed to express it all in a form compatible with scientific wildlife management practice (i.e., as text—especially as numbers and lines on maps).[2] As I show elsewhere (Nadasdy 1999), this process was far from politically neutral. At the same time, however, by rendering the information gathered from these very disparate sources into forms that were mutually compatible with one another, RRSSC members set the stage for their integration. Yet, even then—with the single exception described above—the RRSSC failed to do so. Why?

As we shall see below, the RRSSC's success in translating the experiences of local people into a form compatible with scientific wildlife management did not remove all the obstacles to knowledge integration. Serious methodological difficulties remained. Yet, the fact that RRSSC members did succeeded once (in the case of the missing sheep) proves that these difficulties were not insurmountable. Why, then, did they successfully integrate these different knowledge "artifacts" only once? And is it significant that the one successful case of knowledge integration involved biologists and an outfitter—and not First Nation people? To answer these questions, we must begin by examining those methodological obstacles to knowledge integration that remained even after the translation process. We can then ask how and why these obstacles were overcome in one case, but not others. This inquiry ultimately leads us away from issues of technique and methodology to questions of power. I begin with a very brief background discussion of the RRSSC and the politics of sheep hunting in the Yukon.[3]

The Ruby Range Sheep Steering Committee and the Politics of Sheep in the Yukon

In the fall of 1995 the Kluane First Nation (KFN) hosted a meeting in the village of Burwash Landing, Yukon, to express their concerns about declining populations of Dall sheep in the region. This meeting led directly to the creation of the Ruby Range Sheep Steering Committee. Participants at the meeting selected RRSSC representatives from a wide range of groups with interests in Ruby Range sheep, including local First Nations, the territorial government (Department of Renewable Resources), the federal government (Parks Canada and the Department of Indian Affairs and Northern Development), local big-game outfitters, and members of interested environmental organizations (the Yukon Conservation Society and the Canadian Parks and Wilderness Society). The RRSSC was charged with the task of making management recommendations concerning Ruby Range sheep to the Yukon Fish and Wildlife Management Board, the "primary instrument of fish and wildlife management" in the territory (Council for Yukon Indians 1993:166). To this end, the committee met several times over the next three years.

It became apparent over the course of these meetings that different participants in the RRSSC had radically different ideas about the magnitude of the decline in the sheep population, the reasons for this decline, and potential management solutions. Biologists and outfitters sitting on the RRSSC saw the population decline as relatively minor, a temporary fluctuation caused by several years of unusually bad weather, possibly exacerbated by predation (from wolves and coyotes) and harassment from low-flying aircraft and all-terrain vehicles. Significantly, neither biologists nor outfitters felt that hunting by humans had contributed to the sheep decline. Ultimately, they felt that the sheep population would recover on its own, but they were willing to support management initiatives that addressed the issues of predation and harassment to help speed the population's recovery. Both opposed any restrictions on hunting, the outfitters adamantly so.

Kluane First Nation people, on the other hand, saw the decline in the sheep population as long term and catastrophic. They argued that the population had been declining steadily since the 1960s and that the situation had now reached crisis proportions. They agreed with biologists and outfitters that predation and harassment were factors in the decline, but they vehemently disagreed with them about the role of weather and human hunting. Sheep, they felt, were quite accustomed to Yukon weather, and in any case, a few bad years could not explain a long-term decline of the sort they had seen. Some elders and hunters even found the suggestion that weather was the cause of the decline to be disrespectful to the sheep, implying that they were too "stupid" to take care of themselves in their own homeland. The biggest point of contention between Kluane people and the outfitters and biologists was their disagreement over the significance of human hunting.[4] Kluane people identified hunting—especially by outfitters—as the single most important factor leading to the decline of the sheep population and advocated a total ban on sheep hunting in the region (or, failing that, imposition of a quota on the number of sheep that could be taken).

RRSSC members' different positions regarding the nature of the decline in sheep and its possible remedies arose, at least in part, from the different ways in which each experienced and came to "know" about sheep in the first place. Wildlife biologists, for example, generated knowledge about sheep primarily through a number of formal activities (i.e., "research"), the most important of which was aerial survey conducted by helicopter. The results of this research were then disseminated in the form of written reports and scientific papers. In contrast, First Nation elders and hunters based their understandings of sheep on personal experiences gained over many years spent out on the land: hunting, trapping, fishing, guiding, and traveling. They shared these experiences and the lessons they drew from them orally, in the form of stories, rather than in written form. These differences led RRSSC members to have very different understandings about Ruby Range sheep. At an even more fundamental level, committee members disagreed (at least implicitly) on what constituted valid knowledge about sheep in the first place—and even on the nature of sheep themselves.[5]

The disagreement between First Nation people, on one hand, and the biologists and outfitters, on the other, also had obvious political dimensions. Dall rams, with their large curving horns, are a prized trophy animal for big-game hunters all over the world. As trophy animals, Dall sheep represent a significant potential income for big-game outfitters, who charge hunters quite substantial sums for their hunts, as well as an income source for the territorial government, which sells hunting licenses and collects

trophy fees and taxes. At the same time, Dall sheep have been, and continue to be, an important part of the diet of First Nation people in the southwest Yukon for at least the last two thousand years.[6] Kluane people think
of themselves as sheep hunters. They speak highly of the virtues of sheep
meat and occasionally have gone to great lengths to get it.[7] I was told one
story—from the days before the restoration of KFN people's hunting rights
in the neighboring Kluane National Park and Game Sanctuary—in which
a man risked fines or imprisonment to get sheep for his father's funeral
potlatch, because he felt that a proper ceremony could not be held without
sheep meat. I also heard countless stories about specific sheep hunts, some
of which had occurred as far back as the beginning of the 20th century.[8]
Kluane people have detailed knowledge of where to go to hunt sheep and
know the locations of dozens of traditionally used sheep hunting camps
throughout their traditional territory, quite a number of which are in the
Ruby Range. Finally, on several occasions, I heard KFN members specifically use their self-ascribed status as sheep hunters to contrast themselves
with members of another First Nation, whom they claimed did not traditionally rely on sheep for subsistence.

Struggles between those who see animals as trophies and those who see
them as food have historically played an important role in characterizing
the politics of big game hunting in the Yukon (see McCandless 1985, n.d.). In
the case of sheep, the struggle is especially intense—so intense that despite
overwhelming archaeological and oral evidence, it was not until 1998 that
the territorial government at last formally acknowledged that Dall sheep
should be classified as a traditional subsistence animal under KFN's land
claim agreement.[9] Despite the intensity of the struggle over sheep in the
region, outfitters and First Nation people, the two most important groups
involved in the struggle, have very different degrees of access to state power. Although First Nation people's political presence in the territory has
increased dramatically over the past 30 years, there remains a wide gulf
between First Nation communities and the halls of power in Whitehorse.
Big-game outfitters, on the other hand, have historically had considerable
influence in the territorial government. This is due at least in part to the

financial benefits accruing to the Yukon government as a result of outfitting, but there are other factors as well that contribute to their political clout. For one thing, outfitting is an old and respected (not to mention colorful) tradition in the Yukon, and today's outfitters, as practitioners of that tradition, can draw on powerful historical imagery to justify their positions. Another source of outfitter strength is their political organization. Though there are only 20 outfitters in the Yukon, they present a common front through the actions of the well-organized and very active Yukon Outfitter's Association, a political force to be reckoned with in the territory. Perhaps the greatest source of their political strength, however, is their membership in an elite stratum of Yukon society. Business and government in the territory are dominated by a relatively small number of businessmen who are long-time Yukoners. Outfitters have traditionally been among the members of this group. In 1995, for example, when the RRSSC was formed, at least two members of the Yukon Legislative Assembly—one of whom was the government leader—were ex-outfitters.

Because of outfitters' political power, it would have been difficult for the Yukon Department of Renewable Resources to implement any management initiatives opposed by outfitters (e.g., a ban on hunting)—regardless of any recommendations by the RRSSC. This is not to say that it would have been *impossible*, but at the very least, wildlife managers would have to have had convincing (to Yukon politicians) evidence supporting such action. And despite rhetoric about the value of TEK, this still means evidence produced by biologists, *not* the uncorroborated testimony of First Nation elders—especially if that testimony contradicts the biological evidence.

Such was the political context into which the RRSSC was born. As discussed above, an important part of the RRSSC process was the translation of First Nation elders' and hunters' understandings (and indeed all RRSSC members' understandings) into a form compatible with the reports and published papers of wildlife biologists (i.e., written text, numbers, lines on maps). Despite their common form, however, integration of these knowledge artifacts remained far from straightforward. Many of the obstacles to integration appeared to be technical or methodological. Sheep move around, and population sizes fluctuate over time. Everyone's understanding of sheep, then, is necessarily based on where, when, and how they observed or interacted with them. Thus, it was often extremely difficult to compare one RRSSC member's knowledge of Ruby Range sheep with another's—even after they had been translated into a form compatible with scientific wildlife management. I now turn to an examination of these methodological obstacles to knowledge integration—not because they "prevented" knowledge integration, but because—in one case—they did *not*.

Time, Space, and Knowledge
Differences in Temporal Dimension
The temporal dimension is vital to the practice of wildlife management. Time structures what and how people know about animal populations. Temporal differences in what RRSSC members knew about Ruby Range sheep provided an incentive for knowledge integration. At the same time, however, these differences acted as an obstacle to such integration. Temporal differences existed on a number of different levels—from differences in the length of time (in years) various RRSSC members had been observing sheep in the Ruby Range to what time of year they made these observations. All of these differences played a role in the dynamics of co-management in the RRSSC.

To manage wildlife effectively, one must have good long-term knowledge of wildlife populations. One must know how these populations are changing, why they are changing, and what can be done to effect desired changes. Especially important for management is an understanding of the impact of human activity on animal populations. Since even "stable" wildlife populations experience significant fluctuation from year to year, however, it can often be very difficult to determine the causes—or even the significance— of changes in population size. In an ideal situation—one in which wildlife managers have good long-term data from a population in a fairly "natural" state—they might feel confident in their ability to distinguish the effects of human activity from the stochastic fluctuations experienced by wildlife populations in the absence of humans.

But such long-term data do not exist in the North, where wildlife biology is a relatively recent arrival. The Yukon government, for example, did not hire a wildlife biologist until 1974, the year of the first Ruby Range sheep survey. This problem is further compounded by the expense of conducting wildlife surveys, which has made it impossible for biologists to carry out regular surveys of animal populations—in all but a few relatively small areas—even since their arrival in 1974. As biologists admit, this constitutes a fairly serious limitation to their knowledge of wildlife in the territory, often making it difficult for them to assess the effects of human activity on wildlife populations. To make up for their lack of temporal data on animal populations, biologists focus on maximizing the data obtained from animals taken by hunters and make comparisons between different (spatially separate) populations of the same species.

Ruby Range sheep are exceptional among Yukon wildlife populations for the amount and length of time of data that have been collected about them. Biologists first surveyed this population in 1974 and have been doing so relatively consistently since 1979. Thus, they are in a better position to assess the impact of human activity on the Ruby Range sheep population than they are for nearly any other animal population in the Yukon. Given the history of this region, however, twenty years of data is still quite inadequate. Serious overhunting occurred in parts of the territory at least as early as the Klondike gold rush in 1898. Though the population rebounded (and the pressure on wildlife subsided) somewhat in later years, the rise of the big-game outfitting industry and several subsequent short-lived population booms (most notably during the building of the Alaska Highway in 1941-42) continued to put varying amounts of pressure on wildlife populations in the area. All of these events (especially the building of the highway) directly affected wildlife populations in the Kluane area, sometimes quite significantly (Dick Dickson, personal communication with author, 1996; Hoefs 1981; McCandless 1985). Though biologists use a number of methods to try to "factor out" the effects of human impact on these populations, these are necessarily based on a significant degree of educated guesswork.

In contrast, Native elders and hunters have been in the Yukon for considerably longer than 25 years. There are some elders who have detailed memories of the Ruby Range from as far back as the 1920s, and they heard stories from their own elders about times even longer ago than that. These elders do not depend on costly helicopters to see sheep in the Ruby Range, nor do they have to juggle the need to survey those sheep with the need to study other wildlife populations throughout the territory—all on a single limited budget. Rather, they observed sheep in the Ruby Range as a natural part of their lives hunting and trapping out on the land. As a result, there are no temporal "gaps" in their knowledge of Ruby Range sheep, as there are in the biological survey data.[10]

Such differences in the temporal dimensions of TEK and science are often cited by proponents of knowledge integration as one of the primary reasons for integrating them. They see the long-term observations of First Nation hunters as potentially complementing the more occasional but intensive observations made by biologists and resource managers. By integrating these two sets of information, many resource managers hope to be able to extend their knowledge of animal populations significantly into the past (see, e.g., Ferguson and Messier 1997). Indeed, it is precisely for the purpose of supplementing their inadequate data about animal populations that many resource managers throughout the North have begun turning to TEK. Biologists involved in the RRSSC process explicitly acknowledged this as one of the most important advantages to managing the Ruby Range sheep cooperatively.

Despite this acknowledgment, and the apparent advantages of integrating biologists' and hunters' perspectives on Ruby Range sheep, however, biologists involved in the RRSSC proved unwilling or unable to incorporate First Nation hunters' accounts of past population sizes into their model of the Ruby Range population. According to every single hunter who spoke to the RRSSC, there were once many more sheep in the Ruby Range than there are today, and all agreed that the population decline began well before the first aerial survey was conducted in 1974 (and certainly before these surveys became a regular occurrence in 1979). This would seem to be an ideal situation for the temporal extension of biological data through the use of TEK. Yet, this never happened.

Before RRSSC members could decide what management strategies to adopt, they had to agree on a target population. This entailed long hours of debate over what would constitute a healthy sheep population in the Ruby Range. The committee might have tried to integrate TEK and science by developing a population model based on a combination of testimony by elders and hunters and the aerial survey data (not to mention other inputs, such as those provided by outfitters). Instead, biologists and First Nation people each ended up using their own knowledge of past sheep populations to bolster their arguments over what constituted an appropriate target population. Rather than "integrating" what they knew about sheep, RRSSC members struggled with one another over whose knowledge they should use to set this target level. The RRSSC finally agreed on the objective of restoring the Ruby Range sheep population to its 1980 level, the highest ever recorded by an aerial survey (RRSSC 1996a). According to the survey data, this meant a target population of 1,314 sheep in the survey area. This figure, however, was well below First Nation expectations. Elders and hunters were adamant that the population had once been much higher than this (indeed, they said that by 1980 the population decline had already been well under way). In the end, however, they were forced to agree to this level because biologists (and outfitters) were completely unwilling to entertain the possibility of setting a higher figure. Whether or not they trusted the accuracy of the First Nation testimony (and there were some people on the RRSSC who clearly did not), biologists simply could not accept that testimony as a basis for action because they had no way of independently verifying that the sheep population had ever been any higher than the 1980 level. Given the sensitive political nature of sheep management, and the much greater weight accorded to scientific evidence than to First Nation testimony by the powerful interests involved, biologists needed to be able to back any recommendations with scientific evidence. As a result, biologists could not (and did not) accord the testimony of elders and hunters the same status that they did their own survey data. It is perhaps not so surprising, then, that very little knowledge integration actually occurred. The First Nation settled on the 1980 population as the target level because it was the highest that biologists would go, and biologists would go that high because they themselves had counted that many sheep there.

Biologists were not the only members of the RRSSC to question or undervalue other people's knowledge about sheep in the Ruby Range. First Nation people, for their part, often criticized the knowledge of biologists as part of their effort to establish their own knowledge as legitimate. They frequently contrasted biologists' (and current outfitters') status as relative newcomers to the area with their own personal and family histories. They referred to the many years that they or their parents and grandparents had hunted in the area, claiming that this wealth of experience gave them knowledge of the sheep that far surpassed any that might be gained from a dozen or so annual surveys from a helicopter. In making this argument, First Nation hunters were saying more than simply that they had spent more time observing sheep than biologists had, though this was certainly part of their point. They were also making a comment on the quality of those observations. They claimed that over the course of many years spent hunting out on the land they had also learned *how* to observe animals. This may seem an odd argument to someone who has never hunted. Whenever I went out with experienced hunters, however, I was always impressed by First Nation hunters' ability to spot animals. I was always the last to see them, usually after someone pointed them out to me. And, of course, a good hunter does not need to see animals to know they are there. By noting tracks and other signs, he or she can get a fairly good sense of what animals are in the area, without ever actually seeing them. It became clear to me, as I spent time with these hunters, that it would indeed take many years of studying animals out on the land before I could hope to even approach their powers of observation. First Nation elders and hunters are justifiably proud of their abilities in this regard, and elders and hunters on the RRSSC felt uniquely qualified to comment on the state of the sheep population in the Ruby Range. At the same time, they mistrusted the observations of biologists, whom they saw as lacking the very kinds of experiences they considered essential to being a good observer. As one elder and hunter put it:

I do look at sheep when I go up the valley. Lots of time I never see any. I cover lots of country, I never see nothing. Just what we seen last year, is what I seen up in the Ruby. Head of Marshall Creek, I never seen no sheep there. My cousin went in there with Junior Moose; he saw two rams. . . . Where I went myself, I never seen any. People say they're all around. With the plane they seen lots of sheep. When I was there I look around. I look pretty good around there. I'm used to looking for the game; I'm trained for that. Can spot a sheep or bear, anything, moose, caribou anywhere in the bush. Can spot it from here to across the lake. Sheep, I never seen any. (Frank Joe in Kluane First Nation, and Yukon Territorial Government 1996:12)

Because of the vastness of the territory and the time and expense involved in conducting wildlife research, biologists can at best hope to survey a given animal population once a year. In fact, even in the case of Ruby Range sheep, one of the most studied animal populations in the territory, biologists have fallen short of this modest ideal. Faced with this reality, they are careful to time their surveys so as to maximize the data they can collect. In the Ruby Range, for instance, they have traditionally flown their surveys in June, so they could count the number of yearlings that survived the winter in addition to the number of lambs born. Also, since sheep have seasonal movement patterns, biologists must fly their annual surveys at the same time every year, or they would be unable to compare their results from year to year.

By contrast, elders and hunters do not cover as much ground in a single day as do biologists in a helicopter perhaps, but they see animals all year round and have a good idea of what the animals do and where they are throughout the entire year, rather than on a single day in June. In the Ruby Range, elders and hunters see sheep not only on the lambing cliffs in springtime (where biologists see them) but in their winter and summer ranges as well. They watch the sheep come down to mineral licks, note where they cross between mountain ranges, and watch them in the rut. Whereas biologists know the sheep population through a series of detailed but static and temporally isolated "snapshots," elders and hunters experience sheep more continuously through time. Rather than attempting to integrate these two different views into the lives of sheep, however, RRSSC members used these differences to deny the validity of one another's knowledge. First Nation people claimed that biologists' lamb counts gave an inaccurate picture of the population because of high mortality rates in the period immediately following the counts. Biologists felt that because First Nation people do not systematically count sheep at the same time every year, they do not have an adequate basis for identifying changes in the population.

Differences in Geographical Dimension

Like time, geography also structures how different RRSSC members viewed the problem of sheep in the Ruby Range. In fact, the different geographical dimensions of their knowledge about sheep played an important role in the very formation of the RRSSC and the creation of its mandate. As it turns out, First Nation elders and hunters did not see the decline in the sheep population as limited to the Ruby Range. In fact, some of the elders and hunters present at the November 1995 meeting (at which the RRSSC had been established) had actually spent very little time personally hunting in the Ruby Range. Though they were aware of the situation there, these elders and hunters were also deeply concerned about what they saw as equally severe sheep declines in other areas where they had hunted extensively. The most important such area was to the north, between the White River and the Alaska border:

> Like, White River, when I first went into that area hunting, that was 1953, I was 13 years old. I could sit on a mountain between Rabbit Creek and Boulder Creek, where Dickie [Dickson] was talking about; I'd count 600 sheep. Two deep valleys like. Twenty years later I came back there, could still count 600 sheep. A lot of time a guy could count 350 sheep in one day. I hunted [as a guide] I'd say 20 trips, and I'd get a sheep in one day. I never ever got skunked

with a hunter. I'd take hunters out and I'd get game, but White
River, it's just a cinch to get a sheep in one day. Now, like David
[Dickson] he says, the last time I hunted up there was in 1988. He's
having trouble getting sheep, the same place. . . . Now David says
he has to hunt like hell to get sheep. (Douglas Dickson in KFN and
YTG 1996:19)

Aside from two large-scale aerial surveys (in 1974 and 1993) and sheep kill data collected from mandatory reports submitted by non–First Nation sheep hunters, however, biologists had very little knowledge of sheep populations in the White River area. As a result, they were unwilling to include this area in the mandate of the RRSSC. At the first meeting of the committee in December 1995, members decided that the committee would limit its activity to that area about which "both government and First Nations have some knowledge" (RRSSC 1995: 3). This decision essentially limited RRSSC activities to the study area used by biologists in their aerial surveys of the Ruby Range. First Nation RRSSC members were not altogether happy about this, since the study area represents just a tiny fraction of the area about which they were concerned; it excludes not only the White River area but the majority of the Nisling Range as well. At subsequent RRSSC meetings elders and hunters occasionally tried to extend the committee's mandate beyond the Ruby Range, but to no avail.

Biologists acknowledged that the decline in sheep was not limited to the Ruby Range, stating that it was occurring in "virtually every accessible population in the territory" and into Alaska (RRSSC 1996b:5). Indeed, they reported to the RRSSC that "Alaska reports a 40–70% decline in almost all of their sheep populations, even in areas with little or no harvest" (Yukon Territorial Government 1997:7). Despite this, however, biologists were unwilling to comply with First Nation requests to expand the RRSSC's mandate into other areas of concern because "there is not enough survey information from other parts of the Yukon to know how widespread the declines are there" (7). Thus, rather than increasing their total stock of knowledge about sheep by integrating the localized knowledge of biologists with the more extensive knowledge of hunters, as they might have done, RRSSC members simply struggled with one another over whose knowledge to use. First Nation people felt that biologists' knowledge about the decline in sheep was too limited geographically. Biologists, for their part, were unwilling to accept hunters' knowledge of sheep outside the Ruby Range study area as the sole basis for a management strategy in those areas.

There were other ways in which geographic differences between how RRSSC members know sheep caused them to question the validity of one another's knowledge. The Ruby Range sheep survey area is crisscrossed by a host of administrative and political boundaries. These include boundaries between game management subzones, outfitter areas (for administering outfitting activities), trapline concessions (for administering trapping activities), and First Nation Traditional Territories. These arbitrary geographical divisions directly affect people's experience of the land and so structure their knowledge of it; yet they overlap with and otherwise fail to correspond to one another. This makes any attempt to compare different people's knowledge of the land very complex. Biologists, for example, conduct their sheep counts by game management subzone. Since the division of the territory into these subzones does not correspond to its division into outfitter areas, and since outfitters count sheep in their area, it is difficult to compare the counts of biologists with those of outfitters.[11]

This lack of geographical correspondence becomes even more pronounced when we consider how individual First Nation elders and hunters experience the land. In the Yukon, there is no formal division of land into different hunting areas (though there is for trapping), but every First Nation hunter does hunt and fish in different places over the course of the year. Though different hunters may share any given place, no two hunters hunt and fish in exactly the same set of places. Thus, each hunter has what we might call a personal hunting area (though I continually refer to a "hunting" area, in it I include everywhere that a hunter goes in the bush, whether to hunt, fish, trap, pick berries, cut wood, etc.). These personal areas may overlap with one another, but no two are identical. Studies mapping the personal hunting areas of individual hunters in the same community (e.g., Brody 1982) have shown that these areas vary significantly in size, shape, and location. This is certainly the case in Burwash Landing as well. Elders and hunters regularly share their observations and thoughts about the land and animals with one another, so that their knowledge of the land extends beyond their own personal hunting area, but when biologists ask them for specific information about animal sightings, such as sheep counts, for example, they necessarily supply this information from their own experiences in their own unique hunting areas. This means that individual First Nation people's testimony, and the numbers that each provides to biologists, may vary considerably from one another's testimony, especially considering the high level of geographical and temporal variation in the boreal forest (Nelson 1983:200-224). Some biologists and resource managers misinterpret these differences between hunters as evidence for the unreliability of TEK and so are suspicious of First Nation people's knowledge altogether.

One biologist told me his misgivings about integrating TEK and knowledge because of the subjective nature of TEK. He said that it was "too fluid and dependent upon individuals" to be integrated with science. Not only does TEK change over time, according to him—perhaps reflecting changes in the world—but it also varies according to the hunter or elder with whom you talk. This, of course, is anathema to scientists. Scientific knowledge must be reproducible; it must be true for everyone, or it cannot be considered "knowledge" at all. When biologists are confronted by inconsistent and conflicting testimony by elders and hunters, some assume that this testimony is unreliable. Others recognize the complexity of the problem but are unsure of how to make use of such knowledge. First Nation people and scientists alike make much of the fact that TEK is inherently local, that it is rooted in a particular place. Yet, by failing to use TEK because of differences between hunters (either because they see it as invalid or because they do not know how to use it) biologists and resource managers implicitly deny the local nature of First Nation people's experiences on the land. The fact that this knowledge is not used (even by those biologists who recognize its validity) because it does not fit easily into the practices of bureaucratic wildlife management emphasizes the biases inherent in the project of knowledge integration.

The lack of geographical correspondence between different people's knowledge is further compounded when we consider its relation to the temporal differences discussed above. We saw that people's knowledge of sheep is constrained by the times they encounter the animals. Biologists count the sheep population in the spring, while outfitters interact with sheep during the licensed hunting season (late summer and early fall). Even First Nation people's observations of sheep are necessarily time dependent, since there are places that they visit more or less frequently, or only for seasonally specific activities, like berry picking or trapping. These temporal differences have an important geographical component, because sheep ignore the arbitrary administrative lines that humans draw on maps as they go about their seasonal movements. Thus, the timing of a sheep count can affect not only *where* one will see sheep, but *whether* one sees them at all. Sheep that have their lambs outside the biologists' study area, but whose summer range is in a part of that study area overlapping an outfitter concession, for example, will be counted by outfitters but not by biologists. This, in fact, is precisely how one outfitter accounted for the discrepancy between his own counts and those of biologists (RRSSC 1996b:3). He argued that it was inappropriate to use the biologists' aerial survey data to manage sheep hunting in his outfitting area, because spring counts do not accurately reflect the population found there during hunting season. As we have seen, however, this temporal/geographical discrepancy was not an insurmountable problem. In fact, biologists and the outfitter subsequently overcame it and integrated one another's sheep counts to solve the problem of the missing sheep.

The Case of the Missing Sheep Revisited:
"Trust" and the Politics of Knowledge Integration

Members of the RRSSC were aware of many of these temporal and geographical discrepancies before the RRSSC process even began. Indeed, the existence of such differences was one of the primary incentives for engaging in co-management in the first place. The fact that different people knew about Ruby Range sheep at different times and places meant that RRSSC members could, in theory, pool their knowledge, creating a collective knowledge base that exceeded any individual's knowledge—not only in quality but also in temporal and geographical scope. At the same time, these temporal and geographical differences made it extremely difficult to compare and integrate different people's knowledge. What exactly is one to make of differences between a June and a July sheep count? Of a count by game management subzone versus one by outfitting area? Of differences in the testimony of various First Nation hunters who have different hunting areas? There is no objective formula into which one can plug such incomparable data. If one is to make sense of these disparities, one must engage in a process of creative interpretation. The case of the missing sheep is a perfect example.

Although the biologists and the outfitter had both counted sheep by game management subzone (thus, there was no geographical discrepancy), there were other differences that made their counts difficult to compare. Biologists had counted sheep from the air in July, whereas the outfitter had counted them from the ground in August. Integrating these two counts required an act of imagination; one had to imagine the sheep leaving the area in June and returning in August. Either party could have rejected this interpretation for any number of reasons (e.g., based on their understanding of sheep behavior). Even more important, biologists and the outfitter had to be willing to accept and act upon the number of sheep reported by the other.

The notion of "trust" occupies a prominent place in the rhetoric of TEK. Government and First Nation participants in co-management processes are routinely urged to "trust one another" and are warned that without such trust co-management cannot succeed. Certainly, biologists and outfitters had to trust one another to be truthful, to accurately report the number of sheep they really saw. Likewise, each had to have confidence in how the other had gone about counting sheep. That is, they had to trust one another's ability to generate accurate data. Without these two forms of trust they could not have integrated their knowledge the way they did. But it was not enough that biologists and the outfitter simply "trust" one another; they also had to be willing to *act* on one another's information (i.e., to modify their own numbers, or at least their understanding of the meaning of those numbers, and to *use* those new numbers and meanings in their management efforts). This is not the same as "trust." Indeed, the notion of "trust" must be viewed within the broader context of power relations. Biologists, for example, may have "trusted" the First Nation elders who said that the sheep population had once been much higher than it was in 1980. That is, they may have believed the elders to be honest and even trusted them to generate accurate sheep counts. But, given the political context of sheep hunting in the Yukon, there is *no way* biologists could have accepted and *acted upon* First Nation elders' accounts of the size of past sheep populations. To do so would have been to endorse the view that there had been a catastrophic population decline requiring drastic and immediate action. Aside from the fact that biologists did not believe this to be the case, for them to have advocated such drastic action (such as a ban on sheep hunting) in the absence of "scientific" evidence to back it up would have been impossible.

Biologists on the RRSSC simply could not support a ban on hunting (or even the imposition of a quota hunt) based solely on Kluane people's arguments, regardless of how well they understood these arguments or how personally sympathetic they might have been. Biologists have to be able to justify (with scientific evidence) the positions they take on wildlife management. They must be able to answer the criticisms of other biologists employed by those with competing political interests. For them to take a position that they could not defend in this way would be viewed as irresponsible. Outfitters and others could then have criticized them for being biased and "unscientific," and they would have been utterly unable to defend themselves from these charges. Their reputations as scientists would have been damaged, and they might conceivably even have lost their jobs. And all of this would have been for naught since, considering the political power wielded by outfitters in the territory, the government could not have implemented a hunting ban (or quota hunt) without incontrovertible "scientific" proof that the sheep population had once been as high as Kluane elders and hunters maintained (it would have been difficult enough even *with* such proof). In the absence of scientific evidence, supporting Kluane people's position regarding the past population size of the Ruby Range sheep population simply was not an option for biologists on the RRSSC. Yet, this is precisely what they would have to have done if "knowledge integration" were to succeed.

In the case of the RRSSC, the committee's failure to successfully integrate knowledge artifacts indicates more than simply a lack of trust between committee members. Indeed, the fact that the only instance of artifact integration in the whole RRSSC process occurred between an outfitter and biologists is quite significant, and this significance was not lost on First Nation people. As we have seen, the integration of biologist and outfitter data that occurred in the case of the missing sheep was far from straightforward; it required a certain amount of creative interpretation to overcome the incomparability of the two counts. The fact that integration occurred in *spite* of these difficulties indicates not only that the outfitter and biologists trusted one another's motives and methods enough to work together to overcome these technical difficulties; it also highlights the political dimensions of knowledge integration. Biologists had accepted the outfitter's numbers at face value and were willing to base their actions (or non-action, in this case) on them—without requiring any additional "proof"—despite the fact that those numbers differed radically from their own. Kluane people felt that by doing this, biologists were extending to the outfitter a degree of trust that they had resolutely refused to extend to First Nation people.

By this time in the RRSSC process, some Kluane people had already begun to suspect that their position regarding sheep was being dismissed on political or racial grounds rather than on intellectual grounds. When they saw that biologists were willing to trust the outfitter, whose economic interests gave him a clear motive for fabricating the results of his sheep count, and yet seemingly refused to trust the word of some of the most respected people in their community, they felt that their suspicions had been confirmed. In addition, the fact that biologists and outfitters could come to such an agreement without the consent, or even the involvement, of Kluane First Nation illustrates the differences in power that existed between committee members.[12] It is almost inconceivable, for example, that First Nation people could have excluded biologists and their knowledge from the process and still have effectively "explained away" such a dramatic change in the sheep population. Yet, biologists were able to use outfitter data in this way because there were no significant political obstacles preventing them from doing so (as there were to the use of First Nation people's testimony). The case of the missing sheep, perhaps more than any other single incident, caused Kluane First Nation people to lose confidence in the RRSSC process.

Notes

1. Game management zones and subzones are administrative units used by the Yukon Department of Renewable Resources for managing wildlife and administering hunting and fishing regulations.

2. See Nadasdy (2003) for a detailed description of these knowledge artifacts and how they were produced.

3. For a more in-depth discussion of the context in which the rrssc operated, see Nadasdy (2003).

4. I don't mean to conflate the interests and positions of outfitters and biologists here. In some ways their positions were quite different (see Nadasdy 2003), but their agreement that hunting had not been a significant factor in the decline of the sheep population—and so did not need to be restricted—had important political implications.

5. For a more comprehensive discussion of the different ways in which various rrssc members constructed knowledge about sheep, see Nadasdy (2003).

6. In the summers of 1948 and 1949, McClellan (1975:120) reports having seen "good numbers of sheep being dried at a Tutchone meat camp on the Big Arm of Kluane Lake." This happens to be in the Ruby Range Dall sheep study area. See also Arthurs (1995) for archaeological evidence of sheep hunting in the area.

7. McClellan (1975:121) also found that Kluane people ate sheep. In addition she discusses their use of sheepskin to make "parkeys" (the local term for parkas) and blankets, babiche (rawhide laces), for snowshoes, horns for ladles, and forelegs for knife scabbards. Though these parts of the sheep are seldom used today, I was told about all of these uses and saw several old objects of this kind.

8. Though I myself never encountered any mythic stories or ritual behavior related specifically to sheep, McClellan found instances of both in the Kluane area (McClellan 1975:121-122).

9. Until that time, the government had refused to consider including sheep with moose and caribou as animals to which First Nation people had special rights in the event of the need to establish a Total Allowable Harvest as per 16.9.0 of the Umbrella Final Agreement (Council for Yukon Indians 1993:176-177).

10. I am speaking here of the community viewed collectively. Certainly there are gaps in specific individuals' personal experiences of the Ruby Range, but it would be difficult to find a long stretch of time in which no one in the community visited the Ruby Range. And Kluane First Nation people regularly share their observations about animals with one another (see Nadasdy 2003). Some might object that in recent years there are such gaps, because Kluane people do not spend as much time out on the land as they used to, but my own experiences in the community do not bear this out. In fact, people continue to spend quite a bit of time in the Ruby Range, especially on the two arms of Kluane Lake and at Cultus Bay, areas that they and their elders also used historically. Although the amount of time they spend in the more remote parts of the Ruby and Nisl-

ing Ranges has declined over the years, there are still those who do spend considerable time in these areas, especially during the winter.

11. However, at least one outfitter had recorded his sheep counts by game management sub-zone, including the outfitter who had "found" the 100 missing sheep.

12. It is true that outfitters and First Nation people are unlikely to trust one another with very detailed information about their sheep sightings. As a result it is not surprising that biologists and outfitters did not invite kfn to participate in these discussions. The fact that Kluane people were also denied the opportunity to question the validity and use of the outfitter's knowledge, however (especially considering the outfitter's obvious motive for fabricating his results), clearly illustrates the political dimensions of the incident.

7. Local Knowledge, Multiple Livelihoods, and the Use of Natural and Social Resources in North Carolina

David Griffith

In one of the photographs in my book on Mid-Atlantic fisheries, *The Estuary's Gift*, a woman and a man sit in a rowboat with a dead eight-point buck between them, the buck's antlers and head protruding over the side of the vessel (Griffith 1999:68). The man, in the bow, is handling the oars while the woman reclines in the stern, resting a shotgun across her knees. They look slightly overdressed for hunting, the woman wearing a long-sleeved, ankle-length dress, leather boots, and a hat that resembles a beret, and the man wearing what looks like a dark suit and a whaleboat captain's cap. In the background, the riverbank is forested with sweet gum and pine, and the caption reads, "Woman with shotgun ferrying deer on the New River, North Carolina, c. 1895."

Though taken in the latter part of the 19th century, this photograph could have been taken a hundred years later, of Jesse and Helen McMillan, who live down a rutted dirt road on a small plot of land where a muddy neck of creek offers access to the Pamlico River and Sound. Calling the McMillans' land waterfront property is something only an unscrupulous realtor might do. The water is so still it is practically stagnant, the docks look rickety, and the bank is littered with eel and crab pots, old fishing nets, lines, and other remnants of fishing. Jesse McMillan sets crab pots during the summer months, keeps eels in tanks, hunts, sets flounder nets, and scavenges lumber he finds drifting downriver or across the sound after a storm.

With the scavenged lumber he adds on to a workshop where he builds traps and repairs his motors and fishing equipment, making it about three times the size of the small, one-room trailer where he and Helen live. The workshop reflects his attachment to the estuary and its resources as well as his craftsman's past. Like many fishers, although he prefers fishing, he is able to fall back on welding, mechanical work, carpentry, pipe fitting, and other skills when he must. Like fishers elsewhere, he falls back on these skills when developments, whether natural or social, prevent him from earning enough income from fishing. Like fishers elsewhere, too, he returns to fishing whenever he can, adding to a corpus of knowledge seated in multiple ways of making ends meet (Griffith and Dyer 1996; Griffith and Valdes Pizzini 2002).

Typically, families of fishers, farmers, and foresters in North Carolina and other parts of the Mid- and South Atlantic coastal plain rely on multiple livelihoods to meet household food and income needs. In their households, like urban couples who combine two or more incomes to survive, people in rural areas of the Mid-Atlantic mix different natural resource extraction activities with reliance on social support networks and work in the formal economy. This has been true for the past three hundred years, or since early Europeans displaced Algonquin, Tuscarora, and Siouxian groups from the coastal plain, and many parts of the South have retained large stretches of wilderness and forest because of the importance of hunting and forestry throughout the region.

West of the barrier islands and the fringes of development immediately adjacent to the oceans and parts of the sounds, large areas of coastal North Carolina are still home to abundant wild fish stocks, deer, black bear, and vast stretches of wetlands and nursery areas that provide estuarine havens for juvenile fish and shellfish. Pine forests cover much of the coastal plain, although pines today differ from the native long-leaf pine forests that once carpeted the state. North Carolina's coastal ecology and the proximity of urbanized and gentrified segments of coast have created a social and ecological context where multiple livelihoods are, to many of its long-time Native inhabitants, preferable to specializing in either wage work or the exploitation of a single resource. The continued reliance on multiple livelihoods that mix natural resource exploitation with work in the formal economy has created local knowledge bases that include information about ecological relationships as well as information about relations between environmental health and political and economic processes. Unfortunately, much of the most relevant and interesting work being done today on local knowledge, such as ethnobiology or the focus on traditional ecological knowledge (TEK), either ignores or pays little attention to the economic and political contexts in which hunters, fishers, and others who possess vast stores of TEK operate. These knowledge bases—combining ecological, geographical, historical, and socioeconomic information—stand in contrast to the specialized knowledge systems that have developed based on more narrow and intensive exploitation and observation of plant and animal resources, such as intensive agriculture, experimental science, and commodity production.

Here I explore differences between multiple livelihoods and specialized resource exploitation, discussing the implications of multiple livelihoods for local knowledge. I accomplish this through an examination of naval stores production, the state's first most important commodity, commercial fishing, and the water quality debates that have occurred in conjunction with a dinoflagellate called *Pfiesteria* in recent years.

Naval Stores in North Carolina before and after 1830

Naval stores—the collective name for resin, tar, pitch, turpentine, spars, masts, timbers, and other pine-based products used primarily to build and waterproof ships and their riggings—became colonial North Carolina's most important export commodity early in the 18th century, when the colony began supplying naval stores to the British Crown's navy and the empire's mercantile fleet. Because this period was the height of mercantile capitalism, coinciding with the global expansion of the British Empire, the strategic importance of naval stores cannot be underestimated. Domestic British Isles supplies of timber for shipbuilding had been taxed since the mid-16th century, competing with the population's demands for timbers for housing and fuel for iron smelting, and no adequate conifers for turpentine and other waterproofing material were native to the Isles. Supplies from the Baltic region—historically the source of most of Britain's naval stores—were sporadic and forever tied up in tariff disputes and political developments that several times closed off the entrance to the Baltic Sea (Williams 1989: 83). As early as 1726, the North Carolina port of Brunswicktown, on the lower Cape Fear River, began shipping naval stores to England along with ports in New England and other colonies up and down the eastern seaboard; forty-two years later, when the first data on all ports became available, North Carolina ports, and Brunswicktown in particular, were providing over 60 percent of the naval stores consumed by His Majesty's sailors and merchants.

Prior to the American Revolution, the production of naval stores in North Carolina was carried on primarily along the coastal plain south of the Albemarle Sound and up the Cape Fear River valley between Wilmington and Fayetteville (formerly known as Cross Creek). The area north of the Albemarle Sound, between Edenton and Elizabeth City, was the longest settled and the seat of the colony's political power. The Granville District, which ran from the mountains to the coast along today's North Carolina–Virginia state line, was still in the hands of one of the original Lords Proprietors, Lord Granville. Though the most densely populated, longest settled by Europeans, and most developed region of the colony, due to Granville's ownership it generated no revenues for the colony while demanding the lion's share of colonial administrative services and other resources.

Although planters in the Albemarle region produced naval stores, they were more tied to Virginia tobacco growers and produced a variety of forestry, grain, and fisheries products, later embracing cotton as a principal crop. Large herring haul-seining operations up and down the Albemarle Sound and the shores of the Roanoke River, from the mid-18th century to the Civil War, were indicative of the power of large landowners in the region (Griffith 1999: chapter 3). These operations provided seasonal employment and high-quality protein for thousands of families in the area, netting and packing fish for twenty-four hours a day and landing up to 250,000 per haul. These fisheries were only a part of more complex, larger plantations, such as Hope and Sommerset, that produced corn, wheat, cotton, tobacco, and other commodities for export, as well as keeping orchards and gardens for domestic use.

By contrast, naval stores were primarily the business of families of small farmers, many of Highland Scottish ancestry. Prior to the Revolution, North Carolina attracted more Highland Scots than any other colony. Large-scale Scottish immigration into North Carolina, actively encouraged by a Scottish colonial governor, Gabriel Johnston, began as early as 1732 and continued until the American Revolution, in which many Scots fought, and lost, against the Whigs. With German, Dutch, Moravian, and other immigrants to the colony, Scots migrated into what was largely a wilderness along one of three principal routes: directly from the British Isles, landing in Brunswick or Wilmington, or coming overland from elsewhere in the colony, either south along the coastal plain from the Albemarle region and then west into the interior up the Cape Fear River, or south out of Pennsylvania and Virginia through the Shenandoah Valley.

Though Scottish Highlanders initially came because of Governor Johnston's encouragement, later they arrived because of ties of kinship and friendship and the growth of a Gaelic community up and down the Cape Fear River, centered principally around Fayetteville, and increasing persecution in the British Isles after the battle of Culloden in 1746. Thus they were both immigrants and refugees. Others came to North Carolina because the colony offered sanctuary to indentured servants who had defaulted on their terms of their indenture in other colonies. This policy angered landowners and others in neighboring colonies, particularly Virginia (Thomas Jefferson among them), yet it was part of the state's conscious attempt to encourage new immigrants to settle in the state.

These two groups of immigrants—Highland Scots and former indentured servants who failed to complete their contracts—composed a smallholding class of yeoman farmers with little capital and, quite likely, an understory of mistrust of established power, including merchants and large landowners. Although they may have longed for large landholdings, families from these backgrounds were more likely to engage in a mixed domestic economy of farming, hunting, and gathering, with little more to market than resin, tar, pitch, turpentine, staves, spars, and other naval stores.

Through much of the 18th century and into the 19th century, these yeoman farmers thus produced naval stores as parts of household economies. Extracting naval stores from North Carolina's heavy forests involved several unpleasant, difficult tasks. First, to stimulate the flow of resin, longleaf pines were scored, diagonally, as high up on the trunk as one could reach. The cuts slanted down and inward, from the left and right, making V-shaped impressions along the face of the tree. This was called "boxing" the tree, and at their base the trees were fitted with pans or cups to catch the sap. Every ten to fifteen days in the summer, and less often in the winter, men scraped the scored face of the tree with a wooden or metal blade mounted on a long pole, channeling the sap into the pan. They carried the heavy and sticky resin to large central distilleries that distilled turpentine through an unhealthy and hazardous process, the air around the distilleries heavy with the lingering fumes and odors of turpentine and the distilleries themselves explosive.

For tar and pitch manufacture, both fresh trees and, most commonly, the trees that the farmers had bled to death for the turpentine were piled in a donut-shaped pit, between 10 and 20 yards across, set on fire, and covered with grass and dirt in a manner similar to the manufacture of charcoal, creating a smoldering mound. Workers then opened a hole and a ditch to drain off the tar that slowly oozed from the smoldering wood. Tar from trees used for turpentine was usually of slightly higher quality, fetching higher prices at market. Farmers could either sell the tar or add value to it through a rendering process that reduced the tar to pitch, requiring two units (usually barrels) of tar to make one unit of pitch.

Barrels of finished resin, tar, and pitch made it to Wilmington and Brunswick over a network of streams, dirt roads, and plank roads connecting the interior with the Cape Fear River. The barrels were literally rolled to market, often pulled behind horses or mules, in pairs, with short axels fitted to the lids and bottoms of the barrels. In Brunswick and Wilmington, tar and pitch were shipped out, and the resin was distilled into turpentine. Between 1726, when Brunswick was founded, and the American Revolution, when the

British market dried up for several years, the Cape Fear region was exporting between 50,000 to 65,000 barrels of tar, pitch, and turpentine per year, around half of the total for all North Carolina ports.

Though remarkable, this level of production was not sufficient to decimate the longleaf pine forests. That naval stores production was largely embedded in domestic economies, with multiple livelihoods, kept production at levels that the forests could sustain. Most of the work was accomplished through household labor, without the use of slaves. Slave labor was not common in the yeoman households of the piney woods. From 1755 to 1769, for example, in New Hanover County, slave-owning households made up between 26 and 30 percent of the total households; over half of those had only 1 to 4 slaves, and households with more than 4 slaves made up only 10 to 13 percent of the total (Merrens 1962).

It was not until after 1830 that specialized pine plantations emerged and, over time, greatly advanced the decimation of longleaf pine forests (Outland 2001). In the 1830s, two new uses for turpentine were developed: as a solvent for rubber production and in camphene, an illuminant that was less expensive and burned longer and brighter than lard oil. Turpentine also had medicinal uses. Shortly after these discoveries, turpentine production began to interest men with substantial capital and large numbers of slaves, and there was a shift from small- and medium-sized farm families exploiting the longleaf pine as part of a varied household economy to large, specialized production.

Other technological developments complemented this shift. In 1834 the copper still was developed, moving distilling turpentine from port cities and other central locations to deep within forests. In 1840 developers completed a 126-mile railroad, crossing the coastal plain from Weldon to Wilmington (the longest in the world in its day), which facilitated access to more forested acreage and eased transporting barrels of tar, pitch, and, increasingly, finished turpentine. In the 1850s the Cape Fear and Deep River Navigation Company made the Cape Fear River more navigable, further extending the reach of planters exploiting the pine.

Finally, a few less aggressive human endeavors also facilitated the slow decimation of this natural resource. Beginning with European settlement, use of the pine for construction timber began. More damaging, however, was the general suppression of forest fires in the colonies. Longleaf pine ecological communities depend on fire to clear away understory and remain healthy. The Tuscarora, Sioux, and Algonquin peoples who inhabited the forests prior to European contact set fires every fall, primarily for deer hunts and to make forests easier to walk through, encouraging longleaf pine growth (Frankenberg 1997; Williams 1989). When suppressed, however, particularly in the turpentine-producing areas, the buildup of wood chips, sap, and other residues of the process caused any fires that did occur to be particularly devastating.

In addition to the suppression of fire and logging, the specialized slave plantations devoted to turpentine production practiced what Outland called, appropriately, a "suicidal harvest," decimating the longleaf pine. "A shift to planter control of production accompanied the turpentine industry's expansion," he writes (2001:313). "Since the late 1720s, small and middle-sized farmers had manufactured a significant portion of naval stores. But as the industry spread along the Cape Fear River in the 1840s and continued its dramatic growth into the 1850s, men with capital and many slaves entered the manufacture on a grand scale."

Similarly, historian David Cecelski questioned whether the Owens plantation went bankrupt because of fiscal mismanagement or environmental disaster. He writes, "In the 1840s and 1850s, the naval stores industry was rapidly destroying the long-leaf pine forests. . . . When Wilmington's exports [of turpentine] rose from 7,218 barrels in 1847 to more than 120,000 a decade later, every 50,000-barrel increase in output came at the expense of another 250,000 acres of piney woods" (1997:18–19). After the mid-19th century the longleaf pine forests were decimated in North Carolina, and turpentine manufacturers moved on to rape the forests of South Carolina, Georgia, Alabama, and other southern states.

One final point about naval stores production in colonial North Carolina concerns its possible influence over local, regional, and American history. American history, of course, has been a building block of nationalism since 1776, and the ways that Americans remember national and regional history reflects upon, and influences, local knowledge, memory, and history. Remembering American history is an inherently political project, the active business of statesmen and legitimate, credentialed scholars. Immediately following the American Revolution, perhaps no one was more influential than Thomas Jefferson in how the Revolution, and hence the birth of a nation, was represented and portrayed—its heroes, its important battles, the individuals and groups responsible for its success. What and who were listed in the first and most enduring accounts of the conflict was a subject of deep concern for Jefferson.

Jefferson's dedication to science and education was evident from his own writings, his legendary personal library holdings, his support and personal mentoring of Meriwether Lewis, and his role in the creation of the University of Virginia and, by extension, his promotion of the state-supported university and public education in general. Given his strong dedication, it may be somewhat disquieting to many Americans to learn that the former education-oriented third president of the United States was, late in life, accused of engaging a campaign of biased historical reporting and censorship.

In 1819, the same year the University of Virginia was chartered, Jefferson wrote a letter to two newspapers, the *Raleigh Record* in North Carolina and the *Essex Register* in Salem, Massachusetts, in which he denounced the papers' coverage of the so-called Mecklenburg Declaration. This was a declaration of independence that supposedly was made by North Carolina statesmen on May 20, 1775, preceding Jefferson's declaration by over a year. Whether or not the Mecklenburg Declaration ever occurred was a matter of controversy among historians for over a century. Most now agree with a 1909 analysis of historical documents that it was a conflation of the Mecklenburg resolves, a series of quite radical statements approximating a declaration of independence by denying the British Crown's authority over the North Carolina colony (Ganyard 1963:151). In 1834, however, Jo. Sewell Jones wrote *A Defense of the Revolutionary History of the State of North Carolina from the Aspersions of Mr. Jefferson*, arguing not only that the Mecklenburg Declaration occurred but that North Carolina's contributions to the Revolution had been neglected by historians in general, due largely to the influence of Thomas Jefferson.

The Mecklenburg Declaration aside, one critical revolutionary moment has received short shrift in American history books: the Moore's Creek Bridge Campaign. Though it was the first decisive Whig victory of the American Revolution, the battle at Moore's Creek, which prevented Loyalist forces from joining other British forces who were trying to suppress rebellion in New England, receives little more than a few lines in standard histories of the American Revolution. It especially pales beside coverage of events such as the skirmish at Concord and the Boston Tea Party.

Neglect of North Carolina history may, in fact, have a material basis. Serious ethnic and class division separated colonial North Carolina from the colonies north of the Granville District and south of the Cape Fear River valley. These divisions may be traced to typical multiple livelihoods practiced in North Carolina during the colonial period, livelihoods partially dependent on the production of naval stores for the British navy and merchant vessels, as well as to the allegiances that emerged during the Revolution. The Highland Scots were not only among the principal suppliers of naval stores to the British, hence having a material stake in their victory; they were also forced to swear loyalty oaths to the Crown before settling in North Carolina. While many swore these oaths reluctantly, and others placed little store in them, some Scots took them seriously enough to fight on behalf of the British during the Revolution; in fact, the majority of loyalist combatants at Moore's Creek were Highland Scots.

Two other groups may have been seen by Jefferson and other members of the large planter class as unfit for history: the Moravians, who attempted to remain neutral during the war, and those former indentured servants who defaulted on their terms of indenture and, because of colonial policy, were offered sanctuary in North Carolina. Along with the Highland Scots and those who forged the policy of offering sanctuary to fugitive indentures, these groups were not highly regarded by those colonies dominated by large planter classes to the north and south of North Carolina. This may (and I emphasize the word *may*) account for giving North Carolinians little credit, and hence little history, for the success of the American Revolution. In any case, diverting the colony and state from the course of national history had a potentially chilling and isolating effect that I have noted in my book on Mid-Atlantic coastal populations (Griffith 1999: chapter 8) and that Jo. Sewell Jones noted in his 1834 treatise: "Extinguish this feeling of veneration for our ancestors, and you vitally assail the honor of the state, corrupt and degrade the people, and by degrees inure them to the control of a foreign demagogue" (1834:vi).

Flexibility in North Carolina Commercial Fisheries
The Albemarle-Pamlico Estuarine System (APES) is the second largest estuarine system on the eastern seaboard; though smaller than the Chesapeake Bay, the system supports an equally diverse set of fisheries that are similar in a number of respects. Blue crab production is the largest fishery in the state, which has several components, but the system also supports a large shrimp fishery and several kinds of finfish. Although some fishing families specialize in one fishery, it is common for families to rely on a primary fishery for most of the year while moving into other fisheries during other parts of the year (Griffith 1999: chapter 5). Equally common is the practice, based on repeated observation, of moving in and out of fisheries from year to year, as the following two quotes—one from a crabber and the other from a shrimper—illustrate:

> Pamlico River Crabber: I never go past Gun Point on the north side. I just never do. If I can't catch them there, I do something else. I go to flounder fishing totally or something like that. In fact, in 1988 I quit crabbing for five years and just flounder fished in the spring, summer, and fall. Spring, summer, and fall because it got where—the price of flounder went up and it was starting out 30 cents. And the Washington Crab Company, they didn't have but like three or four guys they let grade. And he wanted picking crabs and get a straight price, and it dropped down to like 18 cents or 19, and I just went to flounder fishing. It had been sort of a bad year that year. We were catching a lot more crabs per pot than we are now, but it was considered a bad year back then. So I went to flounder fishing;

I flounder fished all over the place—Albemarle Sound. And I mullet fished in the wintertime. And I started back crabbing about six or seven years ago.

Cape Fear Shrimper: Well, you know, this year, I started back to oystering. And it seems like this year the oysters are ready to come back. . . . It's surprising how big the oysters have grown since last year. For some reason, they made a comeback. But you know, I believe this seafood comes in cycles. Take, for instance, shrimp in the Pamlico Sound. About every seven or eight years they'll have a tremendous season; this year they had one of the best they've ever had. Next year will probably be one of the sorriest. But five or six years from now they'll have another big season. It seems like it comes in cycles. Last spring, year before last, in the Cape Fear River, February, March, and April, we were catching 16 and 20 count shrimp in the Cape Fear. What them shrimp were doing is they were going outside and they would come back in that river on that rising water and work their way back.

I chose these two passages not only because they illustrate the practice of moving among different fisheries, but also because they suggest that ecological knowledge is seated in personal experience and, by extension, local history. Interviewing fishers across North Carolina, I have been struck by how little, for example, crab fishers in the Albemarle Sound know about shrimping even in the Core Sound, despite that the waters of both the Albemarle and Core Sounds join with the Pamlico Sound. Problems with developing more comprehensive knowledge systems, or knowledge that is as geographically broad as it is locally textured, contextualized, and deep may stem from the complexity of knowledge that fishers obtain in the local setting, its specific nature, and the problems of applying that knowledge to other areas where it, in fact, may not apply. In other words, the tendency to place natural and social processes into larger contexts has been limited geographically, including primarily those areas that fishers experience directly.

Specific Dimensions of Local Environmental Knowledge

> *Everything runs in cycles and it all works by the moon.*
>
> North Carolina crabber

Fishers in North Carolina develop knowledge systems that are both more and less applicable to estuarine environments in general. Their TEK is, like the estuarine system they know so much about, layered. Open-ended, ecological narratives with fishers reveal that they believe the conditions that influence the behaviors of fish and shellfish include, first, several natural phenomena working in conjunction with one another. I include some of these phenomena (not necessarily in order of importance) in the following list:

Phases of the Moon	Substrate features
Wind speed and direction	Shoreline characteristics
Salinity levels	Time of year (season)
Oxygen levels	Food web dynamics (predation)
Water temperature	Water depth

Fishers then consider these phenomena against backgrounds of specific geographical formations, recent events, and other natural and social phenomena that make their knowledge difficult to generalize to other environments. A few examples of this follow:

> *Core Sound Shrimper: Because you take a tide—the only time a channel netter can catch one is at tide. And when they're moving, I don't know as they don't work right on that way. I know when we do our best shrimping in that channel is on a flood tide. When that moon starts to shell, it's about four or five after is the very best time, whenever you see her start to shell a little over yonder and then they're going to show up overnight.*

> *Pamlico Sound Shrimper: Everything can affect it [the catch]. You usually figure on a full moon, or just after a full moon, three or four days after the full moon we'll usually get some shrimp. June*

and July. A full moon in July is usually always the best you're going to get out of brown shrimp. But if you hit a real big weather change or something before that, that's going to take it's place. Basically, you ain't going to figure the mess out unless you're going every night.

Pamlico River Crabber: They [blue crabs] go in these creeks and they won't leave unless it's bad water, that's what a jimmy crab does. He comes up to this brackish water / fresh water and he'll die here. Everybody knows that. Unless the pollution is real bad and he'll go on back out. That's what they like; this is where they go. If the water is good, they'll go way up past the trestle. They've been caught up there in Greenville, you know, crabs, big jimmies. Some of the biggest crabs around are in Lake Mattamuskeet.

Jarrett's Bay Crabber and Clammer: Pocosin is a swamp on a hill. It was just a 60-square-mile piece of swamp out there, all bayberry and brush and stuff. The rain would trickle off, it would trickle off for a week after a heavy rain. Now it's all ditches. You could drive a steamboat through it. And after a heavy rain, it just rushes out of there. I've had salinities in here where I grow my clams. I've got them out there now, we'll take a look at them when we go outside. I've had salinities go down to zero, and my normal salinity in here is probably between 22 and 26, which is very—the ocean, you know, is 31. That's pretty saline; it's excellent salinity. But after a heavy rain, it will plummet in here.

While key natural phenomena are seated within more specific information, they are also seated within larger understandings, or folk theories, that aid in their interpretation. The idea of fish populations occurring in cycles is probably the premier example of this, noted by nearly all the fishers we encounter in North Carolina, but another is the notion (confirmed by estuarine ecologists) of the water having layers:

Pamlico Sound Crabber: I'll tell you right now—every crab, they just migrate away as far as they can get from that dead water.

They know, they know. And sometimes it's layers, the way they get trapped in it. So the fresh water will be on top of the salt water, and that dead water will sometimes be six feet deep. So the fish are trapped down into a hole that's, say, 20 feet deep. And all around that hole will be six feet of water and it'll be all dead water. And after awhile, they'll run out of oxygen in that hole and they'll die; they won't be able to get out. That's how things like that happen. After hurricanes you really see some strange stuff going on. The bottom gets all torn up and you see the methane and all that stuff comes bubbling up to the surface. Wow. After a big storm, you see all those organic materials that's been laying on the bottom for years being all tore to pieces, you know.

Others folk theories are more complex, combining a variety of the features in the list above with human phenomena to make judgments about the fish movements, water quality, and other factors influencing their decisions about where and when to fish and their explanations of why the resource is in the condition it is in.

Fishers' TEK never develops in a social or cultural vacuum. Indeed, human dimensions of TEK include ideas about relations between nutrient runoff from agriculture and water quality, dredging, management decisions that influence drag times and other fishing effort, coastal tourist development, and other social and economic phenomena. As noted earlier, part of this stems from their participating in other components of the coastal economy by combining multiple livelihoods and moving among various fisheries. Other dimensions of the fishing industry around them are more specialized, provide the larger social context in which many management decisions are made, and many fishing practices, and their TEK, develop.

Larger Social Context

While most of the fishing families in the state operate on a relatively small scale, in part confined by the movements of fish and shellfish into the shallows during portions of the year, alternatives to family fisheries exist. I discuss, briefly, four such alternatives.

Processors' fleets: Fleets established by blue crab processing houses assure supplies of crab to their plants. Fishers who work for processing fleets can be owner-operators, who receive trip expenses for fishing, slip space for their vessels, or other services. Other fishers in this group collect wages on fishing vessels. Many of the Mexican and Vietnamese fishers in the region began by working for processors, who helped set them up in business in return for marketing their catch with them.

Part-time fishers: Part-time fishing has increased in the Mid-Atlantic over the past decade, with people using primarily stationary gear, such as crab pots or nets, that they check less often than full-time fishers. Most of these individuals have ties to fishing families or used to be full-time fishers, but some are retirees or others who don't know any of the informal rules of soaking gear. Many full-time fishers regard them as a nuisance and view their practices as environmentally harmful.

Recreational fishers, including charter and party boat captains and crew: Research conducted during the mid-1990s revealed three important categories of recreational fishers: those affiliated with fishing clubs, those not affiliated with fishing clubs, and "professional" recreational fishers, such as charter boat and party boat captains and crew (Griffith 1996, 1999). Recreational fishing interests have held more sway among lawmakers in recent years, and organized recreational fishers pose one of the primary threats to commercial fishers, attempting to impose net bans and other regulations that would devastate Mid-Atlantic commercial fisheries. Not all recreational fishers back such proposals, and many—principally charter boat captains—tied to commercial fishing families through kinship or friendship ties, oppose them as actively as commercial fishers.

Industrialized fisheries: These are large vessels that fish primarily in ocean waters as opposed to the sound. The largest industrialized fishery is the menhaden fleet. Menhaden oil has industrial uses, principally as a rustproofing agent. Most of this fleet, which used to be much larger than it is today, is now concentrated in Reedsville, Virginia. These vessels are large (more than 60 feet) and have African American crews. The vessels at Wanchese also tend to be somewhat larger, between 40 and 60 feet, and fish up and down the eastern seaboard. Many are long liners or roller net fishers, similar to the fishers of New Bedford and Gloucester, Massachusetts. Some of this fleet, along with the major processors, has moved to Norfolk, given the instability and occasional treacherous waters of Oregon Inlet.

The existence of each of these fisheries has implications for fisheries management and for the continued development of local knowledge. Management decisions affect different parts of Mid-Atlantic fisheries differently, and most focus on either individual species or specific gear types rather than acknowledging the complexities of fishing operations that move among various species and gear from day to day and season to season. In the Albemarle Sound, for example, striped bass have been strictly regulated for several years, the regulations primarily spearheaded by recreational fishers who want the species protected. Currently their commercial harvest is restricted to five fish per commercial fisherman per day, despite the fact that longtime herring fishers in the sound argue that, based on their observations, striped bass populations (locally known as "rock" or "rockfish") are more than healthy and that they are upsetting the ecosystem's health by their predation, most of which is directed toward young blue crabs (Griffith 1999:111–113).

> They've made it where you can't even think about catching enough [rockfish] to survive on. But we have these huge schools of them. I mean, they're just overpopulated. They're rundown and they look bad. They started eating the little rockfish. And they eat crabs. Crabs are already down. And the fishermen have to stay on the crabs because they can't catch the rockfish. If the fishermen could have jumped off these crabs onto the rockfish the last two years and got the rockfish down a little bit, that would have saved the crabs that the crabbers have been catching, and some of what the rock have been eating.

Even some of those involved with the recreational fishery agree with this, as the following quote from a local charter boat captain shows:

> We're now seeing rockfish in places nobody's ever seen them before,
> and I think that supports the theory that there's getting to be so
> many of them that they're leaving their normal environment look-
> ing for food. We had a big fish kill last July, I guess. I know the fish
> habitat, the water that they showed up dead in, but we had a heat
> spell. In my opinion, there were too many fish in water that was
> stagnant on a dead tide, extreme heat. But you probably wouldn't
> have such a big kill if they weren't so over-populated.

Unspecialized strategies and management efforts focusing on individual species have important implications for local knowledge and the environment. Moving among different fisheries allows fishers to develop complex knowledge bases about the behaviors of fish, shellfish, and other marine life while distributing fishing pressures over a number of species instead of only one. They are often among the first to recognize problems with water quality and other problems, natural and human, with the estuary. The following quote from a longtime crabber indicates some of the ecological relations they consider in estimating estuarine health:

> The eagle and duck populations haven't been as good around here.
> I think that's due to all the bad water we have on the river because
> I think it's carried all the little clams and stuff from the bottom
> out in deeper water that they feed on, and I don't think that helps
> them. Ducks—I just don't think the feed's here for them. They'll
> come for a little while, then they'll leave and go somewhere else. I
> think water quality is bad, I really do. Especially at the heads of
> creeks and places like that, where all the runoff comes in. That's
> really bad, where all your fish go to spawn. I think all that's due
> to runoff. Back when I was a boy, everything had a chance to filter
> out in sloughs and stuff. Now everything's just carried straight out
> in the rivers and they got all the canals and everything.

Yet another fisher, a shrimper from the southern part of the state, near the state's fastest-growing coastal region, places changes in fishing stocks in the context of a history of changes to the bottom that accompanied chang-ing dredging practices:

> Just like they're getting ready to do in Shell Island with this hotel
> resort about to fall in. See, they're going to dredge from the intra-
> coastal waterway down to that inlet right on out and get the sand
> to go there. That used to be one of the hottest spots, nice spot for
> spotted shrimp was right off Shell Island where that hotel is. And
> all that erosion, that sand, has gone out to that muddy bottom,
> and you can't catch enough shrimp there to eat hardly at times. And
> 25 years ago, we used to shrimp out there every night and catch
> them spotted shrimp at night. But that's the way—they're trying
> to save the land. And time will tell, history says in 50 years from
> now they're not going to save it; it's going away from here. And
> they keep building it up and all they're doing is just making it last
> a year or two longer. But the scientist says in 50 or 60 years, may-
> be 100 years from now, Kure Beach down here will be under water.
> And I believe it because you can tell [from] the erosion.

Levels of knowledge like this also make watermen the most skeptical of not only management decisions but also supposedly scientific reactions to water quality problems. Again, their tendency is to place natural and social processes in their larger contexts (even though geographically restricted), something that scientists and managers, focusing on a single species or set of species, often have difficulty accomplishing. How watermen responded to the *Pfiesteria* hysteria of the middle and late 1990s provides an interest-ing illustration of their skepticism regarding scientific research involving an issue close to their hearts: water quality.

Postscript: *Pfiesteria* and Water Quality

Pfiesteria is a marine dinoflagellate, or a single-celled organism believed to release a neurotoxin that kills fish and injures humans, thus falling into that class of water quality problems termed, collectively, Harmful Algae Blooms (HABs). Probably the best known HABs are red tides, although *Pfiesteria* certainly achieved a competitive level of fame during the mid-1990s in the Mid-Atlantic region, when disputes over scientific authority raged across the state of North Carolina, entered North Carolina and Maryland environmentalism and party politics, and contradicted the underlying logic of watermen's ecological knowledge.

The Pfiesteria case is one of focusing on a tiny part of the marine environment to the exclusion of considering that part's relation to the whole or how the whole might influence the part's attributes. It has been, and continues to be, a case of experimental science creating conditions in labs that have limited applicability to the natural environment. The case thus stands in opposition to watermen on two grounds: its removal from the natural landscape and processes that watermen use to understand ecosystems, and its attempt to hold constant attributes of the environment that are continually changing.

Briefly, the Pfiesteria case began in the early to mid-1990s, when a new species of dinoflagellate was discovered in conjunction with several large fish kills (more than 100,000 fish) in the APES, primarily the Neuse River. Scientists working with the dinoflagellate, which they named Pfiesteria, became ill, suffering from a variety of harmful effects from exposure to high laboratory concentrations of Pfiesteria. One lab assistant, after working with fish from fish kills for several weeks, developed symptoms ranging from mild irritability and disorientation to bursts of rage and memory loss. During this same time period other lab workers, and even individuals in offices nearby, began experiencing symptoms of exposure such as headaches and respiratory problems. The list of symptoms associated with Pfiesteria is quite long, ranging from those mentioned above to skin disorders, malaise, and fatigue (Griffith 1999).

While all this was going on, a research team conducted an epidemiological study, interviewing watermen across the Pfiesteria-affected waters and comparing them to two control populations: one of watermen in unaffected waters and another of people without water-based occupations living in watermen communities (Griffith et al. 1998). The study found that, in general, watermen were relatively healthy, but its findings were largely ignored

because they were released at the height of public and political attention to
Pfiesteria as a human health hazard. Watermen remained skeptical, however, and since that time there has been mounting evidence, in fact, that
the afflictions they attributed to *Pfiesteria* were either due to other causes
or exaggerated; an East Carolina University dermatologist has found alternative explanations for the skin disorders attributed to *Pfiesteria*, and a set
of investigations collected together by the Centers for Disease Control in
2000 and published in 2001 present no evidence of a serious health threat.
Long before these findings, however, fishers were highly skeptical of all the
attention on this single-celled organism:

> We have a picture in the house right now, there's a picture of shad
> in a group. There's got to be 500 million in there. I mean, the pic-
> ture taken from the boat, the 100-foot boat looks like a dot com-
> pared to this pile of fish. And they were all dying up there, and it's
> not that far from the beach. And when that happens, after they
> put us out of business and that happens, they're not going to have
> anybody to come clean up their mess for them. They're going to
> be stuck with it and then they're going to have a problem with
> their tourists. Another thing, you see on the television all the time
> about a fish kill up in the Neuse River; you see it all the time. A lot
> of that's been a guy that's crabbing and at the end of the day, he's
> dumping his bait overboard. Dumping two or three boxes of bait
> so you don't have to deal with it. The fish that washes up now
> becomes a fish kill. That happens a lot. So they don't really know
> what's going on.

The skepticism that fishers expressed during the hysteria over *Pfiesteria* is
symptomatic of the way that fishers piece together natural and social phenomena in the context of multiple livelihoods. Their knowledge is complex, acknowledging that water quality and other problems facing the estuary stem from a variety of social and natural factors and take place within
dynamic contexts. They could not accept the laboratory experiments' conclusions about *Pfiesteria* because they were on the water daily and were not

experiencing the myriad symptoms that the algae supposedly induced. Nor could they accept those findings that held constant such factors as wind, runoff, lunar phases, and even the extent to which different groups of fishers and others interact with the marine environment. Mid-Atlantic watermen and their families realize that water quality is, from time to time, threatened by HABs, but just as they refuse to accept total blame for declining fish stocks, they could not accept that a single species of dinoflagellate was responsible for the many human ills and environmental disasters that occur around them.

Combining multiple livelihoods is very much a part of the logic underlying their appreciation of the natural and social environments. Though many fishers target key species using one principal gear, when fishers specialize in one species and one gear, they become overly dependent on, and overly vulnerable to, the set of regulations and natural environmental factors that affect species availability and disposition. Engaging in multiple livelihoods is an extension of engaging in multiple fisheries with multiple gears, reducing their exposure to what has become, more and more, unpredictable marine and social environments.

Note

Thanks to the Wenner-Gren Foundation for Anthropological Research for funds to investigate the naval stores industry.

All interviews in this paper, unless otherwise indicated, are from the 2000–2001 research project "Local Knowledge and Scientific Resource Management in Changing Coastal Communities," funded by the UNC Sea Grant College Program.

8. Integrating Fishers' Knowledge into Fisheries Science and Management

Possibilities, Prospects, and Problems

James R. McGoodwin

Beginning in the late 1970s, and gathering momentum through the 1980s, social scientists and others interested in the fisheries published a growing array of papers that urged bringing localized fishers' knowledge into modern fisheries management. Doing this, it was generally assumed, might help to break the deadlock that had arisen in many fisheries, where fishers, scientists, and managers were unable to work together constructively, while the fisheries with which they were concerned were either declining or had already collapsed. One study recommending the integration of fishers' knowledge stated, "Western scientific understanding is more subject to challenge than in the past, and many now accord it a status as only one among several equivalent ways to generate understanding and knowledge. ... This more egalitarian conception of knowledge frameworks is visible in a wide array of arenas" (McGoodwin, Neis, and Felt 2000:249).

Locally developed fishers' knowledge held out several promising features: for one, its inherent emphasis on flexibility. Rigidly conceived, fine-tuned, and bureaucratic management regimes, it was thought, were not as able to adapt to changing conditions as localized peoples were, while the continuation of current approaches to management practically guaranteed ineffectual management, especially in fisheries that were already highly pressured.

Underlying the optimism about incorporating fishers' knowledge into modern fisheries science and management were assumptions that this would capitalize on naturally arising processes, rather than complicating, confounding, or opposing them. Considerable economies of managerial effort might thus be realized, as well as a reduction of conflict between fishers, scientists, and fisheries managers. Heretofore, most fisheries' scientists and managers had regarded as particularly problematic the tendency of fishers to ignore or circumvent fisheries regulations. Thus, early students of fishers' knowledge and management systems urged scientists to undergo fundamental shifts in thinking, urging, for example, a more sympathetic understanding that even considered finding fault with management regimes that compelled fishers to become lawbreakers (e.g., McGoodwin 1990:183–184).

Another presumed benefit of integrating fishers' knowledge into contemporary fisheries science and management was that it might help prevent the "tragedy of the commons" situation from developing. Experienced social scientists who had studied fisheries problems, including Berkes (1989b), Berkes, Feeny, McCay, and Acheson (1989), Cordell (1989), McCay and Acheson (1987:34), and Vayda (1988), all asserted that when the approach to managing a commons ignored or superseded local management approaches, instead emphasizing either government intervention or privatization, this usually weakened or destroyed local institutions that were effective in preventing the "tragedy" and instead encouraged it. Indeed, while Garrett Hardin's paradigm for the "tragedy" had assumed that the users of common property resources could do little to change the system of exploitation themselves, several studies of local fishing peoples published between the 1960s and 1980s suggested the contrary (e.g., Berkes 1977, 1987, 1989a; Cordell 1989; Klee 1980; Kottak 1966; Leibhardt 1986; Morauta et al. 1982; Poggie 1978; and Ruddle and Johannes 1985).

The optimistic fervor about integrating fishers' knowledge with contemporary fisheries science and management was fueled by the foregoing scholars' work, as well as the work of many others. It proclaimed their discovery of rich systems of localized knowledge deriving from fishers' experience as they exploited marine resources in certain regions. Not only that, much of this localized knowledge explicitly underscored fishers' knowledge about their fisheries' ecological systems, as well as their ideas about the best ways for utilizing and managing them.

Practically all of these scholars also brought to this new era of studies a greater-than-ever stress on humanitarian concerns, coupled with a growing realization that, ultimately, the fisheries are human phenomena, and strictly speaking there cannot be a fishery without human fishing effort. Therefore, they stressed, to predicate the management of a fishery mainly on the basis of biological, ecological, and state-level economic concerns, while essentially ignoring or discounting fishers' knowledge, one risked instituting a management policy that might be doomed to fail, and that at the same time would work serious hardships on fishing peoples.

Not incorporating fishers' knowledge into management regimes, several of these scholars asserted, was also tantamount to denying recognition of important components of fishers' cultural heritage and self-identity. Ignoring these might not only severely disrupt customary patterns of work and social organization, but it might also prompt resistance or non-cooperation with the management regime, while locally prompting heightened levels of competition and effort, socioeconomic atomism, anxiety, disaffection, and other social and economic ills. Clearly, if there were to be more effective fisheries-management regimes in the future, these would have to incorporate fishers' knowledge to a greater degree than had been seen heretofore.

Yet in the wake of these discoveries of the existence and richness of fishers' knowledge, a huge question remained unanswered: how should this localized knowledge, and the people having it, be incorporated into contemporary fisheries science and management? As Berkes (1987:90) noted, fishers' knowledge does "not mesh comfortably with government regulations," partly because, unlike scientific knowledge, fishers' knowledge is predicated mainly on the utilitarian aim of maximizing catches, and less often with regard for bio-ecological understanding per se. Consequently, reconciling fishers' knowledge with scientifically predicated fisheries management would have to depend on the ability of the bio-economic model of fisheries management to accommodate differing kinds of human-ecological relations, while also incorporating social concerns.

A formidable barrier to incorporating what had been learned about fishers' knowledge was the variety of methods that had been utilized to elicit and describe this knowledge. The studies did not lend themselves readily to making comparisons. Their diverse concerns, approaches, methodologies, and findings made comparing among them not merely analogous to comparing apples and oranges, but more like attempting to compare beef stew with fruit salad! Moreover, few of these studies had the barest quantitative salience or potential for replication, and practically none offered even the crudest estimates of how the fishers' knowledge being described was instrumental in ensuring stock sustainability. Imagine, then, the difficulty of drawing generalizations from these disparate studies that might be incorporated into contemporary fisheries science. Hence, these early and rather disparate studies were mostly "existence demonstrations," which showed that indeed fishers' knowledge existed in certain communities. But otherwise they offered few clues regarding how this knowledge might be integrated into contemporary science and management (McGoodwin 1990:110).

Prospects and Problems Stemming from
Attributes of Fishing Peoples and Societies

Practically all fishing people have strong opinions—which indeed are an integral part of their "fishing knowledge"—about the ecology of the marine resources they exploit and what they feel are the best ways to exploit and manage them. Moreover, generally speaking, fishers' knowledge of this type will be easier to incorporate into contemporary fisheries science and management when it has come about over long periods of time, and when it has arisen among people who have been relatively stable over several generations. Important attributes of such stability are longstanding residence in the same region, stable population size, or at least a population that has not been growing so rapidly that it has upset long-standing traditions, and stability regarding the basic methods and technologies that are utilized to exploit the fisheries, as well as stability concerning the species that are customarily targeted.

This is not to imply that for fishers' knowledge to be capable of incorporation into contemporary fisheries science and management the fishing societies must have had fixed and unchanging cultures over many generations. Rather, it is only to suggest that formal incorporation will usually be easier to accomplish when community-based traditions surrounding utilization of the fisheries have existed for a long time, and when the fishing communities have not experienced any radically transforming social and economic change. (This seems the case in the rural-coastal small-scale fishing communities in the Dominican Republic as described by Stoffle et al. 1994; in Kerala and along the Coromandel Coast in India as described by Kurien 2001 and Bavinck 2001, respectively; in Louisiana as described by Dyer and Leard 1994; and in Nigeria as described by Ben-Yami 2001. Problematically, on the other hand, this seems not the case among the rural-coastal fishing communities in Mexico as described by McGoodwin 1994; nor those in Newfoundland as described by Palmer 1994.)

Additionally, in general, fishers' knowledge that has come about as a result of the fishing people having adequate time to experiment with and shape their particular adaptations to local marine environments will not only be generally easier to incorporate into fisheries science and management; it will also usually have a greater impact in these contexts than will knowledge that has arisen only recently. Longer-standing knowledge usually enjoys a greater degree of consensus among community members, especially when they feel this knowledge and their customary fisheries-use practices stemming from it have sustained them for several generations and up to present times.

To the contrary, the localized knowledge of comparatively new arrivals in a fishery—such as new immigrants, members of a burgeoning populace who have recently turned to fishing, or any others who have taken up exploitation of a fishery only recently—will not usually be as rich and detailed as that of longer-resident fishers. Nor can more recent arrivals' knowledge be expected to be as well informed about the hypothetical sustainable yield of the fishery that is being exploited. Thus, while the more recent arrivals will undoubtedly assert strong opinions about how the fisheries they utilize should be exploited and managed, their knowledge will be generally less dependable where it asserts the fishery's sustainable yield. Otherwise, new arrivals' strong opinions must still be taken into consideration when developing a fishery's management policy.

Moreover, regarding fishing societies that have been stable for many generations, the purported sustainability of their practices over a long term must still be weighed in light of another question: was it their knowledge and associated practices that were decisive in sustaining their resources over a long period of time, or was it merely their inability—given their numbers, the demands they placed on the resources, and the technologies they utilized for exploiting the resources—that prevented them from exceeding their resources' sustainable yields or long-term carrying capacities? In other words, if they have never experienced a dramatic decline or collapse of the resources they exploit—and which they acknowledge was clearly brought about by their collective efforts—their "knowledge" concerning the hypothetical sustainable yield of the fishery they exploit may not be particularly well informed. In that case, their "knowledge," strictly speaking, is not based on empirically derived experience concerning what the limits or carrying capacity of their fishery actually is. Yet even then, if they have fished a particular marine ecosystem for some time, they will still likely have at least a rough idea of what its limits are—even if they have never experienced an object lesson such as a near or total collapse.

Thus, as Pinkerton (1994:319) notes in a related vein, fishers' knowledge is more amenable for incorporation into contemporary fisheries science and management when the historical record shows that the group having this knowledge responded constructively to resource depletions in the past. Evidence of constructive responses might include, for example, willingness to participate in self-enforcement and self-monitoring, as well as willingness to work cooperatively with regulatory authorities (e.g., as in the rural fishing communities in the Dominican Republic described by Stoffle et al. 1994; but problematically lacking in the lobster-fishing communities in Maine described by Palmer 1994).

Incorporating fishers' knowledge into contemporary fisheries science and management will likely also be more effective where local fishing practices and constraints are consciously stressed by local adherents as having explicit conservationist aims. Hence, whereas early studies of localized self-management concluded that most such regimes emphasized regulating or limiting access to fishing space, rather than levels of fishing effort (e.g., McCay 1978), a rich and growing ethnographic record shows that many localized fishers have indeed practiced self-management with regard for sound biological-conservationist principles (e.g., Acheson 1972, 1982, and 1988, describing Maine lobstermen who verbally abuse fellow community members for overzealous attempts to increase production by fishing in bad weather, setting out too many traps, or adopting more effective gear such as metal lobster pots; Anderson, 1994, describing traditional peoples of the Northwest Coast of North America and also Hong Kong, who self-limit fishing effort for conservationist reasons; Berkes 1977, describing self-imposed gear restrictions permitting fish to escape among the Cree Indians of northern Canada, while exercising high degrees of self-restraint and not fishing in sanctuaries containing good supplies of their main targeted stocks; Berleant-Schiller 1982, noting that lobster divers of Barbuda release gravid females and also cease fishing when declining yields indicate their prey is being overharvested; Johannes 1978 and Klee 1980, describing a rich variety of conservationist practices among traditional peoples in Oceania; W. A. Johnson 1980, describing the careful bio-ecological management of aquaculture ponds among traditional peasants of ancient Asia and medieval Europe; McCay 1981:4, reporting instances of voluntary restraint among clam fishers in New Jersey; and Moore and Moore 1903, describing gear restrictions imposed in 13th-century Britain to ensure that adequate numbers of migratory salmon reach their spawning grounds).

Incorporating fishers' knowledge into contemporary fisheries science and management is also more likely to be successful, as Pinkerton (1994:333) states, "either where there are individual economic incentives to cooperate because the costs of going it alone are higher, or where management is invested in knowledgeable local authorities with the power to make the rules and also implement them." Such conditions that can be seen as promising for integrating fishers' knowledge with modern fisheries science and management have been described among fishers in the Dominican Republic, whose customs and the supportive ideologies underlying them bring about compliance with self-imposed rules (Stoffle et al. 1994), as well as among oyster fishers along the coasts of Louisiana and Florida, whose traditionally self-imposed management has successfully constrained effort to sustainable levels, while at the same time limiting access by newcomers (Dyer and Leard 1994).

Obviously, fishers' knowledge that has been self-generated, without significant prompting by external forces, will also be much more amenable for incorporation into contemporary fisheries science and management than will knowledge that has been generated mostly as a reaction or resistance to externally imposed management authority. Truly, therefore, an important advantage to incorporating fishers' knowledge into modern management regimes is that, from the fishers' point of view, it may confer more legitimacy and authority on these regimes and thus higher degrees of compliance.

Most often, the process of incorporating fishers' knowledge will require fishers, scientists, and managers to make important concessions to one another that they can agree will be mutually beneficial. Equally important will be for governmental authorities to assure fishers that they will not later be overwhelmed by others having interests in the fisheries, who may begin to compete with them once new management schemes and policies have improved conditions in the fisheries. After that, there is a better likelihood that the management regime will continue to be successful if localized fishers continue to have ongoing involvement, as well as decisive voting power, in future adjustments to the management regime and policy.

Prospects and Problems Regarding Small- versus Large-Scale Fishers

Small-scale fishers, especially those having traditions of fishing in a particular locale that can be traced back for several generations, will invariably profess to have specialized and intimate knowledge of the marine ecosystems they exploit. Problematically, however, compared with the knowledge of larger-scale fishers, their knowledge will usually be more site specific and self-referring and therefore more difficult to incorporate into contemporary fisheries science and management. The knowledge of larger-scale fishers, by comparison, more often converges with that of contemporary fisheries science and management and indeed has often come about through collaborative efforts between large-scale fishers, fisheries scientists, and managers—such as through stock assessment and monitoring operations. The knowledge of small-scale fishers, on the other hand, is less often informed by such experiences, and instead is mainly informed by experiences stemming from harvesting activities.

Yet, being relatively less mobile and more focused upon one or a few marine ecosystems than are larger-scale fishers, small-scale fishers are motivated to a greater degree to develop knowledge that is concerned with the limits of the systems they exploit. Larger-scale, more mobile fishers are less motivated to develop such knowledge, since they can often merely move on to look for other stocks elsewhere if the limit of the ecosystem they are exploiting is exceeded. Thus, smaller-scale, more localized fishers are generally more concerned with whole or entire marine ecosystems, as well as with a more diverse variety of fish species and fishing gear, than are most larger-scale, industrialized fishers, who often target just one or a few species.

As a result, small- versus large-scale fishers will encourage different emphases in fisheries management policies. And because the components of marine ecological systems are interrelated, fisheries policies that are primarily responsive to the more generalized needs of small-scale fishers will usually go farther toward maintaining the overall health of a marine ecosystem than will those formulated primarily in response to the more narrowly defined needs of large-scale fishers. However, as a fisheries-management report of the Food and Agriculture Organization of the United Nations (FAO) (1983:11) reminds us, "Locals have had more incentive to self-regulate a particular fishery than have nomadic roving fleets. However . . . even locals can over-exploit a stock if there is not adequate social control of the number of local participants."

Prospects and Problems Stemming from Relationships among Fishers, Scientists, and Managers

Incorporating fishers' knowledge into contemporary fisheries science and management will likely be more effective if this knowledge can be corroborated by contemporary scientists and academics. On the other hand, it will likely confound fisheries science and management if local fishers merely appropriate scientific studies to help them legitimize activities that are not approved of in the larger society of which they are a part, or if they merely use these to justify activities that are counterproductive to conservationist aims. Fisheries scientists and managers must also come to terms with the fact that fishers' knowledge may include traditions of political activism, which fishers may assert in order to protect what they feel are their rights to certain marine resources. Thus, fisheries managers who ignore this, and who instead feel their task is merely to manage resources with regard for biological conservation and economic maximization for the region or the state, may find themselves expending inordinate amounts of time dealing with fishers' political activism, not to mention defiant and illegal fishing practices.

Integrating fishers' knowledge into contemporary fisheries science and management will be difficult indeed if the established scientists and managers are not sympathetic with fishers' interests or are already co-opted by other interests in the larger society, or if they regard the integration of fishers' knowledge into contemporary science and management as a threat to their continued employment, authority, or accustomed prerogatives. In those cases their incorporation of fishers' knowledge may not improve overall science and management, especially if it is motivated mainly by desires to avoid conflicts with fishers, rather than by a sincere regard for their knowledge. Even more problematic will be situations where scientists and managers are mainly responsive to whichever groups they feel assert the greatest political power, rather than to those having the most knowledge or the greatest personal stake in the fisheries.

Because of their long association with a particular fishery, or worse, because historically they have never had to work cooperatively with fishers, scientists and managers may assert proprietary interests in fishery resources, feeling such resources are "theirs," while regarding fishers as threats to these. In such cases they are not likely to be forthright about sharing what they know about the fishery, yet at the same time may demand that fishers fully disclose the extent of their knowledge and actual fishing practices (see Ward and Weeks 1994, for example, for an illustration of how most of the foregoing problems among fishers, scientists, and managers concerned with oyster fisheries in Texas greatly impeded the incorporation of fishers and their knowledge into contemporary science and management).

Fishers and the State

Particularly in developing countries, which may otherwise lack resources for managing and developing their fisheries, fishers' knowledge can play an important role in developing locally relevant fisheries science, management, and policy. In these situations the most important role of governmental authority usually will be to protect fishers from incursions by new competitors coming from both within and outside the state.

On the other hand, incorporating fishers' knowledge in developing as well as developed countries may be impeded by the manner in which the state defines participants and permits their participation in fisheries policy formulation. Permitting elites from the national society, or other nonlocal interests to benefit from the fisheries, for example, while not holding them responsible for deleterious changes resulting from their participation, can be disastrous for local fishers. Thus, local fishers will have a better chance of representation in state-supervised policy formulation where both their membership and geographical boundaries are clearly defined, and where they are acknowledged by the state as important—if not the primary—stakeholders in the fisheries (e.g., as in the case of localized lake-fishing communities in Mexico described by Pomeroy 1994, where the state generally agrees they are important stakeholders, as well as with their assertions regarding relevant geographical boundaries). At the minimum, the main role of governmental authorities should be to protect localized fishers from incursions by other fishers external to their communities in order to prevent the development of heightened competition that might lead local fishers to abandon their customary approaches and instead begin to "fish as if there were no tomorrow." To do this, governmental authorities should focus their efforts on limiting access so that localized traditional users can pursue their customary fishing techniques and work out their own systems of self-regulation. Where governments are willing to do this, incorporating local fishers' knowledge into contemporary fisheries science and management offers a promising prospect indeed.

Otherwise, where the state is reluctant or unwilling to defend local fishers against competing interests, they will likely have a difficult time getting their knowledge, including their ideas concerning how the fisheries should be utilized and managed, to be acknowledged as instrumental in scientific discourses about the fisheries (e.g., as is problematic for the oyster fishers in Mississippi and Alabama described by Dyer and Leard 1994, commercial salmon fishers in Newfoundland described by Felt 1994, localized Norwegian fjord fishers described by Jentoft and Mikalsen 1994, lake fishers in Mexico described by Pomeroy 1994, and rural fishers in the Dominican Republic described by Stoffle et al. 1994).

Even when the state expresses good intentions in behalf of localized fishers, powerful groups such as fishers' unions, cooperative associations, large-scale seafood producers, processors, marketers, and other powerful interests in the national society may have greater abilities to influence fisheries policy, drowning out fishers' specialized knowledge and swaying governmental decisions against them. Nationally organized unions, for instance, are usually driven by majority pressures within them and may not fairly represent the interests of smaller groups of localized fishers when their interests are opposed to their majority's desires.

Similarly, powerful groups may decisively define not only the management issues in a fishery but also the knowledge (i.e., data) necessary to resolve them, with local fish harvesters relegated to the sidelines (e.g., Felt 1994). Indeed, as Jentoft and Mikalsen (1994) concluded in their study of this problem in certain Norwegian fisheries, it would be simplistic to conclude that fishers' knowledge was merely drowned out by more powerful interests. Rather, the heart of the problem was the state's construction of the advisory and policymaking apparatuses, which situated local fishers some distance from center stage. Thus, local fishers' knowledge and corresponding aims regarding exploitation of their fisheries will have a better chance of incorporation into contemporary fisheries science and management where, as Pinkerton (1994:333) notes, "the state has not constructed representation only from nationally based organizations, but has allowed locally based representation that is not bound by national organizational ideology to arise" (a promising example of this is discussed in Felt 1994 regarding salmon fishers in Newfoundland).

Therefore, a fundamental, indeed crucial, precondition to integrating localized fishers' knowledge into contemporary fisheries science and management is not only an earnest commitment on the part of fisheries scientists and managers to better understand and incorporate that knowledge, but also a similar commitment on the part of the state. Dyer and Leard (1994), for example, describing oyster fishers who receive such state support in Louisiana, and Stoffle et al. (1994), describing rural fishers in the Dominican Republic who are similarly supported, both outline conditions that argue well for the successful incorporation of fishers' knowledge into the fisheries policies that are being developed by those states. Pomeroy (1994), on the other hand, has reason to be skeptical about the chances that local lake fishers' knowledge will decisively influence fisheries management around this large lake in Mexico, where state agencies may instead be eager to back new competitors.

Incorporating fishers' knowledge into contemporary fisheries science and management will also have a better chance of success where state regulations are consistent with local understandings of resource problems or actual local practices (e.g., in the lobster fisheries of Newfoundland as described by Palmer 1994, but not in the oyster fisheries of Texas, as described by Ward and Weeks 1994). Moreover, as already mentioned concerning relationships between fishers, scientists, and managers, the state will be more motivated to incorporate fishers' knowledge into management schemes when it perceives that doing so will help it to avoid management conflicts, as well as decrease potential costs associated with the management effort (e.g., as in oyster fisheries in Florida and Louisiana described by Dyer and Leard 1994, as well as in behalf of rural fishers in the Dominican Republic, as described by Stoffle et al. 1994). Indeed, many localized groups of fishers have won state support simply by threatening conflict, disruption, and even violence if the state does not bend to their desires.

Experimenting with Cooperative Co-management

Cooperative co-management, which empowers fishers to share in decision making with fisheries scientists and managers, is not to be confused with consultative management, in which fishers are merely consulted. In theory, when cooperative co-management is instituted in a fishery, its producers will perceive their mutual stake in sustaining resources at healthy and acceptable levels and will be more motivated to police fishing effort among themselves. Theoretically, this should also reduce their conflicts with fisheries managers, as well as among themselves, while effecting savings in costs associated with the managerial effort (see Jentoft 1989). As Courtland Smith (1988:134) stresses, "For all users to feel the impact of their own actions on the whole, they must have some stake in the management of the resource. To develop incentives for resource conservation, harvesters must collectively experience feedback as to how their individual actions affect the resource." Smith adds that those who feel fishers cannot manage their own fisheries base their skepticism "on the current system of fishery management which promotes rather than reduces conflict," and which therefore also inadvertently elevates the costs of management (136).

Cooperative co-management, a rather novel suggestion just two decades ago, and which to many merely seemed a commonsensical solution for managing fisheries where more orthodox approaches had failed, has seen many subsequent successes (e.g., in southwestern Japan as described by Akimichi 2001; in Iceland as described by Durrengerber and Pálsson 1987; in Norway as described by Jentoft 1985; in Iceland and Norway as described by Jentoft and Kristoffersen 1989; in inshore mid-Atlantic United States as described by McCay 1980; in Alaska as described by Langdon 1984; in British Columbia, Canada, as described by Hilborn and Luedke 1987; and in Shetland Island fisheries as described by Goodlad 1986).

However, cooperative co-management has also revealed situations in which its institution seems ill advised. High degrees of diversity or heterogeneity among users, for example, will greatly increase the difficulty and complexity of developing it. In such situations the fishery may be exploited by people having different ethnicities, religious orientations, or other important socioeconomic or sociocultural orientations. High degrees of diversity may also be present where fishers exploiting a particular fishery utilize different harvesting methods or gear, or where they differ significantly in terms of the scale of their capitalization or levels of effort. Moreover, even where fishers are otherwise very homogeneous with respect to the foregoing attributes, cooperative co-management will be difficult to institute where there has been long-standing, "almost ritualistic hostility" between government officials and users, where there has been long-term factionalism among users themselves, or where fishers have been geographically dispersed and have little tradition of face-to-face relationships and working together (see McCay 1988:327–334).

Nevertheless, these may be the very situations that are most in need of cooperative co-management and that may ultimately benefit the most from it—if it can be developed carefully and appropriately. Indeed, cooperative co-management may hold great potential for mitigating long-standing conflicts in fisheries by acknowledging, legitimizing, and formalizing the participation of various stakeholders who had been heretofore excluded from the fishery, or who had been heretofore marginalized by various management policies.

Summary
The key points in the foregoing discussion are these:

1. Fishers' knowledge will have better prospects for incorporation into contemporary fisheries science and management when it has developed over relatively long and stable time periods.
2. Fishers' knowledge will have better prospects for incorporation into contemporary fisheries science and management when fishers have experienced resource depletions in the past and have acknowledged a role in bringing them about, as well as when fishers already have experience working with management authorities to address fishery problems.

3. Fishers' knowledge that has explicit conservationist aims will have the best prospects for incorporation into contemporary fisheries science and management.

4. Fishers' knowledge that has been self-generated, without significant prompting by external forces or events, will usually have good prospects for incorporation into contemporary fisheries science and management.

5. The knowledge of small-scale as compared with larger-scale fishers is more likely to stress concerns for the sustainability of whole marine ecosystems.

6. Fishers' knowledge that is corroborated by contemporary fisheries science, while being consistent with prevailing public policy, has better prospects for incorporation into contemporary fisheries science and management than does knowledge that cannot be corroborated by contemporary fisheries science.

7. Essential preconditions for the incorporation of fishers' knowledge into contemporary fisheries science and management include scientists and managers being sympathetic with fishers' interests and knowledge, while higher governmental authorities are similarly committed not only to protecting fishers' interests but also to developing fisheries policies that are consistent with their knowledge.

Conclusion and Recommendations

First, scientists and managers should carefully study the rich and growing ethnographic record concerning fishers' knowledge, focusing especially on people whose knowledge seems rooted in biological and conservationist concerns. Next, they should conduct collaborative studies with such peoples with the aim of formalizing their knowledge in ways that will be meaningful and useful for contemporary fisheries science and management, as well as for the fishers themselves.

Second, because the most pressing need in the fisheries today is to reconceptualize management policies in a way that makes human concerns paramount, it is essential that the processes of fisheries science and management incorporate experienced fishers. What is most needed now is a shift away from autocratic and paternalistic modes of management to modes that rely on the collaborative efforts of fishers, scientists, and managers. Regulatory agencies should bring more expert fishers on staff, while granting them authority to participate in scientific studies of particular fisheries and influence management decisions and policy formulation.

Third, radical changes must be undertaken in fisheries science and education. For example, where appropriate, fishers should be required to complete course work in fisheries science and management in order to obtain certification or entitlement to harvest certain fisheries resources. At the same time, fisheries scientists and managers should also be required to complete course work concerning fishers and fishing societies in order to obtain their professional credentials. In this regard it might be beneficial to require internships during the education and professional certification of all three groups—fishers, scientists, and managers—such that each would spend some time in the other's working and living environments. In such a situation, cooperative co-management might spontaneously develop as a natural extension of those processes.

In other words, fisheries science and management must be reconceptualized as a collaborative process involving fishers, scientists, and managers. No longer should fishers be considered apart from the concerns of fisheries science and management. It must be recognized, once and for all, that the fisheries are a human phenomenon—the articulation of marine ecosystems with human social, ecological, political, and economic systems. Bringing about the foregoing changes will require considerable effort, entailing nothing less than radically changing the face of contemporary fisheries science, education, and management.

Fourth and finally, if the foregoing suggestions are carried out, this will likely help to bring about a convergence of knowledge and methodologies among fishers, scientists, and managers.

There can be no quick fix for developing more uniform and useful methodologies for incorporating fishers' knowledge into contemporary fisheries science and management. Indeed, compatible methodologies will be developed only when fishers, scientists, and managers routinely work together on fisheries problems.

Note

The author wishes to acknowledge Christopher L. Dyer, co-editor of Folk Management in the World's Fisheries: Lessons for Modern Fisheries Management (1994), and Evelyn W. Pinkerton, author of that book's final chapter, whose contributions he has drawn on extensively for preparation of this chapter. He also thanks Professors Lawrence Felt and Barbara Neis, Department of Sociology, Memorial University of Newfoundland, for their earlier encouragement of this study.

III

Learning from Local Ecological Knowledge

9. Honoring Aboriginal Science Knowledge and Wisdom in an Environmental Education Graduate Program

Gloria Snively

Although First Nation residents have long utilized time-tested approaches to sustaining both human communities and environments, academic interest among scientists and science educators in living Indigenous approaches is recent, and science instruction and research have been linked with marginalizing and even alienating Native students and entire communities (Devine 1991; Tehenneppe 1993). Native culture and history are often presented in both university education courses and school curricula as narrow, stereotypical portrayals based on inaccurate accounts of the nature of science, history, and Indigenous culture (Devine 1991; Cajete 1999).

Increasingly, in a postcolonial world beset with ecological and social crises, scientists and science educators are showing interest in traditional cultural approaches that have long been used to achieve and maintain sustainable relations between human communities and environments. Over the past 30 years biologists, ecologists, geologists, and other working scientists have been contributing to the burgeoning branch of scientific research known as traditional ecological knowledge and wisdom (TEKW) (Berkes 1999; Inglis 1993; William and Baines 1993), which only recently has been introduced to educators (Corsiglia and Snively 1997; Snively and Corsiglia 2001).

There is great need for new and creative approaches for teaching Native and non-Native students both the processes and content of science. Because culture shapes the inception and the reception of science, any new approach must include culturally relevant models of instruction and appropriate accompanying materials. According to Micmac scholar Marie Battiste, in most jurisdictions in Canada and the United States, science curricula are developed away from Aboriginal communities, without Aboriginal input, and written in English. In effect, the curriculum often serves as another colonial instrument to deprive Aboriginal communities of their knowledge, languages, and culture (Battiste 1998, 2000).

This chapter challenges the Eurocentric assumptions that have pushed Aboriginal science knowledge to the margins and illustrates attempts at the university level to embrace an approach to school science that gives Aboriginal students access to Western science and technology without diminishing their Aboriginal identities; additionally it provides non-Native students with exposure to cultural and scientific values that encourage respect for the survival of both community and environment. I describe an off-campus Graduate Program in Environmental Education at the University of Victoria that attempts to introduce practicing teachers into First Nations communities in such a way that they would understand a scholarly Aboriginal perspective on nature and receive instruction on Indigenous knowledge, history, and culture from the elders, which is the initial phase of being mentored by elders.

One of the encouraging notes in these times is that in spite of all manner of historic and contemporary violence and aggression, both the Indigenous knowledge stories and the peoples still exist in many parts of Canada and throughout the world. It is given to those of us who work at university settings to create programs and spaces for the stories of Aboriginal practitioners to be told (Hall 2000). Universities can play a powerful role in the legitimation of TEKW in our societies, in developing policy regarding science education at the government ministry level, and in promoting courses, programs, and curriculum materials that reflect a postcolonial approach to science education.

I am an educator of environmental, marine, and science education at the University of Victoria, British Columbia. I am a non-Native female professor teaching in a university that attracts few students outside mainstream white society. I had to ask myself, what does a professor of science education like myself have to contribute to First Nations education and the understanding of First Nations culture? Acknowledging that I cannot speak from a First Nations perspective and honoring the teachings that I have been given by elders and First Nations students over the years, I see myself as being useful in providing opportunities for Native people to articulate their concerns, but to speak for them is to deny them the self-determination so essential to human progress. I also see myself as a professor helping mainstream students to critically analyze how science is presented in schools and to question their own taken-for-granted assumptions regarding the nature of science and science-technology-society issues.

For a long time I have felt a deep concern that the universities, and in particular the sciences, are not attracting First Nations students (Whyte 1986; Battiste 1998, 2000; Cajete 1999), despite the fact that First Nations parents and elders desire their children to receive a university education, including degrees in the sciences. How can students of Indigenous backgrounds identify with science, or even Indigenous knowledge, when they seldom if ever learn about their own contributions to science knowledge, their beliefs about the world, their history, or other values (Snively 1995).

Background

An examination of Aboriginal achievement patterns in British Columbia over the years 1997–2002 indicates that 36 to 42 percent of Aboriginal students graduate from grade 12. Of the Aboriginal students who graduated, 8 to 14 percent have taken 12th-grade biology; 5 to 8 percent took 12th-grade chemistry; and 2 percent took 12th-grade physics. It is important to acknowledge that the average test scores in these three courses range from 63 percent to 73 percent and indicate a high level of achievement for those students who do participate (statistics derived by Ministry of Education performance data, as yet unpublished). This low success rate for the majority of Aboriginal students creates barriers to postsecondary schooling and limits their career opportunities. Similarly, according to Indian and Northern Affairs Canada, less than 3.2 percent of the 27,000 First Nations students going to university or college full-time on federal funding during the year 2000 were enrolled in programs leading to careers in the sciences, including agriculture and biological science, engineering and applied sciences, mathematical and physical sciences, and health professions (DIAND 2002). Many Aboriginal people, including elders, teachers, students, and scientists, claim that their people often have viewed science not only as something unfamiliar and strange but also as something unhelpful and bad because it does not acknowledge Aboriginal science and leads their people away from their own culture.

This situation arises from a type of science education in which Aboriginal contributions to science are rarely acknowledged, and Aboriginal content is seldom if ever legitimized or is considered a token addition. Unless science classrooms and teaching materials provide a meaningful context for Aboriginal students, and unless Aboriginal knowledge coexists with Western science in the science classroom, many Aboriginal students will continue to find the science curriculum inaccessible and culturally irrelevant. The goal is to enable Aboriginal children to be successful in school science without giving up their worldview.

For many students, particularly many Aboriginal students, a Western perspective on nature does not harmonize with their own worldview and seems like a foreign culture (Kawagley 1995; Cajete 1999). According to Hodson (1993) science curriculum content is almost exclusively Western in content and orientation, and some curricula are covertly racist. The image of scientist as controller, manipulator, and exploiter of the environment conflicts with the cultural views of Fist Nations students (Battiste 1998; Cajete 1999). Many Aboriginal parents and elders insist that the practice of Western science trains alien, unfeeling people who bring environmental and human damage in their wake. With ample evidence on their side, Native people may fear Westernization, and the consequent alienation from their communities of young tribal members who become "scientists" in the Western manner, and fear that Natives trained in a Western tradition will lose their respect for "old ways" (Green 1981).

Thus a type of cognitive imperialism pervades school science whenever Aboriginal students are being assimilated into thinking like a Western scientist in their science classes (Aikenhead 1997, 2002). Colonization under the guise of "science for all" undermines students' self-identities as Aboriginal people, identities that are fundamentally essential to economic development, environmental and community sustainability, and the cultural survival of Canadian Aboriginal peoples (Battiste 1998; MacIvor 1995; Mosha 1999). This co-optive approach does not admit to the social construction of science knowledge, how and why research and curriculum topics and approaches are selected, or the possibility of alternative truths or ways of knowing. Furthermore, this position describes science as a culturally neutral search for universal truths, which is reliable and guaranteed by the scientific method itself. As a result of this stance, any knowledge that is labeled "unscientific" is rejected. The major effort has been toward examining access issues regarding multicultural groups and to rid them of unscientific beliefs.

There are a variety of so-called "add-on approaches" that can be described as Aboriginal enrichment of existing curricula and pedagogy. It is basically the "dressing up" of textbooks, programs, and teaching strategies to make them appear to be more culturally appropriate for First Nations people. Using First Nations culture as contextual background for the teaching of science, or adjusting the pedagogical approach to include traditional First Nations methods such as storytelling, the use of a talking circle, and inviting an elder into the classroom are some of the methods used by this approach. The advantage of this approach is that it is not threatening and does not demand fundamental change.

Canadian science educators can either colonize students by attempting to enculture them into Western science, or we can begin to embrace a decolonizing approach to school science that gives Aboriginal students access to Western science and technology without diminishing their Aboriginal identities. According to Aboriginal scholars such as MacIvor (1995) and Cajete (1999), this can be done by enculturing students into their own community.

> Native science evolved in relationship to places and is therefore instilled with a "sense of place." Therefore, the first frame of reference for a Native science curriculum must be the "place of the community,

its environment, its history and its people." Native students must be made to feel that the classroom is reflective of "their place." Indeed, relationship to place occurs in a greater context as MacIvor states, "Respect for Native spirituality and for Native nature-wisdom embedded within it, is inseparable from respect for the dignity, human rights, and legitimate land claims of all Native peoples." Given this orientation, stewardship of place is an important part of Indigenous science education. (MacIvor 1995, as quoted in Cajete 1999, p. 47)

Cajete goes on to say that the "transformational process must be a part of the development of contemporary science education for these students" and will be a direct result of the "full integration of Indigenous knowledge, orientation and sensibility into the teaching of science" (47).

Because of power relationships MacIvor (1995) concluded that we should embrace a postcolonial model she called "co-existence," which promotes functioning side by side. This model of coexistence between two worldviews, which encourages equality, mutual respect, and cooperation, is supported by MacIvor 1995, Cajete 1999, and Battiste 1998, 2000. The model posits that Aboriginal children are not disadvantaged by their own cultural identity and language, but are advantaged by it.

Putting together a cross-cultural or coexisting approach requires a common interest and willingness to collaboratively construct a curriculum that addresses the particular needs of a community. Many of the new genera of creative science methodologies that incorporate sense of place, experiential education, ecological understandings, and aesthetic (or spiritual) appreciation have been spurred on by the basic tenant that if you want to understand a West Coast old-growth forest, talk to the people who have been living in it for thousands of years.

Some scholars (Battiste and Henderson 2000) have identified traditional ecological knowledge and wisdom (TEKW) more closely with Aboriginal science:

The traditional ecological knowledge of Indigenous people is scientific, in the sense that it is empirical, experimental, and systematic.

It differs in two important ways from Western science, however: tra-
ditional ecological knowledge is highly localized and it is social. Its
focus is the web of relationships between humans, animals, plants,
natural forces, spirits, and landforms in a particular locality, as
opposed to the discovery of universal "laws." (p. 44)

Acknowledging the contributions of traditional science is a first step in enabling students to learn from groups outside the dominant culture who have made contributions to medicine, agriculture, geology, biology, ecology, habitat and resource management, and community environment relationships (Snively 1995; Snively and Corsiglia 2001). This is a major intellectual, political, and moral challenge for Canadian science educators today.

Alert Bay Field School in Culture and Environment Education

This chapter describes a combined off-campus TEK-enriched graduate-level Environmental Education Program offered in a total emersion summer format in Alert Bay, British Columbia, during July 2001. The University of Victoria program is part of a three-summer offering by the Faculty of Education, University of Victoria. We had been invited by the Namgis First Nation, located on Cormorant Island, which lies off the northeast corner of Vancouver Island in the beautiful Inside Passage, British Columbia. Alert Bay is a fishing community and gateway to the Knight Inlet and the Broughton Archipelago.

The aim of the program, as described in our vision statement, was to draw people from diverse backgrounds to work together in learning about the forest and ocean environments, respecting cultures of Aboriginal people, and educating future citizens to make wise decisions regarding long-term sustainable communities and environments. We had access to the U'mista Cultural Center, which houses one of the finest collections of historical artifacts on the Pacific Coast, the Marine Research Center, and the North Coast Natural Resources Center. The course combined primary historical documents on Kwagulth history and culture with input from Kwagulth elders and focused largely on topics dealing with community-environment relationships, values, current issues, and the contributions of Indigenous peoples to environmental knowledge and the resolution of resource problems.

Participants included one high school teacher of Native ancestry, one elementary teacher of Métis ancestry, and one park naturalist of Native ancestry. Non-Native participants included two park naturalists, two educators with the Department of Fisheries and Oceans, one anthropology major, and twelve teachers.

The program attempted to incorporate approaches that could help teachers and informal educators to develop programs and curricula that can challenge students to take a culturally sensitive stand on issues of culture, environment, and sustainability. It was hoped that if these environmental educators were provided with rich firsthand experiences in a home community during this first summer, they would later be able to draw upon their experiences when framing their thesis topics and projects.

Alert Bay: The Kwakwaka'wakw People

The traditional Kwakwaka'wakw people (or Kwakwala-speaking people) are located along the west coast of British Columbia, adjacent to the northern half of Vancouver Island. For twelve thousand or more years the region is believed to have been home to the Kwakwaka'wakw people, who within this rich environment developed a unique language and one of the world's most enduring cultures. There are sites through the region, on islands, inlets, and bays, where the Kwakwaka'wakw people have lived, fished, gathered food, collected materials for artistic purposes, and buried their dead. Their unique art forms and spiritual stories depict their close interaction with nature. Like so many West Coast Aboriginal groups, the Kwakwaka'wakw population plummeted by two-thirds of their precontact level before smallpox and other European diseases had run their course. Land was taken away and no treaties made.

"Since time beyond recollection," the Kwakwala-speaking groups had expressed their joy though the potlatch. The potlatch ceremony marks important occasions in the lives of the Kwakwaka'wakw: the naming of children, marriage, transforming rights and privileges, and mourning the dead. The more gifts distributed, the higher status achieved by the gift giver and the greater his ability to provide for the community. With the coming of missionaries and government agents, frustration over unsuccessful attempts to "civilize" the people of the potlatch led officials, teachers, and missionaries to pressure the federal government to pass a series of laws beginning in 1884 banning the potlatch. For many years the potlatch went underground to evade prosecution under the law. The Kwakwaka'wakw reject the legitimacy of many aspects of Euro-Canadian settlement and have a long history of concerns related to treaty rights, fisheries, cultural property, land use, and sustainability issues (Webster 1990).

Alert Bay Field School

Although much of the program was team-taught, the combined program of courses included Community and Culture taught by historical researcher John Corsiglia, Ethnobiology of British Columbia First Nations taught by ethnobiologist Dr. Brian Compton, and Environmental Education, which I taught. A key tenet was that environment and culture could not be considered separately; there could be no course on Kwagulth culture that was not also about the Kwagulth environment. Culture and environment are inextricably linked and must be treated holistically. The concept called for strong collaboration at the community level in identifying the interests and perspectives of the Kwagulth people. Every effort was made to involve elders and community leaders as resource persons, and as such they were our professors.

Course packs were developed for each course in order to provide detailed information on historical, cultural, environmental, and cross-cultural topics. The culture course documents were culled from the anthropological and historical literature with particular emphasis placed on primary government documents held by the British Columbia Archives in Victoria. Documents were selected in relation to issues and priorities identified as important by knowledgeable Kwagult community members and school district personnel who were part of the planning process. The culture course combined culture-specific (Kwagulth) secondary resource materials with key primary historical documents and oral history.

Students were placed on study teams with the assigned task of becoming "experts" on topics of cultural and environmental interest by reading their course packs, interviewing local elders and resource persons, making notes of ongoing events, and presenting seminars at appropriate times and locations during the course. Students were also required to keep a detailed field notebook related to the flora, fauna, and ecology of the region and a reflective journal in which to ponder, consider, speculate, and extract personal meaning from their traveling in Kwagult territory.

Specifically, the topic outline for Community and Culture included the following:

- *philosophical foundations: expansionism and long-resident Indigenous peoples*
- *historical interactions involving Alert Bay and Newcomer interests, including an overview of Indigenous and introduced systems*
- *local efforts to protect culture and environment*
- *traditional ecological knowledge oral information systems*
- *formal and informal knowledge*

The topic outline for Ethnobiology of British Columbia First Nations course included the following:

- *cultural salience of organisms*
- *ethnobiology of the Kwakwaka'wakw and of other British Columbia First Nations*
- *field observations of local biodiversity and ethnobiological species*
- *science as a culture-based phenomenon*
- *culinary and medicinal species*
- *the relevance of ethnobiology and ethnozoology to various academic, environmental, and social issues*

The topic outline of Environmental Education course included these points:

- *an introduction to local ecosystems (pond, seashore, and forest communities)*

- *overview of philosophical, theoretical, and ideological approaches to environmental education and First Nations education*
- *current environmental/cultural issues in Alert Bay and the Pacific coast*
- *the research related to students' environmental knowledge*
- *teaching strategies for understanding environmental education issues and for conflict resolution*
- *teaching strategies for understanding cross-cultural science and environmental issues*

From Alert Bay we traveled by seine boat to Hansen Island, where we set up a base camp and tented for three nights. From our base camp we visited Orca Research Lab and Robson Bight Ecological Reserve, where students experienced direct field observations of sea lions, killer whales, harbor seals, dolphins, porpoises, and bald eagles in their natural habitat. Day hikes allowed the field collection of ethnobiological specimens and other ethnobotanical studies and observations of environmental impacts of natural and human disturbances on hillsides, foreshore, and ocean-bottom ecosystems.

Our day hike through culturally modified trees (CMT) within pockets of "old growth forests" radically adjusted our understanding of so-called pristine forests as "tended forests," the results of centuries of traditional sustainable forestry practices by First Nations peoples. A model of traditional sustainable forest utilization emerged as a management practice deserving scientific attention and respect. Our guide informed us that the study of CMTs is also envisioned as a means to help enable key First Nations leaders and land claims researchers to understand the hidden significance of CMTs as evidence of prior land use and occupancy in traditional territories.

We also traveled by seine boat to several abandoned village sites and stopped on Village Island, where we were honored to have a personal tour by elders of the old community.

Journal Entries
In an attempt to glimpse the student's experiences and viewpoints, I have included several quotes (with permission) from the students' word-for-word

reflective journal entries. The first quote describes Rena's observations and feelings as two elders took us to see the abandoned community located on Village Island. According to our informants, the entire village had been forcibly removed by the Royal Canadian Mounted Police (RCMP) during the 1920s as punishment for continuing the potlatches and to force Native children into missionary schools. Some people said it was because white entrepreneurs wanted cheap labor for the fish cannery in Alert Bay. Many elders had not visited the island since its forced evacuation.

> After days of discussing the concept of "sense of place" in our classroom in Alert Bay, I thought that I understood what it meant. Not until I witnessed the transformation of two Elders into young giggling girls did I begin to understand. Vera and Wata stepped onto the beach at Village Island as two women hurting over the knowledge of what had become of their childhood village. They prayed to be blessed as they visited the site, and as I held Wata's hand during the prayer circle, I could feel her tremble (That was Wata's first visit to the island in 50 years). She had already shared with us her apprehension of returning to the village, and I know we were all afraid that it would be too hard for her. I worried that we were intruding on what was a very personal and emotional experience for her.
>
> We stepped up from the beach onto the forest path and began the walk up the hill toward the abandoned village site. Fortunate to be near the front of the group; I walked directly behind Vera and Wata. I listened as they talked—slowly at first—"here we go. . . . How are you doing?" As we neared the crest of the hill, Vera started to point out the old buildings: the school, the site where the church had been, houses of friends and family. The transformation was amazing. The two women became little girls again, giggling as they remembered the sledding hill, the games of Indian baseball, all the nights they were out past curfew and their parents worried. As we listened to the ladies reminisce, the village became alive for us. We could smell the wood smoke pouring from the chimneys, hear

the laughter of children and see a vibrant, loving community. Village Island was no longer abandoned. It was alive, and healing the hearts of these two women.

Rena Sweeny (teacher of Native and non-Native
elementary students in a one-room schoolhouse,
Simoom Sound), journal entry, 2001

Following the potlatch on Village Island, 45 people were charged under Section 149 of the Indian Act, and 20 men and women were sent to Oakalla Prison to serve sentences of two months to three months. The people of Village Island were lucky; other Kwagult villages were burned by the RCMP, and nothing remains, not even the charred ashes of old buildings or the occasional totem pole.

As Jackie Howardson, one of the students put it: "Shame was the gift bestowed upon the First Nations people by the colonizer." For many years the potlatch went "underground" to evade further prosecution under the law. In isolated locations, people favored stormy weather as a suitable time to hold potlatches, knowing that neither the police nor the Indian agent could travel in such weather. At the field school, Chief Bill Cranmer explained, "I was ashamed to dance and speak my own language, but there were those who were not ashamed and refused to let the old ways die. The Elders continued to secretly practice their language and customs. Even though the children were not allowed to be present, the Elders rightly predicted that this would be their gift to ensure that the ways of the people were kept alive" (Howardson (anthropology major and consultant), journal entry, 2001).

Reflections on Fisheries Issues

One aspect of our program focused on fisheries issues. Chief Edwin Newman, hereditary chief of the Namgis and chief of Bella Bella, honored us with a presentation. Newman had been president of the Native Brotherhood and a longtime spokesperson and negotiator for the Native Fishing Association. The following quote is taken from Lenny Ross, an elementary school teacher who has lived for over twenty-five years on the British Columbia coast, where he worked as a logger and fisher and then as a teacher to create an award-winning environmental education program:

> The salmon fishery! Here was a topic I thought I knew well from many perspectives. I knew about the problems with declining stocks, over-fishing, and loss of habitat. I was aware of the devastating impacts on small, Aboriginal and non-Aboriginal coastal communities resulting from the cuts to fishing quotas, but I thought of the government regulations as a necessary evil if we were to save the fish. I felt certain my beliefs were accurate, fair, and well grounded in reality, and I was more or less proud and content with the response by our society to these issues. Chief Edwin Newman began his talk by simply explaining the situation from his First Nations' perspective.

> The village Elder detailed a long process of subjugation and discrimination, such as a 1914 law that excluded Indians from getting fishing licenses that had worked consistently to remove opportunities for west coast Native people to participate in commercial fisheries. While his examples given from long ago were harsh and disturbing to hear, I understood them to be products of a meaner, less aware time, and thus I accepted them as a tragic part of our history. But when he continued with current examples of discrimination that were equally harsh I found them much more disturbing as I could not dismiss them as ignorance of a bygone era. They were the hallmarks of my era. He detailed government policy that I was aware of, but pointed out that they not only consistently ignored First People's concerns, but also actually targeted their participation in the fisheries.

> Buy back programs that concentrated licenses in the hands of corporations, quota systems that excluded locally based fishers, and license boundaries that split traditional fishing grounds into three areas, decimated the economic base for his people and undermined their culture to a degree not felt in non-Aboriginal communities.

Chief Newman summed it up eloquently when he said, "I am an ocean person, and without the ocean we have nothing." Unemployment soared, welfare replaced pride in work, suicide rates increased, and new options were limited. His people could not simply leave and relocate without devastating consequences.

How could I have been so naïve? By telling me his "truth" he shattered my conceptions of the true nature of the situation. He expanded my worldview to include the perception of a non-dominant culture and made me realize that their needs are unique and must be recognized in order to give them the value and consideration they deserve, otherwise the persecution continues. I am no longer so complacent about the society in which I live. I see a greater need for significant changes and I know my life has been altered by this increased awareness.

Lenny Ross
(grade 6 teacher, Victoria), journal entry, 2001

General reflections on TEKW, Indigenous culture, environment, and sustainability:

First Nations people have lived off the land for thousands of years and thus have a better understanding of what it takes to preserve and take care of the environment. Learning about the many uses that different plants provide has certainly had an effect on my outlook regarding the preservation of our forest and plants. If others were enlightened regarding ethno botany it could certainly have an affect on them as well. Having Wata and Vera come and talk to us in Alert Bay sent such a powerful message in terms of the importance of preserving our forests and plants. To see first hand the number of things that a wide variety of plants can be used for and the fact that they are still in use today can change a lot of people's outlook on the destruction of our environment.

Kelly Nelson (high school math and science teacher, Victoria), journal entry, 2001

The components of the First Nations culture are tightly woven together. Wata was not able to speak of her work with the use of plants without relating all of the plants to the cultural roles that they play. For example, the cedar tree is considered the "tree of life," and was traditionally to meet transportation, clothing, food gathering, ceremonial, and artistic needs: "You have to believe in the power, and always give thanks to the highest power." (2001). Vera Newman made the connection clear when she told us "everything we live is culture."

Rena Sweeny, journal entry, 2001

Every aspect of Kwakwa̱ka'wakw culture reaffirms that man, animals and plants all share certain traits and characteristics and are, therefore, equal. . . . The masks, the dances, the potlatch all serve a similar function in that they foster the belief that man and the universe are inseparable and dependent upon the others for survival. Chief Bill Cranmer of Alert Bay told us that the returning of the salmon bones to the sea ensured that the salmon would return. Scientific evidence now supports that there is indeed a biological and ecological reason to do so. It has been determined by scientific means that bears dragging salmon to the forest plays an important part in the nutrient composition of the forest soils encouraging strong vital trees. Traditionally, when the First Nations people walked on their land they had an intimate knowledge of how "systems" were connected and dependent upon the other.

Jackie Howardson, journal entry, 2001

What I lived, with the Kwakwa̱ka'wakw people, was a dramatic change of perspective, from a scientific to a cultural perspective of nature. There is nothing like soaking in a cultural bath. Their culture is not distant like the Mayan's; First Nations live here with us in a multicultural country. Their living culture joins the whole of myself, e.g., my relationship with nature in my childhood and the respect and spirituality that I grant to nature.

Isabelle Morris (French-speaking park interpreter and adult educator), journal entry, 2001

Not only do Indigenous peoples have in-depth knowledge about their local environments; they also honor their environments through daily spiritual practice. When we were in Alert Bay, Vera honored the seals, the whales, the eagles and the salmon by drumming and singing. They have myths and stories that establish respect for other living beings. Is it possible for our modern culture to learn from Indigenous cultures or adapt practices that help us to develop closer emotional connections with our place?

I used to dream of traveling to distant places, thinking that would be the best way to understand the process of living on earth. But perhaps I could learn as much by staying within the horizon visible from this island's edge, focusing on the world close at hand. It's a very old idea, which I never comprehended until now.

Laena Garrison (park interpreter and adult educator), journal entry, 2001

Future Teaching

What specifically can long-term resident peoples like the Kwakwaka'wakw teach us about achieving sustainability and developing a view of a lasting relationship with one's own place? How might this exposure to a timeless way of doing things affect our teaching and professional work in the future? Can Native and non-Native teachers and students learn to recognize the knowledge of the elders and be mentored by them? The following journal entries are the participants' thoughts and feelings toward the summer institute, future teaching, and the teachings of the elders:

Throughout this summer, I have been given a multitude of opportunities to experience things by "doing" rather than just by reading about them. I have never in my life been so excited about learning as I was this summer. I feel like I was a sponge absorbing everything! My level of excitement and increased knowledge in environmental education has made me more confident in what I want to teach. I have gathered so many ideas from this course which I plan to take back to my classroom.

If we could all see the interesting cultural aspects of people from around the world, we would see a lot more tolerance. Appreciation for one's own past, as well as others, is crucial to promoting a tolerant and accepting society. I vow to do the best in my own classroom as a starting point!

> Lisa Kelly (non-Native teacher of Native and
> non-Native students, Sechelt), journal entry, 2001

My immersion into environmental education this summer has been an experience I will never forget. I have been exposed to a wide range of environmental literature, knowledge, opinion and perspective all in an effort at bridging this exposure from awareness to action. I have had the privilege to hear traditional ecological knowledge (tek) from Elders in Alert Bay, allowed to enter a sacred Big House and witness generations of song, dance and custom of the Kwakwaka'wakw peoples. . . .What do I do with all this knowledge that I have been exposed to?

My experiences in Alert Bay furthered by sense of affiliation with First Nations people and of their culture. It also opened my eyes to many truths about what has happened to them at the hands of European colonization. I appreciated the blunt and honest approach in sharing their pain at what they had lost and were trying to hang on to. My job as an educator is to spread those truths. There is an inevitable sense of guilt that accompanies those emotional responses. The challenge is to refocus those emotions into a sense

*of empowerment to better what has happened. By studying mul-
ticultural educations, students become aware of other cultures and
the potential they might have in correcting our current environmental problems. Exposing students to traditional ecological knowledge in science class adds validity to those cultures and an understanding that our culture has its limitations.*

Tye Swallow *(non-Native teacher of Native and non-Native
students, Bella Bella, and teacher of all Native adult students,
Saanich), journal entry, 2001*

Bowers (1995) points out that elders play an important role in the trans-
generational renewal of knowledge that is, over generations of experience,
raised to the level of wisdom. He suggests that traditions are an exceeding-
ly complex and important aspect of Indigenous cultural life and contribute to a form of consciousness that resists being manipulated by the media,
promoters of consumerism, or other forms of modernity. He also suggests
that students need to learn to recognize elder knowledge and the advice of
older people who are interpreting the stories of their people in modern context. In this case, both Native and non-Native teachers learned to recognize
the knowledge and wisdom of the elders in a modern time and learned to
interact with them, which is the initial phase of being mentored by elders.

In light of world ecological crises and recent events with the Nisga'a land
claims, the Delgamuukw decision, the Oka standoff, the Makah whaling controversy, the land claims referendum in British Columbia, climatic changes
affecting the Inuit, and ongoing fishing and forestry disputes, it becomes
increasingly necessary for universities and schools to present the First Nations
experience past and present. This program attempted to immerse teachers and informal educators in a "cultural bath" that would enable them to
experience the life ways, viewpoints, and culture of the Kwakwaka'wakw
people—their response to oppression, triumphs, resiliency, and determi-
nation to rejuvenate their culture.

Discussions of differences in the ways in which societies view plants and
animals and harvest resources over time establish a basis for discussion of

environment, appropriate technology, justice, and sustainable societies. It becomes important to recognize the magnitude of problems caused by our incomplete appreciation of the complexity of the biosphere and the scope of Indigenous knowledge. Unwillingness to recognize Indigenous knowledge as science skews the historical record and restricts approaches to some of our most debilitating environmental and socioeconomic problems (Snively and Corsiglia 2001). Who knows what strategies may be required for resolving environmental, resource management, and sustainability problems in the future.

The participants in the Alert Bay program were selected from a large number of applicants with proven track records of environmental concern and achievement. As such, they had already questioned mainstream cultural assumptions regarding power, justice, sustainability, and community-environment relationships. Our experiences in the home place of the Kwakwa̱ka̱'wakw allowed us to more easily break through cultural assumptions by opening doors of communication. Cultural barriers and borders were broken down by communication and access to information, and beliefs and attitudes were changed. We were all teachers and learners with profound concerns and future aspirations. I believe that in touching our hearts, the elders allowed us to develop that deep sense of oneness and belonging that we all seek.

Protocols and Reciprocity

Gaining entry into a community and relating to elders and community leaders is a complex social process. As is well documented, many elders were victimized by harsh government legislation and missionary schools, and the result is a generation of elders living lives of great personal pain. This pain may result in blocked or distorted traditional teachings that are passed on to the next generation, or feelings of insecurity and alienation that stifle the mentoring process, even blocking many elders from teaching their own children.

In the Alert Bay situation, I had been privileged to have a 17-year relationship with several elders, teachers, and community leaders. As a marine and environmental educator I had walked the beaches, explored the surrounding islands and inlets, and provided workshops for Alert Bay teachers, elders, and community members. It was this relationship of trust, mutual respect, and reciprocity that enabled the graduate program entry into the Alert Bay community.

The process of inviting elders, chiefs, and community leaders into the Alert Bay classroom or along with us on trips taught the graduate students the protocols that are necessary for establishing a relationship with an elder, modeled the process of gift giving and receiving, and demonstrated the proper addressing of names and places. Through this process, trust is established, and a genuine interest in the welfare of the elder and the local community is promoted. This is important; the elder is about to share information that is personal, powerful, and possibly sacred—the recipients must be prepared. In addition, the process of the visits teaches the students the qualities that are necessary for being mentored by the elders. These qualities include patience, a willingness to share, self-discipline, and a deep respect for the spiritual beliefs of others.

It is important to acknowledge that the elders and community leaders had a mutually positive experience, as the following two descriptions indicate:

> For so many years I was angry and resentful because of what the white people did to my people, and I spent many years fighting for my people, I never acknowledged the importance of other people.

> Even today I'm always putting myself down because I'm not educated. For so many generations our people couldn't read. It was hard to be educated in the white man's way. We felt foolish and inferior, and so we didn't speak out. I think it's important that our people tell our stories about what happened to us, because it will teach others in the community to get involved. So by us teaching in the graduate program, it is a way of empowering and encouraging others in our community to get involved. Now I'm able to open my heart and mind.

It has been experiences like the one when your graduate students came to Alert Bay, that I realize that we have to take care of everybody. For some time now I've been trying to look at life in a different way. We all must be respectful of others, and look after one another. It comes from the heart.

Vera Newman, *personal communication*, 2001

All students are really important to me. It doesn't matter what race. I was honored to tell the university students what my elders taught me. I'm planting seeds so that one day they will bloom.

I really enjoyed going to the old villages. It brought back a lot of memories, and I really never thought about going there again after what happened to our people there. Teaching others of the value of First Nations knowledge makes me happy because a lot of that knowledge was taken away, and its coming back strong. It was an experience for me too. Finding our truths uplifts others. The value of our knowledge allows the outside world to know our people were educated without going to university. They lived their education every day, they lived it, breathed it, ate it.

Our territory is our drug store. I just came back from doing a workshop on Quadra Island for 80 French physicians who came here to learn about our medicines. I'm happy that the outside world is learning about our knowledge of medicines and foods. I'm happy for our children because they will have these medicines in their lives that were lost to so many of our people.

Wata Christine Joseph, *personal communication*, 2001

We were the grateful recipients of many kindnesses, but in keeping with traditional "protocol" we did not arrive empty-handed. John Corsiglia's collection of archival material relating to postcontact Kwakwaka'wakw–government relations was genuinely appreciated by leaders interested in issues around control of lands and resources. Dr. Compton's knowledge of the ethnobiology of the Kwakwaka'wakw people was a great source of interest, and we hoped it would provide a catalyst for locally based curriculum development. We treated chiefs, elders, and community leaders like faculty and paid them faculty honoraria. Also, since we were aware of recent research into problems of social polarization and tension that frequently plague small British Columbia school districts, we constantly explored cross-cultural strengths while simultaneously examining ethical and historical issues factually. We hoped that our work would make a difference in schools where children must make their way through the complexities they meet in their own communities.

The Uniqueness of the Graduate Program
From their field experiences, archival research, input from First Nations elders, and seminars the students analyzed, debated, and attempted to understand complex issues relating to community, culture, and environment. By bringing together acknowledged specialists in the key interrelated disciplines, the program provided a unique interdisciplinary starting point for developing educational programs and curriculum materials. In short, the program

- *drew people together of diverse backgrounds from the local Native and non-Native communities and from scientific, environmental, political, student, and research communities to learn about ecosystems and long-term sustainability, providing an interdisciplinary approach*
- *appealed to people who wanted to learn about long-term sustainable communities and environments as a common goal that would help to minimize tensions among various interest groups*
- *helped to integrate knowledge and values, a necessary step in making sustainable land use decisions by providing an ecosystem-based approach*
- *provided students with an opportunity to interact with leaders and*

*negotiators who know the history of First Nations issues from a
First Nations point of view*

- *encouraged an interactive relationship between local communities
and the university*
- *provided access to elders and community leaders and opportunities
to be mentored by elders*
- *sought out local scientists and resource persons to teach topics of
interest*
- *was collaborative and transcultural in nature; through joint projects
between equal partners, the program provided for environmental
and cultural understandings from two worlds*
- *was holistic, integrated, and experiential in nature*
- *called for knowledge and skill in human interaction and interpersonal dynamics, as well as group development and cooperative learning—living together as a family*

Conclusion

Although I consciously avoid teaching science and environmental education courses in an assimilative way, my students are expected nevertheless
to understand the world through the eyes of the Western scientist, just as we
would expect students to understand various points of view toward an environmental issue. Similarly when we deal with Aboriginal science and TEKW,
students are expected to understand the world through the eyes of Aboriginal peoples but not necessarily to believe it. This distinction is important.

In this project the chiefs and elders welcomed the opportunity to theo-
rize and interact with university professors and students, to instruct, and
to tell their stories. This is important. There is a perception that Indigenous
science is not as valuable as Western science, and teachers may see the need
for students to understand "real science" as a justification for not adding the
Indigenous component. A lesson learned in Alert Bay is that the people who
achieved the Indigenous knowledge may be willing to pass it on because
they understand its potential, and the non-Native educators can be receptive and deeply grateful to receive it. Additionally, the elders saw their par-

ticipation in a university-based program as a way of enabling other community members to overcome the bonds of Eurocentric supremacist education and reaffirm the value of their own traditional knowledge.

The study of science and environmental education in my program is framed by questions linked to bringing our cultural practices back into balance with the planet. Questions include the following: What are the origins and consequences of our practice of viewing Western science as superior to other forms of knowing? Where did we get the idea that humans have a legitimate right to have domination over the earth and all its living creatures? What are the consequences? What are examples of Indigenous knowledge and wisdom that could be included in mainstream science and environmental education curricula? How does Western commitment to almost continuous innovation and expedience relate to long-term survivability? What can long successful resident peoples like the Kwakwaka'wakw teach us about sustainability and a view of a lasting relationship with one's "home place"? How might this exposure to a timeless way of doing things affect our teaching and professional work in the future?

Because responsibility for developing culturally appropriate curricula has largely been left to social studies and multicultural teachers, the development of appropriate teaching and learning strategies for science teachers remains pressing. This chapter has presented examples of Indigenous science and technology within particular cultural contexts where learning of applied science takes place. Within a science or environmental education curriculum a few examples might include a herb-gathering walk with a grandparent, making medicines, a pit cooking event, harvesting seaweed, a child watching a parent catch fish, the community eulachon-rendering party, a child walking a streambed with a parent to clear it of debris prior to the spring salmon returning, a parent or other relative explaining the migration patterns of Dungeness crabs. Cross-cultural studies have shown that science learning should be highly kinesthetic and activity oriented, using a variety of sensory modalities in creative combination. This is the way both science and art are learned within a traditional cultural context (Cajete 1999). Seeing, tasting, feeling, smelling, and manipulating have all been used by various cultures to teach what was felt to be important to know about the natural world. It is premature at this time to describe the pedagogical consequences to ongoing practicing teachers and adult educators or the effectiveness of the methods and curriculum materials they develop. This graduate program is a departure from present university programs in science and environmental education.

We stand to learn from the honesty and forthrightness with which the Kwakwaka'wakw people tell their stories. We need a similar candor and directness in addressing the roots of non-Natives' shortcomings, which are traceable one way or another to how we think and how poorly we think about concepts such as time, home place, the limits of natural systems, economic growth, power, wealth, and justice. This failure is reflected in that portion of our sciences, humanities, and social studies that deal with (or ignore) the relation between humanity and environment. Ultimately, our shortcomings can be traced to our schools and to our most distinguished universities.

10. Traditional Wisdom as Practiced and Transmitted in Northwestern British Columbia, Canada

John Corsiglia

Traditional ecological knowledge and wisdom (TEKW) arises in long-resident oral societies where humans live by sustaining both human communities and environmental resources. TEKW practitioners gather, analyze, and share complex sensory information that they use to formulate and encourage workable relationships between humans, other life forms, and the environment, creating values, concepts, roles, responsibilities, and strategies for utilizing, sharing, and protecting resources. During recent decades scientists, philosophers, and educators concerned with environmental management or the threat of environmental collapse have begun to acknowledge the importance and reliability of TEKW observational data and ecological strategies, and the possibility of abstract wisdom regarding human communities and the environment has been considered and demonstrated (Knudtson and Suzuki 1992). At its core, TEKW has a wisdom dimension that encourages the formulation of values and attitudes, as well as day-to-day habits of mind and action that foster respectful life-sustaining interactions and relationships with the environment. This hardworking wisdom component is responsible for maintaining the transmission of the TEKW system from generation to generation and ensures that a community populace perceives crises and threats and deals with them skillfully and diligently. The traditional wisdom component of the TEKW lifeway is particularly important as it identifies and addresses the very environmental problems that appear to mystify modern empire-building societies (EBS). This chapter considers how TEKW can be seen as different from EBS wisdom through an exploration of the Nisga'a culture—a successful and viable TEKW society—takes meaningful steps to utilize traditional wisdom and transmit its perspective, values, and skills from older to younger generations.

Simply put, TEK wisdom places a high value on stability and balance between community and environment and ensures that attitudes, values, and strategies that serve to prevent waste, hoarding, and environmental degradation are communicated between generations. As delineated in the Nisga'a Txeemsim oral story cycle, humans participate in the creation as equals with plant, animal, mineral, and spirit beings. As equals among the many, we are obliged to respect all relations and share without generating disruption or waste. Practices that stand the test of time are more valuable than radical approaches that may bring ridicule or, by failing, put entire communities at risk. Those who take too much or waste the community's resources may be counseled and corrected, but if they will not mend their ways they could be left behind and forgotten. In his earliest incarnation as the ultimate comic neophyte, the youthful the Nisga'a culture hero Txeemsim is afflicted by a netherworld demon and becomes consumed by ravenous hunger, lust, and continuous cravings for stimulation and advantage. It is a long journey to maturation and enlightenment, and the leader-to-be must learn to respect other beings and diligently strive to improve the lot of all.

EBS, however, generally operates by expanding into the homelands of others, especially TEKW peoples, managing populations and modifying lands and resources to enrich urban centers. EBS wisdom is not generally conceptualized as relating to ecological and environmental concerns; instead, EBS wisdom facilitates EBS objectives by managing interpersonal difficulties and problems relating to ownership and control of wealth and property.

Despite extensive non-Native newcomer reliance on TEKW discoveries and innovations, EBS has generally given TEKW intellection a rough ride. In the course of establishing itself in the Americas EBS "borrowed" the use of some five hundred traditional TEKW medicines and traditional crops that supply three-fifths of the world's food supply as well as rubber, long staple cotton, and numerous democratic governance concepts (Weatherford 1988). The extensive "borrowings" are more accurately considered a form of valuable (intellectual) property that was appropriated along with lands, resources, and labor—with little or no recognition or compensation. At the same time EBS developed stratagems for marginalizing and even killing Indigenous peoples, typically after first defining them as legal nonpersons or wards of the state. In the *Long and Terrible Shadow*, Justice Thomas Berger delineates the convolutions of five hundred years of negative stratagems perpetrated by EBS in the Americas (1992). While the practitioners of TEKW have been exploited, marginalized, and ignored by EBS, Indigenous societies such as the Nisga'a have persevered in their TEKW. For community leaders such as Semo'ogit Eli Gosnell and those who have followed in his path, the value and the importance of this knowledge has never been in doubt.

Examples from the Nass Area of Northern British Columbia

During the 1880s the Nisga'a leaders determined that the only way to protect Lisims lands and resources from newcomer encroachment was to negotiate a treaty with the governments of British Columbia and Canada. What is remarkable about this community's subsequent efforts and leadership is that during the ensuing 120-year struggle, the Nisga'a wisdom requirement to protect the home place and respect the decisions of past leaders was heeded, and the leadership stood firm—overcoming very considerable efforts to "break" the community's resolve. The diligence called for by the Nisga'a traditional wisdom was maintained, and the Nisga'a Treaty was finally signed in 1998.

Example 1

The impetus for this chapter evolved from a somewhat jarring challenge presented to the author by the Nisga'a spiritual and political leader Eli Gosnell in 1977: "When are your people [Whites] going to start behaving as if you live here?" The late Sim'oogit Eli Gosnell, father of Dr. Joseph Gosnell, president of the Nisga'a Nation, was a spiritual, cultural, political, and religious leader as well as a Nisga'a historian.

"When the Ts'eax volcano lava flow blocked the Ts'eax River [historical evidence suggests in the late 1700s] the salmon were prevented from ascending to the spawning grounds. We dealt with this situation by put spawning salmon in waterproof boxes and packed them up to the head of the new lake to reestablish breeding runs. This introduction of salmon was successful" (Chief Eli Gosnell, personal communication with author, 1976).

Sim'oogit Gosnell also related how in precontact times "The Nisga'a used fishwheels mounted on floating platforms to catch fish without harming them. We fished selectively to ensure that the finest fish could spawn." He explained how the mesh vanes of the fishwheel were turned by the current and how as they rose upward they scooped up salmon ascending the river. As fish slipped down the vanes toward the horizontal axle of the cylindrical fishwheel, they contacted baffles that guided them out the sides of the fishwheel into submerged holding baskets. "The river was like a moving highway for us and it was convenient and efficient to create stationary wheels to allow the river's power to lift the fish and place them into our baskets. The flowing river kept salmon alive until they were either harvested or released—we always took only the fish we needed and no more." Sim'oogit Gosnell's comments and recent Nisga'a application of the fishwheel for conservation purposes are detailed with photographs and a diagram elsewhere (Corsiglia and Snively 1997). The Nisga'a Fisheries Department now employs fishwheels to catch spawning salmon for lower river tagging and upper river recapture together with sophisticated statistical analysis to determine highly accurate fish counts (Harry Nyce Sr., personal communication with author, 1996).

Example 2

The oil-rich Oolichan fishery of Lisims was certainly one of the most concentrated sources of wealth in Indigenous North America, and even after the ravages of disease during the contact period, some five thousand souls converged on the lower Nass River annually to render the Oolichan oil that made the winter diet of dried salmon digestible. "Without Oolicahan grease it would have been impossible to survive the harsh winters of Northern British Columbia" (James Gosnell, personal communication with author, 1980).

Nisga'a diplomatic, organizational, and entrepreneurial skills were honed and perfected in the course of managing this resource so that many thousands of fishers could assemble in an orderly way on the lower Nass to partake in the late winter harvest and prepare "grease." Used as a matrix for food preservation, Oolichan grease facilitated the winter storage and transport of such easily spoiled foods as berries and smoked cockles (Dr. Bertram McKay, personal communication with author, 1979). The hundreds of uses for Oolichan grease and other Oolichan products formed a very highly articulated Oolichan technology that was supported by diplomatic acumen as well as managerial controls of production and distribution, which have yet to be documented.

Although the ethnology reflects a long history of protecting the area and fending off would-be encroachment, newcomer traders, missionaries, and Indian Department officials brought disruption to the area during historic times and the TEKW obligation to protect animal communities and resources inspired vigorous and relentless political action. When Anglo-Canadian entrepreneurs and even the superintendent of British Columbia Indian Affairs became interested in the Lisims Oolichan and salmon fisheries, pressure on the Nisga'a became very considerable. In 1886 Judges Cornwall and Planta reported on their Public Inquiry "to enquire as to whether any and if, any, what causes of complaint exist among the Indians of the North-West coast of British Columbia":

> The oolichan fishery is of great value. . . . Each man engaged in the fishing expects besides providing for himself and family enough grease for annual consumption, to put up ten boxes for sale; each box is of a certain size and shape and is of the average value of seven dollars. . . . The number of Indians assembling on the Naas for fishing is estimated by thousands, and so the enormous value of the fishery may be seen at a glance.
>
> The value of the fishery thus demonstrated, it must follow that the enjoyment of it should be confined to our own people." (Cornwall and Planta 1886)

The archival record of the late 1800s and early 1900s is replete with such instances of blatantly racist and self-serving statements made by newcomer government officials, judges, missionaries, and entrepreneurs.

The Nisga'a did succeed in protecting the Oolichan from commercialization and destruction—they received an exclusive right of access to this fishery in 1886. Excerpts from the Nisga'a Oolichan Petition, which was probably printed at Gitlaxdamiks for the edification of the government of Canada during the 1880s, demonstrates a thorough understanding of the biology of anadramous fishes, an astute assessment of the nature of commercial enterprise based on greed and racial bias, and a capacity for utilizing formal communication and skillful lobbying:

> There is much uneasiness in the minds of our people, owing to the fear that Commercial Enterprise may one day step in and annex the Oolachan to its own purpose.

> We beg to enunciate our conviction, based upon long observation and close knowledge of this fish, that it would not long survive the denuding processes of commercial operations. Any systematized endeavor to place the oolachan on the market would result in its extinction. We believe the oolachan could be fished out of existence in four or five years.

> From what we have seen of the Salmon Fishing Industry we fear that Commercial Enterprise, if allowed to do so, would fish every river in the province dry of salmon without any regard to the Indian or the future. It has been done on the Fraser; it is being done on the Naas. Hence our plea for the oolachan.

> Other natural sources of food supply have practically passed out of our possession: our berry patches have gone, because we may no longer maintain them by quadrennial burnings. Our ancestral hunting grounds have become common land, free and open to all. Our salmon fishing camps have been abandoned for the employment afforded us by the salmon canneries. The oolachan and its

grease alone remain to us intact, and these we wish to retain, the
goodwill of the Government of Canada prospering us." (Nisga'a
Oolichan Petition, c. 1880, Nisga'a Lisims Government)

Example 3

During the late 1860s Anglican missionaries Doolan and Tomlinson encouraged some Laxgalts'ap residents to form a mission community at Gingolix, which is located at the mouth of the Lisims (or Nass) River. Since time
immemorial, the Nisga'a chiefs have begun the day with a period of morning contemplation on the bank of the Lisims. One morning in 1980 a Gingolix chief observing the river noticed a single Dungeness crab (*Cancer magis-
ter*) swimming out of Alice Arm upriver into Lisims (Dr. Bertram McKay in
Corsiglia and Snively, 1997). When this man saw other crabs moving in the
same direction, he reported his observations to the Gingolix Village Council and raised the alarm. The chiefs returned with him, and all agreed that
the crabs had never been seen to travel in this direction at this time of year.
The chiefs inferred that the crabs were being driven out of Alice Arm by the
tailings plume already seen to be flowing from the new molybdenum mine
at Gitsault. The Gingolix chiefs conferred with the Nisga'a Tribal Council
leaders, who acted immediately. By the end of the day the Nisga'a Nation's
Vancouver lawyers had been contacted. Soon after they were involved in
conducting research regarding the details of permits granted to the mine
and also began to assemble teams of scientists. Within weeks oceanog-
raphers, marine biologists, and ocean pollution scientists ascended the
inlet with the necessary personnel and sampling equipment and were able
to document the presence of highly concentrated and toxic mine tailings.
The Honorable Jim Fulton MP discovered that a federal cabinet minister
had signed "Order in Council SOR-79-345 permitting the dumping of 400
grams of tailings per liter of water . . . a concentration 8,000 times greater than the allowable limit set by the Parliament of Canada" (Raunet 1996).
The scientists studied the situation and were able to demonstrate serious
environmental degradation and confirm the inferences made by the Gingolix man and the chiefs. After intensive legal and political work coupled

with a fall in the value of molybdenum, the company closed the mine rather than install a tailings pond (Raunet 1996).

Over the decades the writer has spoken with many knowledgeable Nisga'a educators and leaders, but never once has he heard a statement to the effect that the integrity of the environment could be compromised for entrepreneurial benefit. Extracting the molybdenum ore body might some day be worth the cost of erecting a proper tailings pond. In the mean time, so far as the elders and chiefs are concerned, that ore body and any profits can wait. The destruction of the marine habitat would be disrespectful to the life forms that exist in the area and could be dangerous to all participants in the food chain.

How May TEKW Assumptions and Attitudes Be Communicated in a Culture?

There are many ways to encourage and introduce children to the wisdom of traditional elders—this is a vast topic that can occupy young scholars long into the future. In the Tχeemsim stories, the most difficult possible feral child, Anmogamhaat is "tamed" through the wisdom of a chief and kindness of an entire village.

Communicating values and approaches: Sometimes the teaching is by example, sometimes by reference to ancient stories, sometimes, when inference and metaphor may fail, there is a possibility of direct explanation. Numerous modes of communicating information are used. Background information and teachings are included with instruction in tasks while the feasting system is itself a vast training ground. Young people may be called upon to secure, transport, cure, or prepare and serve food, prepare gifts, or carry messages. Everything about the public feast carries meaning: where and how and even in what direction people sit all carry meaning. The way people move, speak, and communicate carries meaning. What is said, what is not said—both can be extremely important and may relate to such important issues as resource ownership or leadership status. This extensive "world" of relationships can best be explained by First Nations persons who have training and insight into such matters. These glimpses into the vast domain of First Nations child rearing and encouragement are included to show that well-developed techniques for transmitting respectful attitudes toward community and environment do exist and are certainly a fit topic for interesting and important study. One of the most important features of TEKW wisdom may involve raising children to understand some leaders are particularly trustable and have been carefully trained to avoid making mistakes.

Training the mind: Another branch of TEKW teachings involves training individuals to be in control of their minds. In an environment where humans regularly negotiate dangerous waters and coexist with sea lions, grizzly bears, and government authority, mental acuity and concentration can become matters of survival. As in Vedanta and Buddhism, First Nations teachers sometimes describe the mind as an organ, rather like a muscle that we can discipline and train. The mind should not be allowed to take charge and simply lead us into ego gratification—the mind is only an instrument; it is not our being, essence, or identity. Thus, when the mind rages or entices us with shifting desires, we need not take its manifestations too seriously or allow it to disturb our equanimity. It is best to learn to control the mind-muscle so that it does not behave erratically and cause our destruction.

The River Otter Story: Stories used to encourage proper mind use are important for several Nisga'a people known to the author. For example, there are many versions of stories about the Watzq (River Otter). Versions are told that are suitable to the differing interests of more or less mature children. The deadly River Otter destroys people foolish enough to let their minds stray from the task at hand by taking the form of their stray thoughts and luring them into the river and to their deaths.

> There was a child who was told to take a message to his uncle. He was cautioned to think only about the message, because if he allowed his mind to wander and began thinking about some sweets that his uncle might give him, it could happen that a Watzq might take the form of those sweets and appear along the trail—then the child might try to take hold of those sweets and be lured or dragged into

the river. When we forget to focus on our thoughts the River Otter can take the form of our thoughts and lure us into the river to be dragged under the water to our death and the loss of our spirit.

When the story is told to older boys it can be altered considerably:

A young man was carving a canoe across [the river] from the old village. He had completed the outside shape of the canoe and was engaged in adzing out the interior. This was difficult and repetitive work and he let his mind wander to his girlfriend and what he would do to her if she were present.

Soon he saw that she was approaching from the river bank. At first he was pleased to see her, but he quickly noticed that she was overly complimentary in praising the workmanship and the lines of the canoe. Also he noticed that her ears seemed small and he saw that behind them he could see a very light shadow that looked quite like fur. He then paid closer attention to her hands and noticed an unusual trace of fur on the backs of her hands. Also, her fingers seemed short and very strong with unusually long and thick fingernails that seemed curved and sharp—like those of a predatory animal.

When he observed that her teeth were quite pointed and that her eye teeth were particularly long, he knew without doubt that he was dealing with the deadly Watzq which had taken the form of his girlfriend. He also knew that he was in grave danger. When she invited him to lie down and make love he became alarmed— but he kept his composure and focused on overcoming this monster. Finally he said to her, "Before we lie down together, first turn toward the village and call out to make sure that no one is watching us." She did not want to do this, but he insisted and so she relented [and] turned away from him.

She called out once, "Is anybody there?" There was no answer and she turned back to him. He asked her to call again, this time loud-

er. At that moment, when she called out as loud as she could, he used the adze he still held in his hand and struck her with all his might on the dibble, the bony point at the base of the skull. She fell to the ground and writhed in her death agony. As she lay on the ground bleeding and shrieking she changed into her true form—that of the Watzq, the giant River Otter.

After this event the young man was a changed person. He learned to concentrate on his work completely—never losing his focus and eventually he became well known as a very important and highly valued craftsman who was widely respected and highly sought after.

(Harold Wright, personal communication with author, 1978)

Many lessons of philosophy and psychology are interwoven in such a story: we live in a world of energies where appearances may not always reveal underlying realities; our thoughts represent a way of connecting with this world of energies; there are clues about us that we may see if we use our minds properly; if we indulge in fantasy or allow our minds to be lulled away with desires, we can lose our ability to discern the essence of events; our minds and senses can either save us or destroy us so we must trust the teachings and stay alert; we are personally responsible for keeping our thought processes clear to avoid our undoing; clear thinking people cannot be led down the garden path.

Training a leader: How do TEKW leaders encourage community values developing around knowledge of the community's resources, sincerity, diligence, respect for all life forms, sharing, and harmony, and how does this leadership contrast with that of empire-building societies?

In cultures where values of respect and sharing are encouraged, the author has observed that children seem to be raised most respectfully and lovingly. "A Nisga'a child's feet should not touch the floor until s/he is two years old—until then they are carried about and doted on in the extended family and the whole village" (Dr. Bertram McKay, personal communication with author, 1977). If a child exhibits persistent and excessive self-interested behavior, he or she may be obliged to give away some valued possession to persons outside the immediate family. The giving of objects to siblings and others is encouraged, and the child raised in a matrilineal family may be obliged to give gifts to the father's side if an offense of some sort must be righted (Audrey McKay, personal communication, 1981). Older children are encouraged to tend toddlers, and responsible eight- or nine-year-old children may undertake the care of infant siblings.

One instructive incident involves a twelve-year-old Laxgalts'ap schoolboy being trained by his uncle, the late chief Bill McKay. After school the nephew arrived with four friends and went into Chief McKay's house, where the writer happened to be visiting. Chief Bill invited his nephew to sit on his knee and gave him a double handful of candies "To give out later." Chief Bill then asked his nephew a number of questions that are reconstructed here with names changed:

> How many people smiled at you while you were going to school this morning?" [Answer: "Five."] "Was there smoke coming out of Robert's chimney?" [Answer: "No."] "What was your grandfather doing?" [Answer: "Working on his boat."] "Was he painting it?" [Answer: "No. He was still sanding it."] (Bill McKay, personal communication, 1976)

Later Chief Bill's brother, Dr. Bert McKay, explained to me that the nephew was being trained to become a village chief, and he had to learn to observe and remember what everyone was doing and planning to do in the village: "Someone must know what everyone needs—otherwise there can be a lot of waste. Instead of three boats going on a trip with one man in each it is almost always better for all to go in one boat—it saves fuel and it's safer. The old teaching was that once a village gets to be larger than 200 to 250 people one chief simply might not be able to receive and retain all the details so when a village population reaches those numbers it was better to divide the community and start a second village" (Bertram McKay, personal communication with author, 1976).

Lessons from the Txeemsim cycle: Stories about cultural heroes can guide the development and maturation of leaders within a culture. The path to becoming a fully functioning and enlightened TEKW culture person or leader is revealed in the great Nisga'a Txeemsim story cycle (Boas 1902), where groups of stories relate to different stages of development. Persons suited to this path can be guided by the great story cycle toward spiritual, psychological, and temporal evolution. When William Duncan, the first Anglican missionary to ascend Lisims, was told about Txeemsim in 1859, he noted in his diary that Txeemsim was a miracle worker who seemed to be very like "the Saviour."

The stories of Txeemsim take place over the heroic protagonist's three succeeding incarnations. Initially he is an absolutely feral child of semi-divine parentage who can be subdued and brought to live in association with others only through gentle treatment. Afterward he is contaminated by a Laxwoosa, a mysterious netherworld creature that places a scab in his mouth and infects him with insatiable cravings for sensory pleasure. Once "infected," the young Txeemsim is at the mercy of gluttony and lust, which propel him through the adventures of his first punishing and hilarious incarnation. His youthful quest for sensory gratification brings endless adventure, challenge, and at least as much crushing pain as fleeting pleasure. However, over time and through successive incarnations Txeemsim improves and evolves into a great hero and miracle worker. In 1859 Duncan learned from the Nisga'a about some of Txeemsim's accomplishments. Later, when the missionaries sought to undermine respect for the hereditary chiefs, they sometimes denigrated Txeemsim and described him as a negative figure.

The cycle of the Nisga'a Txeemsim stories summarizes the pitfalls that precede maturation with respect to developing environmentally intelligent attitudes. Like the immature Txeemsim, the immature person may behave egoistically and may suffer very considerably from delusions of grandeur and some belief that being a person means being a superior life form, but through the journey toward enlightenment he will overcome difficulties of perception and eventually serve his people and the entire creation. He evolves not for himself, but for all communities of humans and other creatures. Along his journey Txeemsim is compelled to respect all the communities of both ordinary and supernatural creatures, and astonishingly, he holds even the most powerful supernatural beings to the greatest law, which is the importance of sharing. Txeemsim identifies and conquers a selfish supernatural chief as well as an entire nation of grasping Loolkaks—analogues to the hungry ghosts or Pretas described in Buddhist tradition. The selfish Loolaks attempt to keep the Oolichan harvest to themselves, but when they refuse to believe Txeemsim when he is actually telling the truth, he is able to confound and destroy them. In maturity, as he progresses through these incarnations, Txeemsim's youthful excesses are replaced by the compassion he feels for the people and animals who must strive in semi-darkness. He even charms K'am liggi halhal, the great god of the sky, and succeeds in bringing light [and the possibility of enlightenment] to the world.

The development of proper, trustable leadership takes place over time and involves long years of preparation, which few are called upon to endure. The proper leader must remain aware, diligent, and focused on the good of the community. The lands and resources in the home place are divine gifts and, as an expression of consciousness, must all be respected. Importantly, the Txeemsim stories also apply to day-to-day life, and so they contain highly entertaining lessons that are fundamentally suitable for all.

Conclusion

Traditional wisdom provides time-proven approaches to enjoying renewable resources without destroying them. The above examples indicate something of the depth and range of traditional wisdom as it is preserved and utilized by one British Columbia First Nation—the Nisga'a of Lisims (Nass River). Few deny that the recent experiment with empire building and large human populations causes serious ongoing environmental problems. It is hoped that the fundamental principles imbedded in the wisdom component of TEKW could be an important key to reestablishing workable relations between human communities and the environment. The writer also hopes that First Nations scholars who have themselves grown up exposed to traditional wisdom teachings firsthand will contribute their own observations to a literature of traditional wisdom. The writer was once told of a Hopi teaching about how The wisdom necessary to bring the White People through adolescence is stored in Grandmother Country among the Indian peoples of the Pacific Northwest. Humanity's experiment with empire-building societies has been relatively brief, but it is causing serious environmental problems. It is time for us all to pay closer attention to the proven traditional wisdom concepts and practices that can help us analyze and solve our collective environmental problems.

Note

The observations presented here grow out of some three decades of experience living and working with the Nisga'a, Ahousaht, and Haida people in the fields of community-initiated education and archival research relating to negotiating lands, resources, and human rights issues. The author has been encouraged to write about these topics by Nisga'a leaders and educators, including late Dr. Bertram McKay, Chief Harry Nyce, and Mrs. Deanna Nyce, CEO of the Nisga'a college, Wilp Wilxo'oskwhl Nisga'a. It has long been held by Nisga'a leaders that students of Nisga'a culture, such as Wilp Wilxo'oskwhl Nisga'a scholars, can perform a useful service by "backing up" the oral information system with written observations. It is hoped that this essay will be useful both to the Nisga'a students of culture as well as others who may be concerned with finding relief from some of the environmental problems that threaten us all. The concepts presented here grow out of experience with the way the writer has heard Nisga'a leaders approach culture and action in their communities. It is hoped that some of the analysis here will provide Nisga'a and other First Nations scholars with knowledge categories that may be of assistance when they are considering ways of writing about their own experience.

Anything worthy of consideration in this chapter can be traced to kind First Nations teachers, while any shortcomings of analysis or protocol are entirely my own. The names of some of the mentors who have kindly instructed the writer are referred to. However, it would be impossible to acknowledge all who have shared their observations and have both educated and encouraged the writer.

Afterword

Making Connections For the Future

Charles R. Menzies

There are points in time when the trajectories of independent events coincide in serendipitous and potentially productive ways. Our opening research workshop, which gave birth to this collection, was one such moment. In the room immediately adjoining our session were gathered key representatives of provincial and regional municipal governments, First Nations, forest and mining industries, labor unions, tourism operators, and ecologists. They were meeting to inaugurate the north coast land resource management planning process (NC-LRMP)—the task of which was to find consensus on which pieces of the north coast to "preserve" and which to "develop." Thus, as our presenters discussed the possibilities of linking local knowledge to resource management and planning, the politicians in the next room were issuing statements about the desirability of doing so.

As the NC-LRMP developed, our research was increasingly called upon, and we were invited to participate in several discussions that emerged, particularly those related to the issue of local ecological knowledge: what is it, how can it be understood, how can we study it, and—most importantly for the NC-LRMP—how might it be incorporated into the ongoing planning process. Calling upon on our work was in part a response to the emergence of a core debate among the NC-LRMP table members regarding the relevance of local knowledge in counter-distinction to the quality and efficacy of applied sciences. An undercurrent to this debate manifested itself in an emerging set of tacit and tactical alliances between "locals" on the one side (small business loggers, First Nations, local tour operators, and locally based ecologists) and "outsiders" on the other side (transnational environmental NGOs, large tour operators, and large resources industry processors and their organized labor).

The local/outsider (local knowledge/science) debates resonate well with the core issues raised in the chapters of this volume. From the more pessimistic view (see especially Nadasdy) to the optimistic (McGoodwin), the contributors to this volume have attempted to highlight the particular ways in which locality can be constructed and deployed in the act of regulating, managing, and—ultimately—sustaining natural resources that we all agree are required for the sustenance of our human communities. Here the contributors have attempted to explicate the difficulties of realpolitik. How does one deploy the wisdom of a Nisga'a hereditary leader? In what way is the ecological knowledge of salmon held by Sto:lo fishers constrained and enabled by the history of federal fisheries regulations? In what ways can we teach that values the situated knowledges of Indigenous knowledge holders? In what ways are Indigenous peoples and other wild harvesters developing new knowledges in the contest of traditional methodologies? These questions, as presented, discussed, and debated in this volume, speak directly to the ways in which, as pointed out in Butler's and my chapters, many of our contemporary opportunities to deploy TEK are shaped, and very often constrained, by historical processes. Thus the "local" side of the NC-LRMP divide can be understood as a product of the region's history of resource development and, ironically, the very social factors against which they were arguing. That is, the non-Indigenous coastal communities and the contemporary work and residential opportunities of the Indigenous communities were to a large extent the by-product of a century of industrial resource extractive capitalism.

Elsewhere I have documented the historical development of industry and its implications for Indigenous peoples along British Columbia's north coast (see Menzies and Butler 2001; Menzies 1994, 1996). Suffice to say that this process has been one in which the economies of the chiefly societies have been transformed and that the ecological and economic implications of

Indigenous engagement on and across these lands and waterways has been altered. Furthermore, the non-Indigenous communities that have emerged and disappeared over the course of the past century and a half are also the result of the same processes of industrialization of the landscape. From Ocean Falls to Swanson's Bay, Port Essington, and Annyox, former bustling resource extraction hubs have all but been erased from the landscape and the social memory. Towns that remain, such as Prince Rupert, Bella Coola, and Queen Charlotte City, do so with the economic dynamic that spawned them in retreat. This is the context in which the NC-LRMP participants found themselves debating locality—who is, who is not local, and what is the validity of local knowledge versus science. Locked within a history of resource development, colonial expropriation of Indigenous lands, and environmental practices that have prioritized profit making over sustainability, the NC-LRMP discussions—even as participants attempt to try new approaches—appeared unable to break free from the dead weight of history, and in making their decisions the members drew upon the lessons and expectations of the past.

Perhaps, as Gerald Sider has passionately argued in a discussion of the collapse of Newfoundland fishing outports and struggles over autonomy and economic self-reliance among Lumbee Indian communities of North Carolina, one must consciously act against one's experience (Sider 1997, 2003a, 2003b). That is, the lessons of the past—the historical movements and processes that brought small-scale loggers, First Nations leaders, postmodern eco-warriors, old-time industrialists and their corporate-minded trade unionists, and a host of other players together in one room—need to be turned against and set aside. And, perhaps, this will be the only way that local ecological knowledge can be placed at the center of natural resource planning.

To a certain extent the NC-LRMP process was itself an attempt to do just this—overturn the historical biases and limitations that have accumulated. Although the results are still to be realized in their entirety, the likelihood of actually changing how things are done in British Columbia's forests is not very hopeful. The emerging documents, despite fine introductory words

and important nods to local ecological knowledge, still place the accumulation of profit through resource extraction at the center of the plan. The
question remains—can TEK- and LEK-based approaches actually be realized within the context of overarching processes that maintain accumulation at the center of most forms of societal planning? There are those—
such as Raymond Rogers, for example—who argue that sustainability is
not possible as long as the profit motive remains the driving force of our
society (Rogers 1995).

In the face of this intellectual skepticism I do manage to maintain what
I refer to as an operational optimism. That is, in spite of everything that
might suggest problems and difficulties with TEK and in implementing
or deploying it, I can recognize the clear value in actually listening to the
people closest to the resource, the people who live there, work there, and
know the resource in an intimate and profound fashion. It is very likely
that those who begin from a position of "epistemological skepticism" will
be able to point to errors of logic, fuzzy thinking, or contrary examples. I
share with these fellow travelers a similar skepticism, yet I also draw upon
many years of living and working with First Nations and non-Indigenous
wild plant and animal harvesters—fishermen, hunters, berry pickers, bark
strippers, and so forth.

My operational optimism emerges out of my experience working on the
deck of a fishboat, listening to elders and community members from Gitxaała
and neighboring communities, and observing the many times that my colleagues in the natural sciences simply "get it all wrong." Although this sort
of experience can be problematized and critiqued, it should not be overlooked or set aside. By drawing upon our experiences working with people
whose lives depend upon harvesting wild plants and animals, the contributors to this volume are confident in saying that, despite all of the difficulties, the knowledge held by these people does indeed have something useful for us to learn, something worth understanding.

The many Tsimshian and north coast community members who participated in the workshop and other aspects of the Forests for the Future project share with us this optimistic view. Together we look forward to a future

in which local communities once again locate themselves as a part of, not apart from, the environment within which we must live. We look toward a world in which human sustainability is understood as occurring in concert with environmental sustainability, and the reigning instrumentalist understanding of the environment as natural resources is no longer a paramount value.

References

Aaronson, S. 1986. A Role for Algae as Human Food in Antiquity. Food and Food-
ways 1:311–315.

Abbott, Isabella. 1974. Limu: An Ethnobotanical Study of Some Edible Hawaiian
Seaweeds. Lawai, Kauai HI: Pacific Tropical Botanical Garden.

Acheson, James M. 1972. The Territories of the Lobstermen. Natural History
81(4):60–69.

———. 1982. Metal Traps: A Key Innovation in the Maine Lobster Industry. In Modernization and Marine Fisheries Policy. John R. Maiolo and Michael K.
Orbach, eds. Pp. 279–312. Ann Arbor MI: Ann Arbor Science.

———. 1988. The Lobster Gangs of Maine. Hanover NH: University Press of New
England.

Adams, John W. 1973. The Gitksan Potlatch: Population Flux, Resource Ownership
and Reciprocity. Toronto: Holt Rinehart and Winston of Canada.

Agrawal, A. 1995. Indigenous and Scientific Knowledge: Some Critical Comments.
Indigenous Knowledge and Development Monitor 3(3): 3–6.

Aikenhead, G. 1996. Science Education: Border Crossing into the Subculture of Science. Studies in Science Education 27:1–52.

———. 1997. Towards a First Nations Cross-Cultural Science and Technology Curriculum. Science Education 81:217–238.

———. 2002. Cross-Cultural Science Teaching: Rekindling Traditions for Aboriginal Students. Canadian Journal of Science, Mathematics and Technology
Education 2(3):287–304.

Akimichi, Tomoya. 2001. Species-Oriented Resource Management and Dialogue
on Reef Fish Conservation: A Case Study from Small-Scale Fisheries in
Yaeyama Islands, Southwestern Japan. In McGoodwin 2001, 109–131.

Amoss, Pamela. 1987. The Fish God Gave Us: The First Salmon Ceremony Revived.
Arctic Anthropology 24(1):56–66.

Anderson, Eugene N. 1994. Fish as Gods and Kin. In Dyer and McGoodwin 1994,
139–160.

Arthurs, David. 1995. Archaeological Surveys in the Donjek, Jarvis, Kaskawulsh,
and Alsek Valleys, Kluane Park Reserve, 1993. Winnipeg: Department of
Canadian Heritage, Parks Canada—Archaeological Field Services.

Barnett, Homer G. 1955. The Coast Salish of British Columbia. Studies in Anthropology, no. 4. Eugene: University of Oregon.

Battiste, Marie. 1998. Enabling the Autumn Seed: Towards a Decolonized Approach
to Aboriginal Knowledge, Language, and Education. Canadian Journal
of Native Education 22(1):16–27.

————, ed. 2000. Reclaiming Indigenous Voice and Vision. Vancouver: University of British Columbia Press.

Bavinck, Maarten. 2001. Marine Resource Management: Conflict and Regulation in the Fisheries of the Coromandel Coast. New Delhi: Sage Publications India.

Ben-Yami, Menakhem. 2001. Integration of Traditional Institutions and People's Participation in an Artisanal Fisheries Development Project in Southeastern Nigeria. In McGoodwin 2001, 133–167.

Berger, Thomas R. 1992. A Long and Terrible Shadow: White Values, Native Rights in the Americas, 1492–1992. Vancouver: Douglas and McIntyre.

Berkes, Fikret. 1977. Fishery Resources Use in a Subarctic Indian Community. Human Ecology 5(4):289–307.

————. 1987. Common-Property Resource Management and Cree Indian Fisheries in Subarctic Canada. In The Question of the Commons: The Culture and Ecology of Communal Resources. B. J. McCay and J. M. Acheson, eds. Pp. 66–91. Tucson: University of Arizona Press.

————. 1989a. Co-management and the James Bay Agreement. In Co-operative Management of Local Fisheries: New Directions for Improving Management and Community Development. Evelyn W. Pinkerton, ed. Pp. 189–208. Vancouver: University of British Columbia Press.

————, ed. 1989b. Common Property Resources: Ecology and Community-Based Sustainable Development. New York: Columbia University Press.

————. 1993. Traditional Ecological Knowledge in Perspective. In Traditional Ecological Knowledge: Concepts and Cases. J. T. Inglis, ed. Ottawa: International Development Research Centre.

————. 1999. Sacred Ecology: Traditional Ecological Knowledge and Resource Management. Philadelphia: Taylor and Francis Press.

Berkes, Fikret, David Feeny, Bonnie J. McCay, and James M. Acheson. 1989. The Benefits of the Commons. Nature 340:91–93.

Berkes, Fikret, and Carl Folke. 1998. Linking Social and Ecological Systems: Management Practices and Social Mechanisms for Building Resilience. Cambridge: Cambridge University Press.

Berleant-Schiller, Riva. 1982. Development Proposals and Small-Scale Fishing in the Caribbean. In Modernization and Marine Fisheries Policy. J. R. Maiolo and M. K. Orbach, eds. Pp. 115–139. Ann Arbor MI: Ann Arbor Science.

Berlin, Brent. 1992. Ethnobiological Classification: Principles of Categorization of Plants and Animals in Traditional Societies. Princeton NJ: Princeton University Press.

Berrill, Michael. 1997. The Plundered Seas: Can the World's Fish Be Saved? San Francisco: Sierra Club Books.

Berringer, Patricia Ann. 1982. Northwest Coast Traditional Salmon Fisheries Systems of Resource Utilization. M.A. thesis, University of British Columbia, Vancouver.

Blanchette, Robert A., Brian D. Compton, Nancy J. Turner, and Robert Gilbertson. 1992. Nineteenth Century Shaman Grave Guardians Are Carved Fomitopsis officinalis sporophores. Mycologia 84(1):119–124.

Boas, Franz. 1891. Third Report on the Indians of British Columbia in the Seventh Report of the Committee on the North-western Tribes of Canada. Pp. 408–449. Report of the British Association for the Advancement of Science 61st meeting.

———. 1895. Salishan Texts. Proceedings of the American Philosophical Society 34: 31–48.

———. 1902. Tsimshian Texts: Nass River Dialect. U.S. Bureau of American Ethnology Bulletin no. 27. Washington DC: Government Printing Office.

———. 1921. Ethnology of the Kwakiutl, Based on Data Collected by George Hunt. Bureau of American Ethnology, 35th Annual Report, Part 1, 1913–14. Washington DC: Smithsonian Institution.

Bombay, Harry, ed. 1996. Aboriginal Forest-Based Ecological Knowledge in Canada. Ottawa: National Aboriginal Forestry Association.

Borrows, John. 1997. Living between Water and Rocks: First Nations, Environmental Planning and Democracy. University of Toronto Law Journal 47:417–468.

Bowers, C. 1995. Educating for the Ecologically Sustainable Culture: Rethinking Moral Education, Creativity, Intelligence, and Other Modern Orthodoxies. New York: State University of New York Press.

Boyd, Robert T. 1999. The Coming of the Spirit of Pestilence: Introduced Infectious Diseases and Population Decline among Northwest Coast Indians, 1774–1874. Vancouver: University of British Columbia Press.

Brody, Hugh. 1982. Maps and Dreams. New York: Pantheon Books.

———. 2000. The Other Side of Eden: Hunters, Farmers and the Shaping of the World. Vancouver: Douglas and McIntyre.

Butler, Caroline F., and Charles R. Menzies. 2000. Out of the Woods: Tsimshian Women and Forestry Work. Anthropology of Work Review 21(2):12–17.

Cajete, G. A. 1999. Igniting the Sparkle: An Indigenous Science Education Model. Skyand NC: Kivaki Press.

Carlson, Keith Thor, and Sarah Eustace. 1997. The Lower Fraser Canyon Aboriginal Fishery: An Historical Analysis of Access and Control. Draft paper. Sardis BC: Stó:lo Nation.

Cecelski, David. 1997. Oldest Living Confederate Chaplain Tells All?—Or, James B. Avirett and the Rise and Fall of the Rich Lands. Southern Cultures 3(4):5–24.

Chisholm, Brian, D. E. Nelson, and H. P. Schwarz. 1983. Marine and Terrestrial Protein in Prehistoric Diets on the British Columbia Coast. Current Anthropology 24(3):396–398.

Clayton, Daniel. 2000. Islands of Truth: The Imperial Fashioning of Vancouver Island. Vancouver: University of British Columbia Press.

Compton, Brian D. 1993. Upper North Wakashan and Southern Tsimshian Ethnobotany: The Knowledge and Usage of Plants and Fungi among the Oweeken, Hanaksiala (Kitlope and Kemano), Haisla (Kitamaat) and Kitasoo Peoples of the Central and North Coasts of British Columbia. Ph.D. dissertation, University of British Columbia, Vancouver.

————. 1995. Ghost's Ears (Exobasidium sp. affin. vaccinii) and Fool's Huckleber-
ries (Menziesia ferruginea Smith): A Unique Report of Mycophagy on the
Central and North Coasts of British Columbia. Journal of Ethnobiology
15(1):89–98.

Compton, Brian D., Rolf Mathewes, and Gastón Guzmán. 1995. Puffballs from the
Past: Identification of Gasteromycetes from a Lillooet Archeological Site
and Speculation Regarding Their Prehistoric Use. Canadian Journal of
Archeology 19:154–159.

Copes, Parzival. 1991. An Indian Commercial Fishery for Salmon on the Upper Skeena: Issues and Trade-Offs. Discussion Paper 91–19. Burnaby BC: Institute
of Fisheries Analysis, Simon Fraser University.

————. 1993. An Expanded Salmon Fishery for the Gitksan-Wet'suwet'en in the
Upper Skeena Region: Equity Considerations and Management Implica-
tions. Discussion Paper 93–1. Burnaby BC: Institute of Fisheries Analysis,
Simon Fraser University.

————. 1995. The Profits of Justice: Restoring Aboriginal River Fisheries in British Columbia. Discussion Paper 95–2. Burnaby BC: Institute of Fisheries
Analysis, Simon Fraser University.

Cordell, John, ed. 1989. A Sea of Small Boats. Cultural Survival Reports. Vol. 26.
Cambridge MA: Cultural Survival.

Cecelski, David. 1997., C. F., and J. P. Planta. 1886. Report of the Commission to
Enquire into the State and Condition of the Indians of the North-West
Coast of British Columbia. Province of British Columbia.

Corsiglia, John, and Gloria Snively. 1997. Knowing Home: NisGa'a Traditional Knowledge and Wisdom Improve Environmental Decision Making.
Alternatives Journal 23(3):22–27.

Council for Yukon Indians. 1993. Umbrella Final Agreement between the Government of Canada, the Council for Yukon Indians, and the Government of the Yukon. Ottawa: Minister of Indian Affairs and Northern
Development.

Cove, John. 1982. Gitksan Traditional Concept of Land Ownership. Anthropologi-
ca 24(1):3–17.

Cruikshank, Julie. 1998. The Social Life of Stories: Narrative and Knowledge in the
Yukon Territory. Vancouver: University of British Columbia Press.

Dauenhauer, Nora, and Richard Dauenhauer. 1994. Haa Kusteeyí—Our Culture:
Tlingit Life Stories. In Classics of Tlingit Oral Literature, vol. 3. Seattle:
University of Washington Press.

de Laguna, Frederica. 1960. Story of a Tlingit Community: A Problem in the Relationship between Archeological, Ethnological, and Historical Methods.
Bureau of American Ethnology Bulletin 172. Washington DC: U.S. Government Printing Office.

————. 1972. Under Mount Saint Elias: The History and Culture of the Yakutat Tlingit. Smithsonian Contributions to Anthropology vol. 7. Washington DC:
Smithsonian Institution Press.

Department of Fisheries and Oceans (DFO). 1998. Selective Fisheries Report: June
and December 1998. Electronic document accessed January 31, 1999.

———. 1999a. Electronic document, www.pac.dfo-mpo.gc.ca/ops/fm/afs/default. htm. Preliminary Summaries of Selective Fisheries Projects (accessed October 1999). Hardcopy report prepared by Fisheries and Oceans Canada, Pacific Region. Report distributed at Selective Fisheries Workshop, November 22–24, 1999, Richmond, BC.

———. 1999b. Aboriginal Fisheries Strategy. Electronic document, http://www. pac.dfo-mpo.gc.ca/tapd. Selective Fishing Project List. Prepared by Fisheries and Oceans Canada (accessed February 25, 1999).

Department of Indian Affairs and Northern Development (DIAND. 2001. Overview of DIAND Program Data: Education. Ottawa: DIAND.

Devine, H. 1991. The Role of Archeology in Teaching the Native Past: Ideology or Pedagogy? Canadian Journal of Native Education 18(1):11–22.

Drucker, Philip. 1965. Cultures of the North Pacific Coast. New York: Harper and Row.

Druehl, Louis. 2000. Pacific Seaweeds: A Guide to Common Seaweeds of the West Coast. Madeira Park BC: Harbour.

Duff, Wilson. 1952. The Upper Stalo Indians of the Fraser Valley, British Columbia. Anthropology in British Columbia, Memoir No. 1. Victoria BC: British Columbia Provincial Museum and Archives.

Dunn, John Asher. 1978. A Practical Dictionary of the Coast Tsimshian Language. Ottawa: National Museums of Canada.

———. 1995. Sm'algyax: A Reference Dictionary and Grammar for the Coast Tsimshian Language. Seattle: University of Washington Press; Juneau AK: Sealaska Heritage Foundation.

Durrenberger, E. Paul, and Gísli Pálsson. 1987. Ownership at Sea: Fishing Territories and Access to Sea Resources. American Ethnologist 14:508–522.

Dyer, Christopher L., and Richard L. Leard. 1994. Folk Management in the Oyster Fishery on the U.S. Gulf of Mexico. In Dyer and McGoodwin 1994, 55–89.

Dyer, Christopher L., and James R. McGoodwin, eds. 1994. Folk Management in the World's Fisheries: Lessons for Modern Fisheries Management. Niwot: University Press of Colorado.

Edenso, Christine. 1983. The transcribed tapes of Christine Edenso. Recordings in Haida by Christine Edenso; translation of Haida into English by Robert and Nora Cogo; edited by Tupou Pulu. Anchorage AK: Materials Development Center, Rural Education, University of Alaska.

Ellen, Roy F. 1993. The Cultural Relations of Classification: An Analysis of Nuaulu Animal Categories from Central Seram. Cambridge: Cambridge University Press.

Emmons, George T. 1991. The Tlingit Indians. Frederica de Laguna, ed. Vancouver: Douglas and McIntyre.

Felt, Lawrence F. 1994. Two Tales of a Fish: The Social Construction of Indigenous Knowledge among Atlantic Canadian Salmon Fishers. In Dyer and McGoodwin 1994, 251–286.

Ferguson, Michael, and Francois Messier. 1997. Collection and Analysis of Traditional Ecological Knowledge about a Population of Arctic Tundra Caribou. Arctic 50(1):17–28.

Fisher, Robin. 1977. Contact and Conflict: Indian-European Relations in British Columbia, 1774–1890. Vancouver: University of British Columbia Press.

Food and Agriculture Organization of the United Nations. 1983. FAO Yearbook of Fishery Statistics, vol. 31. Rome: Food and Agriculture Organization of the United Nations.

Frankenberg, Dirk. 1997. The Nature of North Carolina's Southern Coast: Barrier Islands, Coastal Waters, and Wetlands. Chapel Hill: University of North Carolina Press.

Ganyard, Robert. 1963. North Carolina during the American Revolution, the First Phase: 1774–1777. Ph.D. dissertation, Department of History, Duke University, Durham NC.

Garfield, Viola E. 1939. Tsimshian Clan and Society. Seattle: University of Washington.

Garfield, Viola E., and Linn A. Forrest. 1948. The Wolf and the Raven: Totem Poles of Southeastern Alaska. Seattle: University of Washington Press.

Gifford, Ferguson. 1989. Indian Fishing Rights in British Columbia. Report prepared for Department of Fisheries and Oceans and Department of Indian and Northern Affairs Canada. Vancouver, BC.

Goldschmidt, Walter Rochs, and Theodore H. Haas. 1946. The Possessory Rights of the Natives of Southeastern Alaska: A Report to the Commissioner. Unpublished document. Washington DC: Bureau of Indian Affairs.

Goldschmidt, Walter Rochs, and Theodore H. Haas. 1998. Haa aaní—Our Land: Tlingit and Haida Land Rights and Use. Thomas F. Thornton, ed. Seattle: University of Washington Press.

Goodlad, C. Alexander. 1986. Regional Fisheries Management: The Shetland Experience. Notes prepared for the Norwegian/Canadian Fisheries Management Workshop, Tromsø, Norway, June 16–21.

Green, R. 1981. Culturally-Based Science: The Potential for Traditional People, Science and Folklore. London: Proceedings of the Centennial Observation of the Folklore Society.

Griffith, David. 1996. Impacts of New Regulations on North Carolina Fishermen: A Classificatory Analysis. Sea Grant Publication UNC-SG-96–07. Raleigh NC: University of North Carolina Sea Grant College Program.

Griffith, David. 1999. The Estuary's Gift: An Atlantic Coast Cultural Biography. University Park: Pennsylvania State University Press.

Griffith, David, and Christopher Dyer. 1996. Appraisal of the Social and Cultural Aspects of the Multispecies Groundfish Fishery in the New England and the Mid-Atlantic Regions. Report submitted to NOAA. Contract no. 50–DGNF-5–00008. Bethesda MD: Aguirre International/NOAA.

Griffith, David, and Manual Valdés Pizzini. 2002. Fishers at Work, Workers at Sea: A Puerto Rican Journey through Labor and Refuge. Philadelphia: Temple University Press.

Griffith, David, Aaron Shecter, Kristen Borre, and Vernon Kelley. 1998. Occupational Health Risks of Crabbing. Sea Grant Publication UNC-SG-98–02. Raleigh NC: University of North Carolina Sea Grant College Program.

Guerin, Kim A. 1999. *Restoring Respect*, VHS. Produced by Blake Coverton and Pro-Plan Services.

Guiry, Michael D. 2002. Welcome to the Seaweed Site. Electronic document, http://seaweed.ucg.ie/.

Guiry, M. D., and G. Blunden. 1991. Seaweed Resources in Europe: Uses and Potential. Chichester UK: John Wiley and Sons.

Guiry, M. D., and C. C. Hession. 1998. The Seaweed Resources of Ireland. In Seaweed Resources of the World. A. T. Critchley and M. Ohno, eds. Yokosuka, Japan: Japan International Cooperation Agency.

Hall, Budd L. 2000. Breaking the Educational Silence: For Seven Generations, an Information Legacy of the Royal Commission on Aboriginal Peoples. In Indigenous Knowledges in Global Contexts: Multiple Readings of Our World. Budd L. Hall, Dorothy Goldin Rosenberg, and George J. Sefa Dei, eds. Pp. 202–212. Toronto: University of Toronto Press.

Halpin, Marjorie M., and Margaret Seguin. 1990. Tsimshian Peoples: Southern Tsimshian, Coast Tsimshian, Nishga, and Gitksan. In Handbook of North American Indians. Vol. 7, Northwest Coast. Wayne Suttles, ed. Pp. 267–284. Washington DC: Smithsonian Institution.

Harris, Cole. 1997. The Resettlement of British Columbia: Essays on Colonialism and Geographical Change. Vancouver: University of British Columbia Press.

Harris, Douglas C. 2001. Fish, Law, and Colonialism: The Legal Capture of Salmon in British Columbia. Toronto: University of Toronto Press.

Heard, William. 1991. Life History of Pink Salmon (Onchorynchus gorbuscha). In Pacific Salmon Life Histories. C. Groot and L. Margolis, eds. Vancouver: University of British Columbia Press.

Hewes, Gordon W. 1947. Aboriginal Use of Fishery Resources in Northwestern North America. Ph.D. dissertation, University of California, Berkeley.

———. 1973. Indian Fisheries Productivity in Pre-Contact Times in the Pacific Salmon Area. Northwest Anthropological Research Notes 7(3):133–154.

Hilborn, Ray, and Wilf Luedke. 1987. Rationalizing the Irrational: A Case Study in User Group Participation in Pacific Salmon Management. Canadian Journal of Fisheries and Aquatic Sciences 44:1796–1805.

Hill-Tout, Charles. 1902. Ethnological Studies of the Mainland Halkomelem, a Division of the Salish of British Columbia. Report of the British Association for the Advancement of Science 72:355–449.

Hodson, D. 1993. In Search of a Rationale for Multicultural Science Education. Science Education 77(6):685–711.

Hoefs, Manfred. 1981. The Dall Sheep Population of Sheep Mountain/Kluane National Park: Review of Natural History, Assessment of Population Dynamics, and Recommendations for Management. Unpublished manuscript. Gatineau QC: Parks Canada. Available at the Yukon Department of Renewable Resources, Whitehorse YT Y1A 2C6.

Horseman, R. 1975. Scientific Racism and the American Indian in the Mid-Nineteenth Century. American Quarterly 27:152–167.

Hunn, E. 1993. "What Is Traditional Ecological Knowledge? In Traditional Ecological Knowledge: Wisdom for Sustainable Development. N. M. Williams and G. Baines, eds. Pp. 13–15. Canberra: Centre for Resource and Environmental Studies, Australian National University.

Hutchinson, Vonnie, and Susan Marsden. 1992. Saaban: The Tsimshian and Europeans Meet. Prince Rupert: The Tsimshian Chiefs and School District no. 52.

Indergaard, M. 1983. The Aquatic Resource. I. The Wild Marine Plants: A Global Bioresource. In Biomass Utilization. Wilfred A. Côté, ed. Pp. 137–168. New York: Plenum Press.

Inglis, J. T. 1993. Traditional Ecological Knowledge: Concepts and Cases. Ottawa: International Development Research Centre.

Jenness, Diamond. 1934. The Indians of Canada. Bulletin no. 65. Ottawa: National Museum of Canada.

———. 1943. Carrier Indians of the Bulkley River: Their Social and Religious Life. Anthropological Papers, no. 25, Bureau of American Ethnology Bulletin no. 133. Washington DC: Government Printing Office.

Jentoft, Svein. 1985. Models of Fishery Development: The Cooperative Approach. Marine Policy 9:322–331.

———. 1989. Fisheries Co-management: Delegating Government Responsibility to Fishermen's Organizations. Marine Policy, April: 137–154.

Jentoft, Svein, and Trond Kristoffersen. 1989. Fishermen's Co-management: The Case of the Lofoten Fishery. Human Organization 48:355–365.

Jentoft, Svein, and Knut H. Mikalsen. 1994. Regulating Fjord Fisheries: Folk Management or Interest Group Politics? In Dyer and McGoodwin 1994, 287–316.

Johannes, R. E. 1978. Traditional Marine Conservation Methods in Oceania, and Their Demise. Annual Review of Ecology and Systematics 9:349–364.

Johnson Gottesfeld, Leslie. 1994. Conservation, Territory, and Traditional Beliefs: An Analysis of Gitksan and Wet'suwet'en Subsistence. Human Ecology 22(4):443–465.

Johnson, Leslie M. 1999. Gitksan Plant Classification and Nomenclature. Journal of Ethnobotany 19(2):179–218.

Johnson, Martha. 1992. Lore: Capturing Traditional Environmental Knowledge. Yellowknife: Government of the Northwest Territories.

Johnson, Warren A. 1980. Europe. In World Systems of Traditional Resource Management. G. A. Klee, ed. Pp. 165–188. New York: John Wiley and Sons.

Jones, Jo. Sewell. 1834. A Defense of the Revolutionary History of the State of North Carolina from the Aspersions of Mr. Jefferson. Raleigh NC: Turner and Hughes.

Joyce, Amy. 1998. A Research Design for Archaeology at Hope Plantation. M.A. thesis, Department of Anthropology, East Carolina University, Greenville NC.

Kawagley, A. Oscar. 1995. A Yupiaq Worldview: A Pathway to Ecology and Spirit. Prospect Heights IL: Waveland Press.

Kew, Michael, and Julian Griggs. 1991. Native Indians on the Fraser Basin: Towards a Model of Sustainable Resource Use. In Perspectives on Sustainable Development in Water Management: Towards Agreement in the Fraser River Basin. Anthony H. J. Dorcey, ed. pp. 17–48. Research Program on Water in Sustainable Development, vol. 1. Vancouver: Westwater Research Centre, Faculty of Graduate Studies, University of British Columbia.

Klee, Gary A., ed. 1980. World Systems of Traditional Resource Management. New York: John Wiley and Sons.

Kluane First Nation, and Yukon Territorial Government. 1996. Ruby and Nisling Range Wildlife Meeting—November 8, 1995. Report prepared for the Ruby Range Sheep Steering Committee by the Kluane First Nation and the Yukon Territorial Government, Whitehorse.

Knudtson, P., and D. Suzuki. 1992. Wisdom of the Elders. Toronto: Stoddart.

Kottak, Conrad Phillip. 1966. The Structure of Equality in a Brazilian Fishing Community. Ph.D. dissertation, Columbia University, New York.

Kuhn, Richard, and Frank Duerden. 1996. A Review of Traditional Environmental Knowledge: An Interdisciplinary Canadian Perspective. Culture 16(1):71–84.

Kuhnlein, Harriet V. 1990. Nutrient Values in Indigenous Wild Plant Greens and Roots Used by the Nuxalk People of Bella Coola, British Columbia. Journal of Food Composition and Analysis 3(1):38–46.

Kuhnlein, Harriet V., and Nancy J. Turner. 1991. Traditional Plant Foods of Canadian Indigenous Peoples: Nutrition, Botany, and Use. New York: Gordon and Breach.

Kurien, John. 2001. The Socio-Cultural Aspects of Fisheries: Implications for Food and Livelihood Security: A Case Study of Kerala State, India. In McGoodwin 2001, 195–217.

Langdon, Steve J. 1977. Technology, Ecology, and Economy: Fishing Systems in Southeast Alaska. Ph.D. dissertation, Stanford University, Stanford CA.

———. 1979. Comparative Tlingit and Haida Adaptation to the West Coast of the Prince of Wales Archipelago. Ethnology 19(2):101–119.

———. 1984. The Perception of Equity: Social Management of Access in an Aleut Fishing Village. Paper presented at the Annual Meeting of the Society for Applied Anthropology, Toronto, March 14–18.

———. 1997. Efforts at Humane Engagement: Indian-Spanish Encounters in Bucareli Bay, 1779. In Enlightenment and Exploration in the North Pacific, 1741–1805. Stephen W. Haycox, James Barnett, and Caedmon Liburd, eds. Seattle: University of Washington Press. Published for the Cook Inlet Historical Society, Anchorage Museum of History and Art.

Langdon, Steve J., Douglas Reger, and Neil Campbell. 1995. Pavements, Pounds, Pairs, Piles and Puzzles: Research on the Estuarine Fishing Structures of Little Salt Lake, Prince of Wales Island. Paper presented at "Hidden Dimensions: The Archeology of Wet Sites," University of British Columbia, Vancouver, April 27–30.

Langdon, Steve J., Douglas Reger, and Christopher Wooley. 1986. Using Aerial Photographs to Locate Intertidal Fishing Structures in the Prince of Wales Archipelago, Southeast Alaska. Public Data File Document no. 86–9. Anchorage: Alaska Department of Natural Resources, Division of Geological and Geophysical Surveys.

Legat, Alice. 1991. Report of the Traditional Knowledge Working Group. Yellowknife: Department of Culture and Communication, Government of the Northwest Territories.

Leibhardt, Barbara. 1986. Among the Bowheads: Legal and Cultural Change on Alaska's North Slope Coast to 1985. Environmental Review 10:277–301.

Lerman, Norman. 1950. A Collection of Folktales of the Lower Fraser Indians. Typescript.

———. 1976. Legends of the River People. Vancouver: November House.

Lindstrom, S. C., and K. M. Cole. 1991. A Revision of the Species of Porphyra (Rhodophyta: Bangiales) Occuring in British Columbia and Adjacent Waters. Canadian Journal of Botany 70:2066–75.

Lui, Joyce. 1995. The Use of Local Knowledge and Expert Opinion in Resource Planning. Victoria BC: Ministry of Forests.

MacIvor, M. 1995. Redefining Science Education for Aboriginal Students. In First Nations Education in Canada: The Circle Unfolds. Marie Battiste and Jean Barman, eds. Pp. 73–98. Vancouver: University of British Columbia Press.

Madlener, Judith C. 1977. The Seavegetable Book. New York: Clarkson N. Potter.

Marsden, Susan, and Robert Galois. 1995. The Tsimshian, the Hudson's Bay Company and the Geopolitics of the Northwest Coast Fur Trade, 1787–1840. Canadian Geographer 39(2):169–183.

Matson, R. G., and Gary Coupland. 1995. The Prehistory of the Northwest Coast. San Diego: Academic Press.

McCandless, Robert G. 1985. Yukon Wildlife: A Social History. Edmonton: University of Alberta Press.

———. n.d. Trophies or Meat: Yukon Game Management. Whitehorse: Yukon Territorial Archives.

McCay, Bonnie J. 1978. Systems Ecology, People Ecology, and the Anthropology of Fishing Communities. Human Ecology 6(4):397–422.

———. 1980. A Fishermen's Cooperative, Limited: Indigenous Resource Management in a Complex Society. Anthropological Quarterly 53:29–38.

———. 1981. Development Issues in Fisheries as Agrarian Systems. In Culture and Agriculture: Bulletin of the Anthropological Study Group on Agrarian Systems. Vol. 11. Urbana-Champaign: University of Illinois.

———. 1988. Muddling through the Clam Beds: Cooperative Management of New Jersey's Hard Clam Spawner Sanctuaries. Journal of Shellfish Research 7(2):327–340.

McCay, Bonnie J., and James M. Acheson. 1987. Human Ecology of the Commons. In The Question of the Commons: The Culture and Ecology of Communal Resources. B. J. McCay and J. M. Acheson, eds. Pp. 1–34. Tucson: University of Arizona Press.

McClellan, Catherine. 1975. My Old People Say: An Ethnographic Survey of Southern Yukon Territory. Ottawa: National Museum of Man.

McDonald, James. 1985. Trying to Make a Life: The Historical Political Economy of Kitsumkalum. Ph.D. dissertation, University of British Columbia, Vancouver.

———. 1994. Social Change and the Creation of Underdevelopment. American Ethnologist 21(1):152–175.

———. n.d. Cultivating in the Northwest: Gleaning the Evidence from the Tsimshian.

McGoodwin, James R. 1990. Crisis in the World's Fisheries: People, Problems, and Policies. Stanford CA: Stanford University Press.

———. 1994. "Nowadays, Nobody Has Any Respect": The Demise of Folk Management in a Rural Mexican Fishery. In Dyer and McGoodwin 1994, 43–54.

———, ed. 2001. Understanding the Cultures of Fishing Communities: A Key to Fisheries Management and Food Security. FAO Fisheries Technical Paper 401. Rome: Food and Agriculture Organization of the United Nations.

McGoodwin, James R., Barbara Neis, and Lawrence F. Felt. 2000. Integrating Fishery People and Their Knowledge into Fisheries Science and Resource Management: Issues, Prospects, and Problems. In Finding Our Sea Legs: Linking Fishery People and Their Knowledge with Science and Management. Barbara Neis and Lawrence F. Felt, eds. Pp. 249–264. St. John's NF: ISER Books, Memorial University of Newfoundland.

McKay, William. 1977. A Socio-economic Analysis of Native Indian Participation in the BC Salmon Fishery with the Proposed SEP. Vancouver: Department of Fisheries and Environment.

Meggs, Geoff. 1991. Salmon: The Decline of the British Columbia Fisheries. Vancouver: Douglas and McIntyre.

Menzies, Charles R. 1990. Between the Stateroom and the Fo'c'sle: Everyday Forms of Class Struggle aboard a Commercial Fishboat. Nexus 8(1):77–92.

———. 1992. On Permanent Strike: Class and Ideology in a Producers' Co-operative. Studies in Political Economy 38:85–108.

———. 1993. All That Holds Us Together: Kinship and Resource Pooling in a Fishing Co-operative. MAST: Maritime Anthropological Studies 6(1–2):157–179.

———. 1994. Stories from Home: First Nations, Land Claims, and Euro-Canadians. American Ethnologist 21(4):776–791.

———. 1996. Indian or White? Racial Identities in the British Columbian Fishery. In Anthropology for a Small Planet: Culture and Community in a Global Environment. Anthony Marcus, ed. Pp. 110–123. St. James NY: Brandywine Press.

———. 2001. Reflections on Research with, for, and among Indigenous Peoples. Canadian Journal of Native Education 25(1):19–36.

Menzies, Charles R., and Caroline F. Butler. 2001. Working in the Woods: Tsimshian Resource Workers and the Forest Industry of British Columbia. American Indian Quarterly 25(3):409–430.

Menzies, Charles R., et al. 2002. Forests for the Future: Integrating Local Ecological Knowledge with Natural Resource Management. Vancouver: Forest Renewal of British Columbia (http://www.ecoknow.ca).

Merrens, Harry Roy. 1962. Colonial North Carolina in the Eighteenth Century: A Study in Historical Geography. Chapel Hill: University of North Carolina Press.

Miller, Jay. 1997. Tsimshian Culture: A Light through the Ages. Lincoln: University of Nebraska Press.

Milliken, William, and Sam Bridgewater. 2001. Flora Celtica: Sustainable Development of Scottish Plants. Electronic document, http://www.scotland.gov. uk/cru/kdo1/orange/sdsp-00.asp. Edinburgh: Scottish Executive Central Research Unit and Royal Botanic Garden.

Mills, Antonia. 1994. Eagle Down Is Our Law: Wet'suwet'en Law, Feasts, and Land Claims. Vancouver: University of British Columbia Press.

Moore, S. A., and H. S. Moore. 1903. The History and Law of Fisheries. London: Stevens and Haynes.

Morauta, L., J. Pernetta, and W. Heaney. 1982. Traditional Conservation in Papua New Guinea: Implications for Today. Monograph no. 16. Boroko, Papua New Guinea: Institute of Applied Social and Economic Research.

Morrell, Mike. 1989. The Struggle to Integrate Traditional Indian Systems and State Management in the Salmon Fisheries of the Skeena River, British Columbia. In Co-operative Management of Local Fisheries: New Directions for Improving Management and Community Development. E. W. Pinkerton, ed. Pp. 231–248. Vancouver: University of British Columbia Press.

Mosha, R. S. 1999. The Inseparable Link between Intellectual and Spiritual Formation in Indigenous Knowledge and Education: A Case Study in Tanzania. In What Is Indigenous Knowledge? Voices from the Academy. L. Semali and J. L. Kincheloe, eds. Pp. 209–225. New York: Falmer Press.

Nadasdy, Paul. 1999. The Politics of TEK: Power and the "Integration" of Knowledge. Arctic Anthropology 36(1–2):1–18.

———. 2003. Hunters and Bureaucrats: Power, Knowledge, and Aboriginal-State Relations in the Southwest Yukon. Vancouver: University of British Columbia Press.

Nelson, Richard K. 1983. Make Prayers to the Raven: A Koyukon View of the Northern Forest. Chicago: University of Chicago Press.

Nelson, W. A., J. Brodie, and M. D. Guiry. 1999. Terminology Used to Describe Reproduction and Life History in the Genus Porphyra. Journal of Applied Phycology 11(5):407–410.

Newell, Dianne. 1993. Tangled Webs of History: Indians and the Law in Canada's Pacific Coast Fisheries. Toronto: University of Toronto Press.

Nuttall, Mark. 1998. Critical Reflections on Knowledge Gathering in the Arctic. In Aboriginal Environmental Knowledge in the North. L.-J. Dorias, M. Nagy, and L. Muller-Wille, eds. Pp. 21–36. Québec City: Groupe d'études inuit et circumpolaires, Université Laval.

Olson, Ronald. 1967. The Social Structure and Social Life of the Tlingit in Alaska. Anthropological Records, vol. 26. Berkeley: University of California Press.

Ostraff, Melinda. 2003. Contemporary Use of Limu (Marine Algae) in the Vava'u Island Group, Kingdom of Tonga: An Ethnobotanical Study. Unpublished Ph.D. dissertation, University of Victoria, Victoria, BC.

Outland, Robert B., III. 2001. Suicidal Harvest: The Self-Destruction of North Carolina's Naval Stores Industry. North Carolina Historical Review 78(3):309–344.

Palmer, Craig T. 1994. Are Folk Management Practices Models for Formal Regulations? Evidence from the Lobster Fisheries of Newfoundland and Maine. In Dyer and McGoodwin 1994, 237–249.

Pálsson, Gísli. 1997. Learning by Fishing: Practical Engagement and Environmental Concerns. In Linking Social and Ecological Systems. F. Berkes and C. Folk, eds. Cambridge: Cambridge University Press.

Pinkerton, Evelyn W. 1994. Summary and Conclusions. In Dyer and McGoodwin 1994, 317–337.

Poggie, John J., Jr. 1978. Deferred Gratification as an Adaptive Characteristic for Small-Scale Fishermen. Ethos 6 (Summer): 114–123.

Pomeroy, Caroline. 1994. Obstacles to Institutional Development in the Fishery of Lake Chapala, Mexico. In Dyer and McGoodwin 1994, 17–41.

Port Simpson Curriculum Committee. 1983. Port Simpson Foods: A Curriculum Development Project. Prince Rupert: People of Port Simpson and School District No. 52.

Raunet, Daniel. 1996. Without Surrender, Without Consent: A History of the Nisga'a Land Claims. Rev. ed. Vancouver: Douglas and MacIntyre.

Richardson, Allan. 1982. The Control of Productive Resources on the Northwest Coast of North America. In Resource Managers: North American and Australian Hunter-Gatherers. Nancy M. Williams and Eugene S. Hunn, eds. Pp. 93–112. Boulder CO: Westview Press for the American Association for the Advancement of Science.

Rigsby, Bruce. 1967. Tsimshian Comparative Vocabularies with Comparative Notes On Nass-Gitksan Systematic Phonology. Ottawa: National Museums of Canada.

Robbins, William G. 1996. The World of Columbia River Salmon: Nature Culture and the Great River of the West. In The Northwest Salmon Crisis: A Documentary History. Corvallis: Oregon State University Press.

Rogers, Raymond A. 1995. The Oceans Are Emptying: Fish Wars and Sustainability. Montréal: Black Rose Books.

Ruby Range Sheep Steering Committee. 1995. Minutes from the Meeting of the Ruby Range Sheep Steering Committee, December 4, 1995. Prepared by Geraldine Pope. Burwash Landing YT.

———. 1996a. Draft Recommendations from the Ruby Range Sheep Steering Committee to the Yukon Fish and Wildlife Management Board, July 1996.

———. 1996b. Minutes from the Meeting of the Ruby Range Sheep Steering Committee, January 10–11, 1996. Prepared by Paul Nadasdy. Burwash Landing YT.

Ruddle, Kenneth. 1994. Local Knowledge in the Folk Management of Fisheries and Coastal Marine Environments. In Dyer and McGoodwin 1994, 161–206.

Ruddle, Kenneth, and R. E. Johannes. 1985. The Traditional Knowledge and Management of Coastal Systems in Asia and the Pacific. Jakarta: Regional Office for Science and Technology for Southeast Asia, United Nations Educational, Scientific, and Cultural Organization.

Salisbury, Oliver M. 1962. Quoth the Raven. Seattle: Superior.

Salmon, David. 1997. Oceanography of the Eastern North Pacific. In The Rain Forests of Home: Profile of a North American Bioregion. Paul K. Schoonmaker, Bettina Von Hagen, and Edward C. Wolf, eds. Washington DC: Island Press.

Schalk, Randall. 1977. The Structure of an Anadromous Fish Resource. In For Theory Building in Archaeology. Lewis Binford, ed. Pp. 207–250. New York: Academic Press.

Scientific Panel for Sustainable Forest Practices in Clayoquot Sound. 1994. Report of the Scientific Panel for Sustainable Practices in Clayoquot Sound. Victoria BC: Clayoquot Scientific Panel.

Seguin, Margaret. 1984. Lest There Be No Salmon: Symbols in Traditional Tsimshian Potlatch. In The Tsimshian: Images of the Past, Views for the Present. Margaret Seguin, ed. Pp. 110–133. Vancouver: University of British Columbia Press.

———. 1985. Interpretive Contexts for Traditional and Current Coast Tsimshian Feasts. National Museum of Man, Mercury Series, Canadian Ethnology Service Paper no. 98. Ottawa: National Museums of Canada.

Sejersen, Frank. 1998. Hunting in Greenland and the Integration of Local User's Knowledge in Management Strategies." In Aboriginal Environmental Knowledge in the North. L.-J. Dorias, M. Nagy, and L. Muller-Wille, eds. Pp. 37–60. Québec City: Groupe d'études inuit et circumpolaires, Université Laval.

Selective Fisheries Review and Evaluation. 1999. Prepared by Edwin Blewett and Associates, Inc. Timothy Taylor Consulting Services, Inc.

Sider, Gerald M. 1997. "Against Experience: The Struggles for History, Tradition, and Hope among a Native American People." In Between History and Histories: The Making of Silences and Commemorations. Gerald Sider and Gavin Smith, eds. Pp. 62–79. Toronto: University of Toronto Press.

———. 2003a. Between History and Tomorrow: Making and Breaking Everyday Life in Newfoundland. Peterborough ON: Broadview Press.

———. 2003b. Living Indian Histories: Lumbee and Tuscarora People in North Carolina. Chapel Hill: University of North Carolina Press.

Sillitoe, Paul. 1998. The Development of Indigenous Knowledge: A New Applied Anthropology. Current Anthropology 39(2):223–252.

Sirota, G. R., and J. F. Uthe. 1979. Heavy Metal Residues in Dulse, an Edible Seaweed. Aquaculture 18:41–44.

Smith, Courtland L. 1988. Conservation and Allocation Decisions in Fishery Management. In Salmon Production, Management, and Allocation: Biological, Economic, and Policy Issues. William J. McNeil, ed. Pp. 131–138. Corvallis: Oregon State University Press.

Smith, Harlan I., Brian D. Compton, Bruce Rigsby, and Marie-Lucie Tarpent. 1997. Ethnobotany of the Gitksan Indians of British Columbia. Hull QC: Canadian Museum of Civilization.

Snively, Gloria. 1995. Bridging Traditional Science and Western Science in the Multicultural Classroom. In Thinking Globally about Mathematics and Science Education. Gloria J. Snively and Allan M. MacKinnon, eds. Pp. 1–24. Vancouver: Research and Development in Global Studies and Centre for the Study of Curriculum and Instruction, University of British Columbia.

Snively, Gloria, and John Corsiglia. 2001. Discovering Indigenous Science: Implications for Science Education. Science Education 85(1):6–34.

Souther, Barbara C. 1993. Aboriginal Rights and Public Policy: Historical Overview and an Analysis of the Aboriginal Fisheries Strategy. M.A. thesis, Simon Fraser University, Burnaby BC.

Stewart, Hilary. 1977. Indian Fishing: Early Methods on the Northwest Coast. Vancouver: J. J. Douglas.

Stoffle, Brent W., David B. Halmo, Richard W. Stoffle, and C. Gaye Burpee. 1994. Folk Management and Conservation Ethics among Small-Scale Fishers of Buen Hombre, Dominican Republic. In Dyer and McGoodwin 1994, 115–138.

Stoffle, Richard, and Michael Evans. 1990. Holistic Conservation and Cultural Triage: American Indian Perspectives on Cultural Resources. Human Organization 49(2):91–99.

Suttles, Wayne Prescott. 1951. The Economic Life of the Coast Salish of Haro and Rosario Straits. Ph.D. dissertation, University of Washington, Seattle.

———. 1987. Coast Salish Essays. Seattle: University of Washington Press.

Tarpent, Mary-Lucie. 1983. Morphophonemics of Nishga Plural Formation: A Step towards Proto-Tsimshian Reconstruction. In Studies in Native American Languages; Kansas Working Papers in Linguistics 8/2.

———. 1997. Tsimshianic and Penutians: Problems, Methods, Results, and Implications. International Journal of American Linguistics 63(1):65–112.

Taylor, Greg. 1993. Proposal for a New Management Regime for the Skeena River. M.A. thesis, Simon Fraser University, Burnaby, BC.

Tehennepe, S. 1993. Issues of Respect: Reflections of First Nations Students' Experience in Post Secondary Anthropology Classrooms. Canadian Journal of Native Education 20(2):193–260.

Thornton, Thomas F. 1995. Place and Being among the Tlingit. Ph.D. dissertation, University of Washington, Seattle.

———. 1999. Tleikw aaní, the "Berried" Landscape: The Structure of Tlingit Edible Fruit Resources at Glacier Bay. Alaska Journal of Ethnobiology 19(1):27–48.

Turner, Nancy J. 1995. Food Plants of Coastal First Peoples: Royal British Columbia Museum Handbook, Victoria BC. Vancouver: University of British Columbia Press. (First published as Food Plants of British Columbia Indians; pt. 1: Coastal Peoples. British Columbia Provincial Museum, 1975.)

———. 1998. Plant Technology of First Peoples in British Columbia. Rev. ed. Vancouver:

University of British Columbia Press and Royal British Columbia Museum, Victoria. (First published as Plants in British Columbia Indian Technology. Royal British Columbia Museum, 1979.)

————. 2003. The Ethnobotany of "Edible Seaweed" (*Porphyra abbottiae* Krishnamurthy and related species; Rhodophyta: Bangiales) and Its Use by First Nations on the Pacific Coast of Canada. *Canadian Journal of Botany* 81(2):283–293.

Turner, Nancy J., Marianne B. Ignace, and Ronald Ignace. 2000. Traditional Ecological Knowledge and Wisdom of Aboriginal Peoples in British Columbia. Theme issue, "Traditional Ecological Knowledge, Ecosystem Science, and Environmental Management"; Jesse Ford and Dennis R. Martinez, eds. Ecological Applications 10(5):1275–1287.

Turner, Nancy J., John Thomas, Barry F. Carlson, and Robert T. Ogilvie. 1983. Ethnobotany of the Nitinaht Indians of Vancouver Island. Victoria: British Columbia Provincial Museum and Parks Canada.

Underhill, Ruth. 1945. Indians of the Pacific Northwest. Washington DC: Education Division, U.S. Bureau of Indian Affairs; Riverside CA: Sherman Institute Press.

Usher, Peter. 2000. Traditional Ecological Knowledge in Environmental Assessment and Management. Arctic 53(2):183–193.

Vayda, Andrew P. 1988. Actions and Consequences as Objects of Explanation in Human Ecology. Environment, Technology, and Society 51:2–7.

Von Brandt, Andres. 1964. Fish Catching Methods of the World. London: Fishing News (Books).

Ward, William, and Priscilla Weeks. 1994. Resource Managers and Resource Users: Field Biologists and Stewardship. In Dyer and McGoodwin 1994, 91–113.

Ware, Reuben. 1983. Five Issues Five Battlegrounds: An Introduction to the History of Indian Fishing in British Columbia, 1850–1930. Chilliwack BC: Coqualeetza Education Training Centre.

Weatherford, J. 1988. Indian Givers: How the Indians of the Americas Transformed the World. Toronto: Random House.

Webster, G. 1990. Kwakiutl since 1980. In Handbook of North American Indians. Vol. 7: Northwest Coast. Wayne Suttles, ed. Pp. 387–390. Washington DC: Smithsonian Institution.

Whyte, K. 1986. Strategies for Teaching Indian and Metis Students. Canadian Journal of Native Education 13(3):1–20.

William, N. M., and G. Baines. 1993. Traditional Ecological Knowledge: Wisdom for Sustainable Development. Canberra: Center for Resource and Environmental Studies, Australian National University.

Williams, M. D. 1979. The Harvesting of "Slukus" (Porphyra perforata) by the Straits Salish Indians of Vancouver Island. Syesis 12(1–2):63–68.

Williams, Michael. 1989. Americans and Their Forests: A Historical Geography. Cambridge: Cambridge University Press.

Wolf, Eric R. 1982. Europe and the People without History. Berkeley: University of California Press.

———. 1999. Envisioning Power: Ideologies of Dominance and Crisis. Berkeley CA: University of California Press.

Yukon Territorial Government. 1997. Information Packet provided to the Ruby Range Sheep Steering Committee by the Yukon Territorial Government, Department of Renewable Resources on January 7, 1997. Compiled by Jean Carey.

List of Contributors

Kimberly Linkous Brown received her Ph.D. in anthropology from the University of British Columbia in 2005. Her research interests are focused on natural resource issues: access and use, regulation, control and management--primarily in regard to Native peoples.

Caroline Butler did her graduate work in anthropology at the University of British Columbia and is currently Adjunct Professor of Anthropology at the University of Northern British Columbia. She has collaborated with First Nations communities in British Columbia, researching natural resource use and employment, Aboriginal fishing rights, Indigenous knowledge, and traditional resource management. She has also worked with commercial fishers and loggers on the north coast of British Columbia, exploring issues of resource regulation and local knowledge.

Helen Clifton is an elder of the Gitga'at Nation of Hartley Bay, British Columbia. Her late husband, Chief Johnny Clifton, was born at the seaweed camp at Princess Royal Island, and Helen has been harvesting seaweed there since she was a young woman, learning about the old ways of seaweed harvesting from her mother-in-law, Lucille Clifton, and other elders of previous generations. A fluent speaker of Smalgyax, she has participated in and witnessed the changes in plant resource harvesting and processing for over five decades.

John Corsiglia has worked on cross-cultural education and land question issues with the Nisga'a, Haida, and Ahousaht First Nations of British Columbia. He is a lecturer at the University of Victoria.

David Griffith is a senior scientist and Professor of Anthropology at East Carolina University. His recent books include *Fishers at Work, Workers at Sea: A Puerto Rican Journey through Labor and Refuge* (with Manuel Valdés Pizzini) and *The Estuary's Gift: A Mid-Atlantic Cultural Biography*. He is currently conducting comparative research on traditional ecological knowledge among Iñupiaq hunter-fishers of Kotzebue Sound, Alaska, and fishing families in Puerto Rico and North Carolina, as well as work on migration into rural America from Latin America and the Caribbean.

Steve J. Langdon is Professor of Anthropology at the University of Alaska Anchorage, where he has taught since 1976. He obtained his doctorate in anthropology from Stanford University in 1977. He has specialized in southeast Alaska on topics related to precontact, historic, and contemporary fisheries of the Tlingit and Haida people. Findings concerning the operation of intertidal fish traps in the Prince of Wales Archipelago are based on a continuing research program he began in 1985. He has served on two National Academy of Science review boards, most recently (1999) examining the Community Development Quota (CDQ) program established for Bering Sea coastal villagers. He is the author of *The Native People of Alaska* (4th ed., 2002) as well as the editor of *Contemporary Alaska Native Economies* (1986).

James (Russ) McGoodwin is Professor of Anthropology at the University of Colorado at Boulder. His research focuses on fishing people and cultures, the human dynamics that drive resource management policies, and the impacts of climatic and global change. Over his career he has conducted research in Alaska, Denmark, Iceland, Japan, Mexico, Newfoundland, Portugal, Spain, and the West Indies.

Charles R. Menzies, Associate Professor of Anthropology at the University of British Columbia, is Gitxaała Tsimshian and an enrolled member of the Tlingit and Haida Indian Tribes of Alaska. He has written and published papers concerning conflicts between Euro-Canadians and First Nations in the context of land claims, issues of resource allocation, and alliances between First Nations and the green movement. He has also published and presented papers concerning the impact of social and ecological crises on fisherfolk in Le Guilvinec, France. He is the project leader of the interdisciplinary research project Forests and Oceans for the Future (http://ecoknow.ca), that explores local ecological knowledge and its application for forest and fisheries management.

Paul Nadasdy, Associate Professor of Anthropology and American Indian Studies at the University of Wisconsin–Madison, has conducted extensive research on the politics of wildlife management and Aboriginal-state relations in Canada's Yukon Territory. He is the author of *Hunters and Bureaucrats: Power, Knowledge, and Aboriginal-State Relations in the Southwest Yukon*, and his writings have also appeared in such journals as *American Anthropologist*, *Ethnohistory*, and *Arctic Anthropology*. He is currently working on an ethnography of First Nations land claim negotiations in the Yukon.

Gloria Snively is Associate Professor in the Faculty of Education at the University of Victoria, where she teaches science, environmental, and marine education. Since 1974 she has taught curriculum development and conducted workshops with First Nations communities on environmental and marine education projects and on the contributions of Aboriginal knowledge to long-term sustainable communities and environments. She is principal investigator for the Aboriginal Knowledge and Science Education Research Project, which is looking at issues related to the underrepresentation of Aboriginal students in high school science and in the sciences generally.

Nancy J. Turner is an ethnobotanist and Distinguished Professor in the School of Environmental Studies at the University of Victoria. She is also a research associate with the Royal British Columbia Museum. She has authored or co-authored more than 18 books (most recently, *Plants of Haida Gwaii* in 2004 and *The Earth's Blanket* in 2005) and many other publications in the area of ethnobotany, traditional ecological knowledge, and sustainable resource use in Canada.

Index

and distillation in, 11–12; education, 195–97, 199–202; evaluating TEK used in, 13; geographical knowledge, 142–46; impact of Europeans on, 16, 90–91; integration of knowledge with other groups, 129–31; oral histories, 47, 48, 51, 58, 62, 63, 229–31; political issues in, 12, 120–21; political structure, language and history of, 89–91, 103n3; reflections on fisheries science, 207–11; selective fishing by, 61–63; surveys of animals, 141–42; training of the mind in, 229. *See also* Indigenous Knowledge; Traditional Ecological Knowledge

fisheries science: cooperative co-management in, 188–89; integrating local knowledge into, 175–92; problems with integrating local knowledge into, 178–82; recommendations for integration in, 190–92; reflections on Aboriginal, 207–11; relationships among fishers, scientists, and managers in, 183–85; small- versus large-scale fishers and, 182–83. *See also* fishers, Aboriginal; fishing

fishers, Aboriginal: characteristics of, 50, 52–56, 63n2, 189–90; competition from non-Native fishers, 119–20; different types of, 167–69; impact of non-Natives on, 117–18; prospects and problems stemming from attributes of different, 178–82; relationships with scientists and managers, 183–85; small- versus large-scale, 182–83; societies stability, 180; state regulation of, 115–17, 185–87. *See also* fisheries science; fishing

fishing: environmental change affecting, 113–15; government regulation of, 115–17, 225–28; integration of indigenous knowledge of, 175–89; live-capture technologies, 56–58; and local environmental knowledge in North Carolina, 165–67, 170–71; multiple livelihoods and, 153–55, 167–71; in North Carolina commercial fisheries, 163–64; selective, 47–63; traps, 31–36, 41–42, 52–56, 57; tribal and village ownership of

sites for, 53–56; water quality and, 171–74; weirs, 29–31, 34–36, 38–39, 52–56, 57; wheels, 57–58, 62, 224. *See also* fisheries science; salmon

fish wheels, 57–58, 62, 224

Florida, 187

forests: culturally modified trees (CMT) within, 205; of North Carolina, 158–60; resin production and, 158–60; seaweed and, 76–77

Forests for the Future, 3–4, 14, 16–17n1

Fort Langley, 112

Fort Yale, 112

Fraser River, 48, 52–56, 125; ecological knowledge about, 119–20; environmental changes affecting, 114–15; selective fishing experiments, 60–61; Sto:lo people and, 111–13

fruits and vegetables, 81–82

Fulton, Jim, 227

fungi, 92–93, 103n8

game birds, 69, 81

Garrison, Laena, 211

geographical dimension in wildlife management, 142–46

gillnet fishing, 50

Gingolix mission community, 227–28

Gitga'at people, 14; changes among, 82–85; seaweed use by, 65–82

Gitksan/Wet'suwet'en people, 49, 54, 55; pine mushrooms harvesting techniques, 96–99; pine mushrooms used by, 91–94; political structure, language and history of, 89–91; selective fishing by, 59

Gitsxan people, 14

Gitxaala people, 1, 9, 14, 16

Gosnell, Eli, 223, 224

Gosnell, James, 224

Gosnell, Joseph, 223

Griffith, David, 15, 109

Guerin, Kim A., 47

Haida Gwaii, 68

halibut, 69, 81

Yakobi Island, 21
Yakutat Tlingit people, 23
Yukon: Department of Renewable Resources, 135; Fish and Wildlife Management Board, 132; Outfitter's Association, 135; political power in the, 131–36